W9-BAK-913

Portuguese

Phrasebook & Dictionary

Acknowledgments
Product Editor Bruce Evans
Language Writers Yukiyoshi Kamimura, Robert Landon, Anabela de Azevedo Teixeira Sobrinho
Cover Image Researcher Naomi Parker

Thanks
James Hardy, Campbell McKenzie, Martine Power, Angela Tinson, Tony Wheeler, Juan Winata

Published by Lonely Planet Global Limited
CRN 554153

4th Edition – September 2018
ISBN 978 1 78657 462 6
Text © Lonely Planet 2018
Cover Image Facade of Capela das Almas, Porto. Hemis/AWL ©

Printed in China   10 9 8 7 6 5 4 3 2 1

Contact lonelyplanet.com/contact

Although the authors and Lonely Planet try to make the information as accurate as possible, we accept no responsibility for any loss, injury or inconvenience sustained by anyone using this book.

Paper in this book is certified against the Forest Stewardship Council™ standards. FSC™ promotes environmentally responsible, socially beneficial and economically viable management of the world's forests.

Look out for the following icons throughout the book:

 'Shortcut' Phrase
Easy to remember alternative to the full phrase

 Q&A Pair
'Question-and-answer' pair – we suggest a response to the question asked

 Look For
Phrases you may see on signs, menus etc

 Listen For
Phrases you may hear from officials, locals etc

 Language Tip
An insight into the foreign language

 Culture Tip
An insight into the local culture

How to read the phrases:
- Coloured words and phrases throughout the book are phonetic guides to help you pronounce the foreign language.
- Lists of phrases with tinted background are options you can choose to complete the phrase above them.

These abbreviations will help you choose the right words and phrases in this book:

a	adjective	**m**	masculine	**sg**	singular
f	feminine	**n**	noun	**v**	verb
inf	informal	**pl**	plural		
lit	literal	**pol**	polite		

Contents

PAGE 6

🎓 **About Portuguese**
Learn about Portuguese, build your own sentences and pronounce words correctly.

PAGE 27

Travel Phrases
Ready-made phrases for every situation – buy a ticket, book a hotel and much more.

 Basics 27

 Practical 39

Social — 109

Safe Travel — 155

Food — 171

PAGE 194

Menu Decoder
Dishes and ingredients explained –
order with confidence and try new foods.

PAGE 208

Two-Way Dictionary
Quick reference vocabulary guide –
3500 words to help you communicate.

INTRO

Portuguese

português poorr·too·*gesh*

Who speaks Portuguese?

OFFICIAL LANGUAGE

PORTUGAL
BRAZIL
CAPE VERDE
GUINEA-BISSAU
ANGOLA
MOZAMBIQUE
SÃO TOMÉ & PRÍNCIPE
EAST TIMOR
MACAU (CHINA)

Why Bother

If it's true that language is the door to a nation's soul, you might get a little closer to grasping the *saudade* – that melancholic longing for something (the 'Portuguese blues'), and its famous musical expression, *fado*.

Distinctive Sounds

Throaty 'r' (similar to French) and nasal vowels (pronounced as if you're trying to force the sound through the nose).

Portuguese in the World

The global distribution of Portuguese began during *Os*

200 MILLION
speak Portuguese as their first language

40 MILLION
speak Portuguese as their second language

Descobrimentos (The Age of Discoveries) in the 15th and 16th centuries, when Portugal was a colonial power with huge economic, cultural and political influence. The empire's reach can be seen in the number of countries where Portuguese or Portuguese-based creoles are spoken today.

Portuguese in Portugal

The Instituto Camões (www.instituto-camoes.pt, in Portuguese), named in honour of Portugal's greatest poet Luís de Camões, was created in 1992 to promote Portuguese language and culture worldwide. The most important literary prize for Portuguese language is also called Prémio Camões.

False Friends

Warning: many Portuguese words look like English words but have a different meaning altogether, eg *salsa saal*·sa is 'parsley', not 'sauce' (which is *molho mo*·lyoo in Portuguese).

Language Family

Romance (developed from the colloquial Latin spoken by the Romans during their 500-year rule of present-day Portugal). Close relatives include Galician, Spanish, Italian, French and Romanian.

Must-Know Grammar

Portuguese has both a formal and an informal word for 'you' (*você* vo·*se* and *tu* too respectively). Verbs have a different ending for each person – like the English 'I do' vs 'he/she do**es**'.

Donations to English

Numerous – you may recognise *albino, port, brocade, dodo, molasses, commando* ...

5 Phrases to Learn Before You Go

 When is admission free?
Quando é grátis a entrada?
kwang·doo e *graa*·teesh a eng·*traa*·da

Try to plan your sightseeing in Portugal around free-admission days (often Sunday mornings).

 Can I have a half-serve, please?
Podia servir-me meia-dose, por favor?
poo·*dee*·a ser·*veer*·me *may*·a·do·ze poor fa·*vor*

Much Portuguese cuisine is served in massive portions – it's often worth ordering a half-serve, especially if you're on a budget.

 Can I get this without meat?
Este prato pode vir sem carne?
esh·te *praa*·too po·de veer seng *kaar*·ne

Vegetarians aren't generally well catered for in Portugal, and they may need to be creative in requesting their dishes.

 Where can we go for 'street fado'?
Onde é que há fado vadio?
ong·de e ke aa *faa*·doo va·*dee*·oo

For an authentic, spontaneous approach to music, seek out places where locals take turns singing the 'Portuguese blues'.

 Where can I find an art exhibition?
Onde é que há alguma esposição de arte?
ong·de e ke aa alg·*goo*·ma shpoo·zee·*sowng* de *aar*·te

There are always interesting cultural happenings in major Portuguese cities, including free fringe-art exhibitions.

10 Phrases to Sound Like a Local

| Cool! | **Óptimo!** | o·tee·moo |

| Great! | **Fantástico!** | fang·*taash*·tee·koo |

| Sure. | **É claro.** | e *klaa*·roo |

| Maybe. | **Talvez.** | taal·*vesh* |

| No way! | **De maneira nenhuma!** | de ma·*nay*·ra neeng·*yoo*·ma |

| Just joking. | **Estou a brincar.** | shtoh a breeng·*kaar* |

| No problem. | **Não há problema.** | nowng aa pro·*ble*·ma |

| It's OK. | **Está bem.** | shtaa beng |

| Of course! | **Claro que sim!** | *klaa*·roo ke seeng |

| Never mind. | **Não faz mal.** | nowng fazh mao |

ABOUT PORTUGUESE

Pronunciation

Vowel Sounds

The vowel sounds in Portuguese are quite similar to those found in English, so you should be able to get talking with confidence. There are some differences, of course. Most vowel sounds in Portuguese also have a nasal version with an effect similar to the silent '-ng' ending in English, such as *amanhã* aa·ma·*nyang* (tomorrow), for example. The letter *n* or *m* at the end of a syllable, or a tilde (~) in written Portuguese indicate that the vowel is nasal (also see **consonant sounds**).

SYMBOL	ENGLISH EQUIVALENT	PORTUGUESE EXAMPLE	TRANSLITERATION
a	among	maçã	ma·*sang*
aa	father	tomate	too·*maa*·te
ai	aisle	pai	pai
ay	play	lei	lay
e	ten	cedo	*se*·doo
ee	feet	fino	*fee*·noo
o	lot	sobre	*so*·bre
oh	oh!	couve	*koh*·ve
oo	book	gato	*ga*·too
ow	cow	Austrália	ow·*shtraa*·lya
oy	boy	noite	*noy*·te

Consonant Sounds

Most of the consonants in Portuguese are also found in English. Note that the *r* rr is similar to the French 'r' sound.

SYMBOL	ENGLISH EQUIVALENT	PORTUGUESE EXAMPLE	TRANSLITERATION
b	bed	beber	be·*ber*
d	dog	dedo	*de*·doo
f	fit	faca	*faa*·ka
g	gap	gasolina	ga·zoo·*lee*·na
k	kit	cama	*ka*·ma
l	let	lixo	*lee*·shoo
ly	million	muralhas	moo·*raa*·lyash
m	mat	macaco	ma·*kaa*·koo
n	no	nada	*naa*·da
ng	sing (indicates nasalisation of preceding vowel)	ambos, uns, amanhã	*ang*·boosh, oongsh, aa·ma·*nyang*
ny	canyon	linha	*lee*·nya
p	pin	padre	*paa*·dre
r	like 'tt' in 'butter' said fast	hora	*o*·ra
rr	as in French 'croissant'	relva	*rrel*·va
s	sad	criança	kree·*ang*·sa
sh	shut	chave	*shaa*·ve
t	top	tacho	*taa*·shoo
v	very	vago	*vaa*·goo
w	water	água	*aa*·gwa
y	yes	edifício	ee·dee·*fee*·syoo
z	zoo	camisa	ka·*mee*·za
zh	pleasure	cerveja	serr·*ve*·zha

Some consonant sounds can change depending on where they appear in a word. For example, an *s* at the beginning of the word is pronounced like the s in 'sea' – eg *sal* saal (salt). When *s* comes at the end of the word, or at the end of a syllable which is followed by a consonant, as in *está* shtaa (are), it's pronounced sh, but if it's surrounded on both sides by vowels (as in *camisa* ka·mee·za), it's pronounced z. Follow the coloured pronunciation guides and you won't have any trouble.

Word Stress

Stress (ie the emphasis on one syllable over another) generally occurs on the second-to-last syllable of a word, though there are exceptions. If a written vowel has a circumflex (ˆ) or an acute (ˊ) accent marked on it, this cancels the general rule and the stress falls on that syllable.

fino	*fee*·no	fine
português	poor·too·*gesh*	Portuguese
cajú	ka·*zhoo*	cashew

Also, if you're reading Portuguese words for yourself, it's handy to know these other exceptions: when a word ends in a written *i, im, l, r, u, um* or *z*, or is pronounced with a nasalised vowel, the stress falls on the last syllable.

beber	be·*ber*	to drink
calor	ka·*lor*	heat
actuação	a·too·a·*sowng*	performance

Don't worry too much about it when using phrases from this book though – if you follow the coloured pronunciation guides you can't go wrong.

You'll notice in conversation with Portuguese speakers that as in English, when certain syllables are given more stress, others are practically unpronounced. For example, unless the final syllable is stressed, the vowel is pronounced very lightly and in conversation may disappear altogether – so *antes* is technically pronounced *aang*·tesh but in practice sounds more like ants. Again, we've always given the correct pronunciation in our coloured guides.

Reading & Writing

Portuguese is written with the Latin alphabet. For spelling purposes (eg if you need to spell your name to book into a hotel), the pronunciation of each letter is provided below.

~ PORTUGUESE ALPHABET ~

A a aa	**B b** be	**C c** se	**D d** de
E e e	**F f** e·fe	**G g** je	**H h** a·*gaah*
I i ee	**J j** *jo*·ta	**K k** *ka*·pa	**L l** e·le
M m e·me	**N n** e·ne	**O o** o	**P p** pe
Q q ke	**R r** e·rre	**S s** e·se	**T t** te
U u oo	**V v** ve	**W w** *da*·blyoo	**X x** sheesh
Y y *eeps*·lon	**Z z** ze		

You'll notice that some letters, usually vowels, have accent marks. The acute (´) accent and the circumflex (ˆ) indicate stress, the grave (`) accent indicates the contraction of two *a*'s, and the tilde (~) indicates nasalisation. You'll also see the cedilla sometimes used at the bottom of the letter 'c' – ç is pronounced as s rather than k (*criança* kree·*ang*·sa).

ABOUT PORTUGUESE

Grammar

This chapter is designed to explain the main grammatical structures you need in order to make your own sentences. Look under each heading – listed in alphabetical order – for information on functions which these grammatical categories express in a sentence. For example, demonstratives are used for giving instructions, so you'll need them to tell the taxi driver where your hotel is, etc.

Adjectives & Adverbs

Describing People/Things • Doing Things

Adjectives are generally placed after the noun. They change form depending on the gender and number of the noun they describe (see also **gender** and **plurals**).

handsome boy	menino bonito (lit: boy handsome-**m-sg**) me·*nee*·noo boo·*nee*·too
handsome boys	meninos bonitos (lit: boys handsome-**m-pl**) me·*nee*·noosh boo·*nee*·toosh
pretty girl	menina bonita (lit: girl pretty-**f-sg**) me·*nee*·na boo·*nee*·ta
pretty girls	meninas bonitas (lit: girls pretty-**f-pl**) me·*nee*·nash boo·*nee*·tash

Adverbs are normally formed by adding *-mente* ·*meng*·te to the end of the feminine form of the adjective.

~ ADJECTIVE ~			~ ADVERB ~		
clear	clara f	*klaa*·ra	**clearly**	claramente	*klaa*·ra·*meng*·te
slow	lenta f	*leng*·ta	**slowly**	lentamente	*leng*·ta·*meng*·te

Articles

Naming People/Things

The Portuguese words *um* oong and *uma* oo·ma correspond to the English article 'a/an'. If what you're referring to is masculine you use *um*, if it's feminine you use *uma*. The plurals *uns* oongsh and *umas* oo·mash correspond to the English 'some'.

~ MASCULINE ~		
sg	um café oong ka·*fe*	**a coffee**
pl	uns cafés oongsh ka·*fesh*	**some coffees**

~ FEMININE ~		
sg	uma sandes oo·ma *sang*·desh	**a sandwich**
pl	umas sandes oo·mash *sang*·desh	**some sandwiches**

There are four words that correspond to the English article 'the'. The form you use is determined by the gender and number of the noun the article is used with (see overleaf).

See also **gender** and **plurals**.

~ MASCULINE ~		
sg	o comboio oo kong-*boy*-oo	the train
pl	os comboios oosh kong-*boy*-oosh	the trains
~ FEMININE ~		
sg	a mochila a moo-*shee*-la	the backpack
pl	as mochilas ash moo-*shee*-lash	the backpacks

Be

Describing People/Things • Doing Things • Indicating
Location • Pointing Things Out

Portuguese has two words which can be translated as 'be' in
English: *ser* ser and *estar* shtaar. They're both irregular verbs
(just like 'be' in English) so you need to learn the various forms
they take by heart. Learning to use them perfectly will take
some time and effort, but the basic difference in their usage
isn't too difficult to grasp.

The verb *ser* refers to states that have a degree of perma-
nency or durability about them.

You also use *ser* to point something out in Portuguese. Just
start your phrase with *É* ... e ... (lit: it-is ...) as in the example
below. See also **demonstratives** and **there is/are**.

That's a beautiful building.	É um edifício lindo. (lit: it-is a-**m-sg** building beautiful-**m-sg**) e oong ee-dee-*fee*-syoo *leeng*-do

~ SER – PRESENT TENSE ~

I	am	eu	sou	e·oo	soh
you sg inf	are	tu	és	too	esh
you sg pol	are	você	é	vo·se	e
he	is	ele	é	e·le	e
she	is	ela	é	e·la	e
we	are	nós	somos	nosh	so·moosh
you pl inf	are	vocês	são	vo·sesh	sowng
you pl pol	are	vós	sois	vosh	soysh
they m/f	are	eles/elas	são	e·lesh/e·lash	sowng

The verb *estar* generally refers to events which are temporary in nature. It's also used to talk about the location of things that are moveable.

~ ESTAR – PRESENT TENSE ~

I	am	eu	estou	e·oo	shtoh
you sg inf	are	tu	estás	too	shtaash
you sg pol	are	você	está	vo·se	shtaa
he	is	ele	está	e·le	shtaa
she	is	ela	está	e·la	shtaa
we	are	nós	estamos	nos	shta·moosh
you pl inf	are	vocês	estão	vo·sesh	shtowng
you pl pol	are	vós	estais	vosh	shtaish
they m/f	are	eles/elas	estão	e·lesh/e·lash	shtowng

Demonstratives

Describing People/Things • Indicating Location • Pointing Things Out • Giving Instructions

To refer to or point at a person or object, use one of the following words before the noun, depending on whether the person or object you're referring to is close or further away, masculine or feminine, and singular or plural.

	~ SINGULAR ~		~ PLURAL ~	
	m	**f**	**m**	**f**
this (close)	este *esh·*te	esta *esh·*ta	estes *esh·*tesh	estas *esh·*tash
that (away)	aquele *a·ke·*le	aquela *a·ke·*la	aqueles *a·ke·*lesh	aquelas *a·ke·*lash

Is this seat free?	Este lugar está livre? (lit: this-m-sg place is free-sg) *esh·*te loo·*gaar* shtaa *lee·*vre

These words can also be used on their own, without an accompanying noun, meaning 'this (one)', 'that (one)', 'these' and 'those'.

Those are Portuguese.	Aqueles são portugueses. (lit: those-m-pl are Portuguese-pl) *a·ke·*lesh sowng poor·too·*ge·*zesh

Gender

Naming People/Things

All Portuguese nouns are either masculine **m** or feminine **f**. This determines the endings on any adjectives you use to describe them, as well as which forms of the Portuguese equivalents of the articles 'a/an' and 'the' are used.

The gender that a given noun takes is often arbitrary: there's no reason why, for example, the noun *sol* sol (sun) is masculine while *praia* prai·a (beach) is feminine. The dictionaries and word lists in this book indicate gender for nouns, but here are some guidelines for taking a guess at gender if you need to:

» nouns referring to male persons or animals, and those ending in -*o*, -*ema* or -*oma* are usually masculine
» nouns referring to female persons or animals, and those ending in -*a* or -*dade* are usually feminine

See also **articles** and **adjectives & adverbs**.

Have

Possessing

An easy way to indicate possession is to use the verb *ter* ter (have), which has different forms for each person.

~ *TER* – PRESENT TENSE ~					
I	**have**	eu	tenho	e·oo	ta·nyoo
you sg inf	**have**	tu	tens	too	tengsh
you sg pol	**have**	você	tem	vo·se	teng
he	**has**	ele	tem	e·le	teng
she	**has**	ela	tem	e·la	teng
we	**have**	nós	temos	nosh	te·moosh
you pl inf	**have**	vocês	têm	vo·sesh	teng·eng
you pl pol	**have**	vós	tendes	vosh	teng·desh
they m/f	**have**	eles/elas	têm	e·lesh/e·lash	teng·eng

Negatives

Negating

To make a sentence negative, just add the word *não* nowng
(no) before the main verb – in the example below, the verb is
vejo ve·zhoo (see).

I see the market.	Vejo o mercado.
	(lit: I-see the-**m-sg** market)
	ve·zhoo oo mer·*kaa*·doo
I don't see the market.	Não vejo o mercado.
	(lit: no I-see the-**m-sg** market)
	nowng ve·*zhoo* oo mer·*kaa*·doo

In Portuguese, the double negative is not only acceptable, but
correct:

| **I can't see anything.** | Não vejo nada. (lit: no I-see nothing) |
| | nowng ve·zhoo *naa*·da |

See also **there is/are**.

Personal Pronouns

Doing Things • Naming People/Things

Subject pronouns corresponding to 'I', 'you' etc are often left
out in Portuguese, as the verb endings make it clear what the
subject is. You only need to use them if you want to empha-
sise who or what is doing the action. You'll also notice that
there are polite and informal versions of 'you' (marked with
pol and **inf**). The polite version, combined with a verb in the
third person singular (he/she), is used with people older than
you or those you don't know very well. In this book we've used
the form that best suits the context – generally this means the
polite form unless the phrase is marked otherwise.

~ SUBJECT PRONOUNS ~

I	eu	e·oo	**we**	nós	nosh
you sg inf	tu	too	**you** pl inf	vocês	vo·sesh
you sg pol	você	vo·se	**you** pl pol	vós	vosh
he	ele	e·le	**they** m	eles	e·lesh
she	ela	e·la	**they** f	elas	e·lash

The direct object pronouns corresponding to 'me', 'you' and so on are listed below.

~ DIRECT OBJECT PRONOUNS ~

me	me	me	**us**	nos	noosh
you sg inf	te	te	**you** pl inf	vos	voosh
you sg pol m/f	o/a	oo/a	**you** pl pol m/f	os/as	oosh/ash
him	o	oo	**them** m	os	oosh
her	a	a	**them** f	as	ash

Plurals

Naming People/Things

If a noun ends in a vowel, you can make it plural by simply adding -s sh.

~ SINGULAR ~		~ PLURAL ~	
book	livro m *lee·vroo*	**books**	livros m *lee·vroosh*
bed	cama f *ka·ma*	**beds**	camas f *ka·mash*

If a noun ends in -s, -z or -r and the final syllable is stressed, the plural is formed by adding -es esh.

~ SINGULAR ~		~ PLURAL ~	
Portuguese	português poor·too·*gesh*	**Portuguese**	portugueses poor·too·*ge*·zesh
nose	nariz na·*reesh*	**noses**	narizes na·*ree*·zesh
flower	flor flor	**flowers**	flores *flo*·resh

Don't forget, you have to change any articles and adjectives you use with a plural noun to their plural forms too.

See also **articles**, **adjectives & adverbs** and **gender**.

Possessives

Naming People/Things • Possessing

There are various ways to indicate possession in Portuguese, for example by using the verb *ter* (see **have**). Simplest of all is to use the preposition *de* de (of), followed by the name of the person who owns the object.

It's Carla's backpack.
    É a mochila da Carla.
    (lit: it-is the-**f-sg** backpack of-**f-sg** Carla)
    e a moo·*shee*·la da *kaar*·la

Also, as you do in English, you can indicate possession using pronouns. The table opposite lists the equivalents for the English possessive adjectives 'my', 'your' and 'our'. They are placed between the article and the noun they describe, and agree in number (singular or plural) and gender (masculine or feminine) with the noun.

It's my ticket.
    É o meu bilhete.
    (lit: it-is the-**m-sg** my-**m-sg** ticket)
    e oo *me*·oo bee·*lye*·te

	~ SINGULAR NOUN ~		~ PLURAL NOUN ~	
	m	**f**	**m**	**f**
my	meu *me·oo*	minha *mee·nya*	meus *me·oosh*	minhas *mee·nyash*
your sg inf	teu *te·oo*	tua *too·a*	teus *te·oosh*	tuas *too·ash*
your sg pol	seu *se·oo*	sua *soo·a*	seus *se·oosh*	suas *soo·ash*
our	nosso *no·soo*	nossa *no·sa*	nossos *no·soosh*	nossas *no·sash*
your pl	vosso *vo·soo*	vossa *vo·sa*	vossos *vo·soos*	vossas *vo·sash*

For the equivalents of 'his', 'her' and 'their', it's a bit different. The adjective goes after the noun, and the gender and number match the owner rather than the noun they describe – eg 'her book' is *o livro dela* oo *lee*·vroo *de*·la (lit: the-**m-sg** book her).

his	dele	*de*·le	**their** m	deles	*de*·lesh
her	dela	*de*·la	**their** f	delas	*de*·lash

See also **gender** and **articles**.

Prepositions

Giving Instructions • Indicating Location • Pointing Things Out

Prepositions in Portuguese can be placed before the noun – eg *com leite* kong *lay*·te (with milk) – or after verbs. Here are some common prepositions:

	~ PREPOSITIONS ~			
between	entre	*eng*·tre	**over**	por cima de	poor *see*·ma de
to/for	para	*pa*·ra	**under**	debaixo de	de·*bai*·shoo de
until	até	*a*·te	**with**	com	kong

Some other prepositions have a standard form, but when they come before an article they combine with the article (which agrees in gender and number with the noun it goes with). 'In the rooms', for example, is *nos quartos* noosh *kwaar·*toosh – *nos* is a combination of *em* eng (in) and *os* oosh (the-m-pl).

	STANDARD FORM	m sg	f sg	m pl	f pl
by/for	*por* por	pelo *pe·*loo	pela *pe·*la	pelos *pe·*loosh	pelas *pe·*lash
in/on	*em* eng	no noo	na na	nos noosh	nas nash
of/from	*de* de	do doo	da da	dos doosh	das dash
to	*a* a	ao ow	à aa	aos owsh	às aash

See also **articles** and **gender**.

Questions

Asking Questions

To ask a question, simply make a statement but raise your voice inquisitively at the end of the sentence, as you would in English.

Do you speak Portuguese?	Fala português? (lit: you-speak-sg-inf Portuguese) *faa·*la poor·too·*gesh*

You can also use one of the question words from the table opposite. They go at the beginning of the sentence, just like in English.

~ QUESTION WORDS ~

How?	Como?	ko·moo
How much?	Quanto?	kwang·too
How many?	Quantos? **m pl** Quantas? **f pl**	kwang·toosh kwang·tash
What?	Quê?	ke
What/Which?	Qual?	kwaal
Where?	Onde?	ong·de
Who?	Quem?	keng
Why?	Porquê?	poor·ke

There Is/Are

Indicating Location • Negating • Pointing Things Out

To say 'there is' or 'there are' in Portuguese, use *há* aa (lit: it-has). Add *não* nowng (no) before *há* to make a negative sentence.

There's a seat available.	Há um lugar vago. (lit: it-has a-**m-sg** seat free-**m-sg**) aa oong loo·*gaar vaa*·goo
There aren't any seats available.	Não há lugares vagos. (lit: no it-has seats free-**m-pl**) nowng aa loo·*gaa*·resh *vaa*·goosh

See also **be**.

Verbs

Asking Questions • Doing Things • Giving Instructions • Making Requests

Portuguese has three types of verbs: those ending in *-ar* aar (*morar* mor·*aar*, 'live'), those ending in *-er* er (*comer* koo·*mer*, 'eat') and those ending in *-ir* eer (*partir* par·*teer*, 'leave'). The present tense verb endings for each person ('I', 'you', 'we' etc) are very similar for all three, so you can recognise them easily.

	~ -AR ~	~ -ER ~	~ -IR ~
I	-o ·oo	-o ·oo	-o ·oo
you sg inf	-a ·ash	-es ·esh	-es ·esh
you sg pol	-a ·a	-e ·e	-e ·e
he/she	-a ·a	-e ·e	-e ·e
we	-amos ·a·moosh	-emos ·e·moosh	-imos ·ee·moosh
you pl pol	-ais ·aish	-eis ·aysh	-is ·eesh
you pl inf	-am ·owng	-em ·eng	-em ·eng
they	-am ·owng	-em ·eng	-em ·eng

As in any language, some Portuguese verbs are irregular. The most important ones are *ser* ser (be), *estar* shtaar (be) and *ter* ter (have). For more details see **be** and **have**.

Word Order

Doing Things • Giving Instructions • Making Requests

Generally, the order of words in a sentence is the same as in English (subject–verb–object).

I'd like a room.   Eu queria um quarto.
(lit: I would-like a-**m-sg** room)
e·oo ke·*ree*·a oong *kwaar*·too

Basics

BASICS **UNDERSTANDING**

Understanding

KEY PHRASES

Do you speak English?	Fala inglês?	*faa*·la eeng·*glesh*
I don't understand.	Não entendo.	nowng eng·*teng*·doo
What does ... mean?	O que quer dizer ...?	oo ke ker dee·*zer* ...

Q Do you speak (English)?
Fala (inglês)?
faa·la (eeng·*glesh*)

Q Does anyone speak (English)?
Alguém aqui fala (inglês)?
aal·*geng* a·*kee faa*·la (eeng·*glesh*)

A I speak (English).
Falo (inglês).
faa·loo (eeng·*glesh*)

A I don't speak (Portuguese).
Não falo (português).
nowng *faa*·loo (poor·too·*gesh*)

A I speak a little.
Falo um pouco.
faa·loo oong *poh*·koo

Q Do you understand (me)?
Entende(-me)?
eng·*teng*·de(·me)

A Yes, I understand.
Sim, entendo.
seeng eng·*teng*·doo

A No, I don't understand.
Não, não entendo.
nowng nowng eng·*teng*·doo

Pardon?
Desculpe?
desh·*kool*·pe

BASICS

UNDERSTANDING

> **LANGUAGE TIP**
>
> **False Friends**
> You can often guess the meaning of Portuguese words, as many are similar to English. But things aren't always what they seem:

constipação	kong·shtee·pa·sowng	headcold (not 'constipation')
depressa	de·pre·sa	fast (not 'depressed')
massa	maa·sa	noodles (not 'Catholic Mass')

What does ... mean?	O que quer dizer ...? oo ke ker dee·zer ...
How do you pronounce this?	Como é que se pronuncia isto? ko·moo e ke se proo·noong·see·a eesh·too
How do you write ...?	Como é que se escreve ...? ko·moo e ke se shkre·ve ...
Could you please repeat that?	Podia repetir isto, por favor? poo·dee·a rre·pe·teer eesh·too poor fa·vor
Could you please write it down?	Podia escrever isso, por favor? poo·dee·a shkre·ver ee·soo poor fa·vor
Could you please speak more slowly?	Podia falar mais devagar, por favor? poo·dee·a fa·laar maish de·va·gaar poor fa·vor

✂	**Slowly, please!**	Devagar, por favor!	de·va·gaar poor fa·vor

Numbers & Amounts

BASICS

NUMBERS & AMOUNTS

KEY PHRASES

How much?	Quanto?	*kwang·too*
a little	um bocadinho	oong boo·ka·*dee*·nyoo
a lot	muito	*mweeng·too*

Cardinal Numbers

0	zero	*ze*·roo
1	um	oong
2	dois	doysh
3	três	tresh
4	quatro	*kwaa*·troo
5	cinco	*seeng*·koo
6	seis	saysh
7	sete	*se*·te
8	oito	*oy*·too
9	nove	*no*·ve
10	dez	desh
11	onze	*ong*·ze
12	doze	*do*·ze
13	treze	*tre*·ze
14	catorze	ka·*tor*·ze
15	quinze	*keeng*·ze
16	dezasseis	de·za·*saysh*
17	dezassete	de·za·*se*·te

18	dezoito	de·*zoy*·too
19	dezanove	de·za·*no*·ve
20	vinte	*veeng*·te
21	vinte e um	*veeng*·te e oong
22	vinte e dois	*veeng*·te e doysh
30	trinta	*treeng*·ta
40	quarenta	kwa·*reng*·ta
50	cinquenta	seeng·*kweng*·ta
60	sessenta	se·*seng*·ta
70	setenta	se·*teng*·ta
80	oitenta	oy·*teng*·ta
90	noventa	no·*veng*·ta
100	cem	seng
200	duzentos	doo·*zeng*·toosh
300	trezentos	tre·*zeng*·toosh
1000	mil	meel
1,000,000	um milhão	oong mee·*lyowng*

Ordinal Numbers

Ordinal numbers are written with a degree sign in Portuguese – 1st is written *1º*, 10th is *10º*, and so on.

1st	primeiro m	pree·*may*·roo
	primeira f	pree·*may*·ra
2nd	segundo m	se·*goong*·doo
	segunda f	se·*goong*·da
3rd	terceiro m	ter·*say*·roo
	terceira f	ter·*say*·ra
4th	quarto m	*kwaar*·too
	quarta f	*kwaar*·ta
5th	quinto m	*keeng*·too
	quinta f	*keeng*·ta

Fractions & Decimals

a quarter	um quarto	oong *kwaar*·too
a third	um terço	oong *ter*·soo
a half	a metade	a me·*taa*·de
three-quarters	três quartos	tresh *kwaar*·toosh

In Portugal, decimals are written – and pronounced – as in English, except that the period is replaced by a comma (*vírgula veer*·goo·la).

3.14	três vírgula catorze (3,14)	tresh *veer*·goo·la ka·*tor*·ze

Amounts

How much?	Quanto? *kwang*·too
How many?	Quantos? m pl *kwang*·toosh Quantas? f pl *kwang*·tash
Please give me ...	Por favor dê-me ... poor fa·*vor* de·me ...

a few	uns	oongsh
	poucos m pl	*poh*·koosh
	umas	oo·mash
	poucas f pl	*poh*·kash
(just) a little	(só) um	(so) oong
	bocadinho	boo·ka·*dee*·nyoo
a lot	muito	*mweeng*·too
less	menos	me·noosh
many	muitos m pl	*mweeng*·toosh
	muitas f pl	*mweeng*·tash
more	mais	maish
some	uns m pl	oongsh
	umas f pl	oo·mash

BASICS NUMBERS & AMOUNTS

Time & Dates

KEY PHRASES

What time is it?	Que horas são?	kee o·rash sowng
At what time ...?	A que horas ...?	a ke o·rash ...
What date?	Qual data?	kwaal daa·ta

Telling the Time

Generally, the 12-hour clock is used for telling the time in Portuguese, though the 24-hour clock is often what you'll see written down.

Q What time is it?	Que horas são?	kee o·rash sowng
A It's (one) o'clock.	É (uma) hora.	e (oo·ma) o·ra
A It's (10) o'clock.	São (dez) horas.	sowng (desh) o·rash
A Five past (10).	(Dez) e cinco.	(desh) e seeng·koo
A Quarter past (10).	(Dez) e quinze.	(desh) e keeng·ze
A Half past (10).	(Dez) e meia.	(desh) e may·a
A Quarter to (11).	Quinze para as (onze).	keeng·ze pa·ra ash (ong·ze)
am	da manhã	da ma·nyang
pm (afternoon)	da tarde	da taar·de
pm (evening)	da noite	da noy·te

Q At what time...?	A que horas ...?	a ke o·rash ...
A At (one).	À (uma).	aa (oo·ma)
A At (five).	Às (cinco).	aash (seeng·koo)
A At (7.57pm).	Às (sete e cinquenta e sete da noite).	aash (se·te e seeng·kweng·ta e se·te da noy·te)
afternoon	tarde f	taar·de
dawn	madrugada f	ma·droo·gaa·da
day	dia m	dee·a
evening	noite f	noy·te
midday	meio dia m	may·oo dee·a
midnight	meia noite f	may·a noy·te
morning	manhã f	ma·nyang
night	noite f	noy·te
sunrise	nascer do sol m	nash·ser doo sol
sunset	pôr do sol m	por doo sol

The Calendar

Monday	segunda-feira f	se·goong·da·fay·ra
Tuesday	terça-feira f	ter·sa·fay·ra
Wednesday	quarta-feira f	kwaar·ta·fay·ra
Thursday	quinta-feira f	keeng·ta·fay·ra
Friday	sexta-feira f	saysh·ta·fay·ra
Saturday	sábado m	saa·ba·doo
Sunday	domingo m	doo·meeng·goo

January	Janeiro m	zha·*nay*·roo
February	Fevereiro m	fe·*vray*·roo
March	Março m	*maar*·soo
April	Abril m	a·*breel*
May	Maio m	*maa*·yoo
June	Junho m	*zhoo*·nyoo
July	Julho m	*zhoo*·lyoo
August	Agosto m	a·*gosh*·too
September	Setembro m	se·*teng*·broo
October	Outubro m	oh·*too*·broo
November	Novembro m	no·*veng*·broo
December	Dezembro m	de·*zeng*·broo

What date?	Qual data?	kwaal *daa*·ta
Q What date is it today?	Qual é a data de hoje?	kwaal e a *daa*·ta de o·zhe
A It's (18 October).	Hoje é dia (dezoito de Outubro).	o·zhe e *dee*·a (de·*zoy*·too de oh·*too*·broo)
spring	primavera f	pree·ma·*ve*·ra
summer	verão m	ve·*rowng*
autumn/fall	outono m	oh·*to*·noo
winter	inverno m	eeng·*ver*·noo

Present

now	agora	a·*go*·ra
today	hoje	o·zhe
tonight	hoje à noite	o·zhe aa *noy*·te
this morning	esta manhã	*esh*·ta ma·*nyang*

this afternoon	esta tarde	esh·ta taar·de
this week	esta semana	esh·ta se·ma·na
this month	este mês	esh·te mesh
this year	este ano	esh·te a·noo

Past

day before yesterday	anteontem	ang·tee·ong·teng
(three days) ago	há (três dias)	aa (tresh dee·ash)
since (May)	desde (Maio)	desh·de (maa·yoo)
last night	a noite passada	a noy·te pa·saa·da
last week	a semana passada	a se·ma·na pa·saa·da
last month	o mês passado	oo mesh pa·saa·doo
last year	o ano passado	oo a·noo pa·saa·doo
yesterday morning	ontem de manhã	ong·teng de ma·nyang
yesterday afternoon	ontem à tarde	ong·teng aa taar·de
yesterday evening	ontem à noite	ong·teng aa noy·te

Future

day after tomorrow	depois de amanhã	de·poysh de aa·ma·nyang
in (six days)	daqui à (seis dias)	da·kee a (saysh dee·ash)
until (June)	até (Junho)	a·te (zhoo·nyoo)

next week	na próxima semana	na *pro*·see·ma se·*ma*·na
next month	no próximo mês	noo *pro*·see·moo mesh
next year	no próximo ano	noo *pro*·see·moo *a*·noo
tomorrow morning	amanhã de manhã	aa·ma·*nyang* de ma·*nyang*
tomorrow afternoon	amanhã à tarde	aa·ma·*nyang* aa *taar*·de
tomorrow evening	amanhã à noite	aa·ma·*nyang* aa *noy*·te

BASICS TIME & DATES

🔍 LOOK FOR

Aberto	a·*ber*·too	Open
Casa de Banho	*kaa*·za de *ba*·nyoo	Toilets/WC
Entrada	eng·*traa*·da	Entrance
Fechado	fe·*shaa*·doo	Closed
Homens	o·mengsh	Men
Informação	eeng·for·ma·*sowng*	Information
Mulheres	moo·*lye*·resh	Women
Não Fotografar	nowng foo·too·gra·*faar*	No Photography
Não Fumar	nowng foo·*maar*	No Smoking
Proibido	pro·ee·*bee*·doo	Prohibited
Saída	sa·ee·da	Exit

BASICS · TIME & DATES

Public Holidays

New Year's Day	Dia de Ano Novo	*dee·a de a·noo no·voo*
Mardi Gras	Carnaval	*kar·na·vaal*
Good Friday	Sexta-feira Santa	*sesh·ta·fay·ra sang·ta*
Liberation Day (25 April)	Dia da Liberdade	*dee·a da lee·ber·daa·de*
Labour Day (1 May)	Dia do Trabalhador	*dee·a doo tra·ba·lya·dor*
Corpus Christi	Corpo de Deus	*kor·poo de de·oosh*
Portugal Day (10 June)	Dia de Portugal	*dee·a de poor·too·gaal*
Assumption (15 August)	Assunção de Nossa Senhora	*aa·soong·sowng de no·sa se·nyo·ra*
Republic Day (5 October)	Implantação da República	*eeng·plang·ta·sowng da rre·poo·blee·ka*
All Saints' Day (1 November)	Dia de Todos-os-Santos	*dee·a de to·doosh·oosh·sang·toosh*
Independence Restoration Day (1 December)	Restauração da Indepen-dência	*resh·tow·ra·sowng da eeng·de·peng·deng·sya*
Immaculate Conception (8 December)	Imaculada Conceição	*ee·ma·koo·laa·da kong·say·sowng*
Christmas Day (25 December)	Natal	*na·taal*

For some holiday greetings in Portuguese, see **well-wishing** (p119).

Practical

Transport

KEY PHRASES

When's the next bus?	Quando é que sai o próximo autocarro?	*kwang·doo e ke sai oo pro·see·moo ow·to·kaa·rroo*
A ticket to ...	Um bilhete para ...	*oong bee·lye·te pa·ra ...*
Please tell me when we get to ...	Por favor avise-me quando chegamos a ...	*poor fa·vor a·vee·ze·me kwang·doo she·ga·moosh a ...*
Please take me to this address.	Leve-me para este endereço, por favor.	*le·ve·me pa·ra esh·te eng·de·re·soo poor fa·vor*
I'd like to hire a car.	Queria alugar um carro.	*ke·ree·a a·loo·gaar oong kaa·rroo*

Getting Around

Which ... goes to (Lisbon)?	Qual é o ... que vai para (Lisboa)? *kwaal e oo ... ke vai pra (leezh·bo·a)*
Is this the ... to (Peniche)?	Este é o ... para (Peniche)? *esh·te e oo ... pra (pe·neesh)*

boat	barco	*baar·koo*
bus	autocarro	*ow·to·kaa·rroo*
train	comboio	*kong·boy·oo*
tram	eléctrico	*e·le·tree·koo*

When's the first (bus)?	Quando é que sai o primeiro (autocarro)? *kwang*·doo e ke sai oo pree·*may*·roo (ow·to·*kaa*·rroo)
When's the last (bus)?	Quando é que sai o último (autocarro)? *kwang*·doo e ke sai oo *ool*·tee·moo (ow·to·*kaa*·rroo)
When's the next (bus)?	Quando é que sai o próximo (autocarro)? *kwang*·doo e ke sai oo *pro*·see·moo (ow·to·*kaa*·rroo)
Where's the station?	Onde é a estação? *ong*·de e a shta·*sowng*
How long does the trip take?	Quanto tempo é que leva a viagem? *kwang*·too *teng*·poo e ke *le*·va a vee·*aa*·zheng
Is it a direct route?	É uma rota directa? e *oo*·ma *rro*·ta dee·*re*·ta
Does it stop at (Amarante)?	Pára em (Amarante)? *paa*·ra eng (a·ma·*rang*·te)
What time does it get to (Porto)?	A que horas chega ao (Porto)? a ke o·rash *she*·ga ow (*por*·too)
How long will it be delayed?	Quanto tempo é que vai chegar atrasado? *kwang*·too *teng*·poo e ke vai she·*gaar* a·tra·*zaa*·doo
Is this seat available?	Este lugar está vago? *esh*·te loo·*gaar* shtaa *va*·goo

✂	**Is it free?**	Está vago?	shtaa *va*·goo

That's my seat.	Este é o meu lugar. *esh*·te e oo *me*·oo loo·*gaar*
Please tell me when we get to (Évora).	Por favor avise-me quando chegamos a (Évora). poor fa·*vor* a·*vee*·ze·me *kwang*·doo she·*ga*·moosh a (*e*·voo·ra)
I'd like to get off at (Cascais).	Queria sair em (Cascais). ke·*ree*·a sa·*eer* eng (kash·*kaa*·eesh)
How long do we stop here?	Quanto tempo vamos ficar parados aqui? *kwang*·too *teng*·poo va·*moosh* fee·*kaar* pa·*raa*·doosh a·*kee*

Buying Tickets

Where do I buy a ticket?	Onde é que eu compro o bilhete? *ong*·de e ke *e*·oo *kong*·proo oo bee·*lye*·te
Where's the ticket machine?	Onde está a bilheteira automática? *ong*·de shtaa a bee·lye·*tay*·ra ow·too·*maa*·tee·ka
Do I need to book (very far in advance)?	Preciso de fazer reserva (muito antecipada)? pre·*see*·zoo de fa·*zer* rre·*zer*·va (*mweeng*·too ang·te·see·*paa*·da)
Can I get a stand-by ticket?	Posso comprar um bilhete de última hora? *po*·soo kong·*praar* oong bee·*lye*·te de *ool*·tee·ma *o*·ra

Buying a Ticket

What time is the next ...?

Quando é que sai o próximo ...?
kwang·doo e ke sai oo pro·see·moo ...

boat
barco
baar·koo

bus
autocarro
ow·to·kaa·rroo

train
comboio
kong·boy·oo

One ... ticket, please.

Um bilhete ..., por favor.
oong bee·lye·te ... poor fa·vor

one-way
de ida
de ee·da

return
de ida e volta
de ee·da ee vol·ta

I'd like a/an ... seat.

Queria um lugar ...
ke·ree·a oong loo·gaar ...

aisle
na coxia
na koo·shee·a

window
à janela
aa zha·ne·la

Which platform does it depart from?

Em qual plataforma parte?
eng kwaal pla·ta·for·ma paar·te

A ... ticket (to Braga).
Um bilhete de ...
(para Braga).
oong bee·*lye*·te de ...
(pra *braa*·ga)

1st-class	primeira classe	pree·*may*·ra *klaa*·se
2nd-class	segunda classe	se·*goong*·da *klaa*·se
child's	criança	kree·*ang*·sa
one-way	ida	ee·da
return	ida e volta	ee·da ee *vol*·ta
student	estudante	shtoo·*dang*·te

I'd like a/an ... seat.
Queria um lugar ...
ke·*ree*·a oong loo·*gaar* ...

aisle	na coxia	na koo·*shee*·a
nonsmoking	de não fumadores	de nowng foo·ma·*do*·resh
smoking	para fumadores	pra foo·ma·*do*·resh
window	à janela	aa zha·*ne*·la

Is there (a) ...?
Tem ...?
teng ...

air-conditioning	ar condicionado	aar kong·dee·syoo·*naa*·doo
blanket	cobertor	koo·ber·*tor*
sick bag	saco para vomitar	*saa*·koo pra voo·mee·*taar*
toilet	casa de banho	*kaa*·za de *ba*·nyoo

🔊 **LISTEN FOR**

agente de viagens m&f	a·*zheng*·te de vee·*aa*·zhengsh	travel agent
atrasado/ atrasada m/f	a·tra·*zaa*·doo/ a·tra·*zaa*·da	delayed
bilheteira f	bee·lye·*tay*·ra	ticket window
cancelado/ cancelada m/f	kang·se·*laa*·doo/ kang·se·*laa*·da	cancelled
cheio/cheia m/f	*shay*·oo/*shay*·a	full
horário m	o·*raa*·ryoo	timetable
plataforma f	pla·ta·*for*·ma	platform

I'd like to cancel my ticket, please.	Queria cancelar o bilhete, por favor. ke·*ree*·a kang·se·*laar* oo bee·*lye*·te poor fa·*vor*
I'd like to change my ticket, please.	Queria trocar o bilhete, por favor. ke·*ree*·a troo·*kaar* oo bee·*lye*·te poor fa·*vor*
I'd like to confirm my ticket, please.	Queria confirmar o bilhete, por favor. ke·*ree*·a kong·feer·*maar* oo bee·*lye*·te poor fa·*vor*
Can I get a sleeping berth?	Tem carruagem cama? teng ka·rroo·*aa*·zheng *ka*·ma
What time should I check in?	A que horas devo fazer o check-in? a ke o·rash *de*·voo fa·*zer* oo *shek*·eeng

Luggage

Where can I find a/the ...?	Onde fica ...?	*ong*·de *fee*·ka ...
baggage claim	o balcão de bagagens	oo bal·*kowng* de ba·*gaa*·zhengsh
lost and found office	o balcão de perdidos e achados	oo bal·*kowng* de per·*dee*·doosh e a·*shaa*·doosh
luggage locker	o depósito de bagagens	oo de·*po*·zee·too de ba·*gaa*·zhengsh
trolley	um carrinho	oong ka·*rree*·nyoo

Can I have some coins/tokens?
Pode-me dar umas moedas/fichas?
po·de·me daar *oo*·mash mo·e·dash/*fee*·shash

My luggage has been damaged.
A minha bagagem foi danificada.
a *mee*·nya ba·*gaa*·zheng foy da·nee·fee·*kaa*·da

My luggage has been lost.
A minha bagagem perdeu-se.
a *mee*·nya ba·*gaa*·zheng per·*de*·oo·se

My luggage has been stolen.
A minha bagagem foi roubada.
a *mee*·nya ba·*gaa*·zheng foy rroh·*baa*·da

That's (not) mine.
Isto (não) é meu.
eesh·too (nowng) e *me*·oo

Bus, Coach & Tram

Is this a bus/tram stop?	Isto é uma paragem de autocarro/eléctrico? *eesh·too e oo·ma pa·raa·zheng de ow·to·kaa·rroo/e·le·tree·koo*
How do I get to the bus terminal?	Como posso chegar á rodoviária? *ko·moo po·soo she·gaar aa rroo·doo·vee·aa·ree·a*
How often do buses/ trams come?	Qual é a frequência dos autocarros/eléctricos? *kwaal e a fre·kweng·sya doosh ow·to·kaa·rroosh/ e·le·tree·koosh*
What's the next stop?	Qual é a próxima paragem? *kwaal e a pro·see·ma pa·raa·zheng*
city bus	autocarro da cidade m *ow·to·kaa·rroo da see·daa·de*
departure bay	portão de embarque m *poor·towng de eng·baar·ke*

PRACTICAL   TRANSPORT

🔍 LOOK FOR

Bilheteira	bee·lye·tay·ra	Ticket Booth
Chegadas	she·gaa·dash	Arrivals
Depósito de Bagagens	de·po·zee·too de ba·gaa·zhengsh	Luggage Check-In
Embarque	eng·baar·ke	Departure
Gare de Embarque	gaa·re de eng·baar·ke	Boarding Area
Passageiros	pa·sa·zhay·roosh	Passengers
Sala de Espera	saa·la de shpe·ra	Waiting Room

intercity bus	autocarro inter-cidades m ow·to·*kaa*·rroo eeng·ter·see·*daa*·desh
local bus	autocarro local m ow·to·*kaa*·rroo loo·*kaal*
(hotel) shuttle bus	carrinha do hotel f ka·*rree*·nya doo o·*tel*
timetable display	horário de partidas e chegadas m o·*raa*·ryoo de par·*tee*·dash e she·*gaa*·dash

For bus numbers, see **numbers & amounts** (p30).

Train

What station is this?	Qual estação é este? kwaal shta·*sowng* e *esh*·te
What's the next station?	Qual é a próxima estação? kwaal e a *pro*·see·ma shta·*sowng*
Do I need to change?	Preciso de mudar de comboio? pre·*see*·soo de moo·*daar* de kong·*boy*·oo
Which carriage is (for) ...?	Qual é a carruagem ...? kwaal e a ka·rroo·*aa*·zheng ...

1st class	de primeira classe	de pree·*may*·ra *klaa*·se
2nd class	de segunda classe	de se·*goong*·da *klaa*·se
dining	restaurante	rresh·tow·*rang*·te
(Faro)	para o (Faro)	pra oo (*fa*·roo)

Taxi

I'd like a taxi at (9am).	Queria chamar um táxi para as (nove da manhã). ke·*ree*·a sha·*maar* oong *taak*·see pra ash (*no*·ve da ma·*nyang*)
I'd like a taxi tomorrow.	Queria chamar um táxi amanhã. ke·*ree*·a sha·*maar* oong *taak*·see aa·ma·*nyang*
Where's the taxi rank?	Onde é a praça de táxis? *ong*·de e a *praa*·sa de *taak*·seesh

Qual é a próxima paragem?
kwaal e a *pro*·see·ma pa·*raa*·zheng
What's the next stop?

PRACTICAL TRANSPORT

Is this taxi available?	Este táxi está livre?	
	esh·te taak·see shtaa lee·vre	
✂ **Is it free?**	Está livre?	*shtaa lee·vre*
How much is it (to Silves)?	Quanto custa (até ao Silves)?	
	kwang·too koosh·ta (a·te ow seel·vesh)	
How much is the flag fall/ hiring charge?	Quanto custa a bandeirada base?	
	kwang·too koosh·ta a bang·day·raa·da baa·ze	
Please take me to (this address).	Leve-me para (este endereço), por favor.	
	le·ve·me pa·ra (esh·te eng·de·re·soo) poor fa·vor	
✂ **To ...**	Para ...	*pa·ra ...*
I don't want to pay a flat fare.	Eu não quero pagar uma tarifa estipulada.	
	e·oo nowng ke·roo pa·gaar oo·ma ta·ree·fa shtee·poo·laa·da	
Please ...	Por favor ...	*poor fa·vor ...*

come back at (10am)	volte (às dez da manhã)	*vol·te (aash desh da ma·nyang)*
slow down	vá mais devagar	*vaa maish de·va·gaar*
stop here	pare aqui	*paa·re a·kee*
wait here	espere aqui	*shpe·re a·kee*

For other useful phrases, see **directions** (p58), and **money & banking** (p92).

Car & Motorbike

I'd like to hire a/an ... car.	Queria alugar um carro ... ke·*ree*·a a·loo·*gaar* oong *kaa*·rroo ...

4WD	com tracção às quatro rodas	kong traa·*sowng* aash *kwaa*·troo *rro*·dash
automatic	de mudanças automáticas	de moo·*dang*·sash ow·too·maa·*tee*·kash
manual	de mudanças manuais	de moo·*dang*·sash ma·noo·*aish*

I'd like to hire a motorbike.	Queria alugar uma mota. ke·*ree*·a a·loo·*gaar* oo·ma *mo*·ta
How much for daily hire?	Quanto custa para alugar por dia? *kwang*·too *koosh*·ta *pa*·ra a·loo·*gaar* poor *dee*·a

PRACTICAL TRANSPORT

🔊 LISTEN FOR

carta de condução f	*kaar*·ta de kong·doo·*sowng*	drivers licence
com ar condicionado	kong aar kong·dee·syoo·naa·doo	with air-conditioning
com motorista	kong moo·too·*reesh*·ta	with a driver
multa f	*mool*·ta	fine
parquímetro m	par·*kee*·me·troo	parking meter
portagem f	por·*taa*·zheng	motorway pass

How much for weekly hire?	Quanto custa para alugar por semana?
	kwang·too koosh·ta pa·ra a·loo·gaar poor se·ma·na
Does that include insurance/mileage?	Inclui seguro/ kilometragem?
	eeng·kloo·ee se·goo·roo/ kee·lo·me·traa·zheng
Do you have a road map?	Tem um mapa de estradas?
	teng oong maa·pa de shtraa·dash
What's the speed limit?	Qual é o limite de velocidade?
	kwaal e oo lee·mee·te de ve·loo·see·daa·de
Is this the road to ...?	Esta é a estrada para ...?
	esh·ta e a shtraa·da pa·ra ...

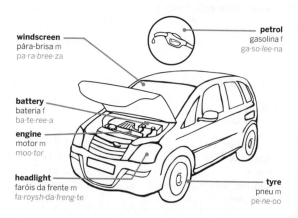

windscreen
pára-brisa m
pa·ra·bree·za

petrol
gasolina f
ga·so·lee·na

battery
bateria f
ba·te·ree·a

engine
motor m
moo·tor

headlight
faróis da frente m
fa·roysh·da·freng·te

tyre
pneu m
pe·ne·oo

🔍 LOOK FOR

diesel m	*dee*·zel	diesel
gás m	gash	LPG
gasolina f **sem chumbo**	ga·zoo·*lee*·na seng *shoong*·boo	unleaded petrol/gas

Where's a petrol/gas station?	Onde fica um posto de gasolina? *ong*·de *fee*·ka oong *posh*·too de ga·zoo·*lee*·na
Please fill it up.	Encha o tanque, por favor. *eng*·sha oo *tang*·ke poor fa·*vor*
(How long) Can I park here?	(Quanto tempo) Posso estacionar aqui? (*kwang*·too *teng*·poo) *po*·soo shta·see·oo·*naar* a·*kee*
Can you check the oil?	Pode verificar o óleo? *po*·de ve·ree·fee·*kaar* oo *o*·le·oo
Can you check the tyre pressure?	Pode verificar os pneus? *po*·de ve·ree·fee·*kaar* oosh pe·*ne*·oosh
Can you check the water?	Pode verificar a água? *po*·de ve·ree·fee·*kaar* a *aa*·gwa
Do I have to pay?	Tenho que pagar? *ta*·nyoo ke pa·*gaar*
I need a mechanic.	Preciso de um mecânico. pre·*see*·zoo de oong me·*kaa*·nee·koo
I've had an accident.	Tive um acidente. *tee*·ve oong a·see·*deng*·te

PRACTICAL TRANSPORT

LOOK FOR

Dar Prioridade	daar pree·oo·ree·*daa*·de	Give Way
Entrada	eng·*traa*·da	Entrance
Pare	*paa*·re	Stop
Portagem	por·*taa*·zheng	Toll
Proibido Entrar	pro·ee·*bee*·doo eng·*traar*	No Entry
Sair da Autoestrada	sa·*eer* da ow·to·*shtraa*·da	Freeway Exit
Sentido Único	seng·*tee*·doo oo·nee·koo	One-Way

The car has broken down (at Setúbal).	O carro avariou-se (em Setúbal). oo *kaa*·rroo a·va·ree·*oh*·se (eng se·*too*·baal)
I've run out of petrol.	Estou sem gasolina. shtoh seng ga·zoo·*lee*·na
Can you fix it (today)?	Pode-se arranjar (hoje)? *po*·de·se a·rrang·*zhaar* (*o*·zhe)
How long will it take?	Quanto tempo vai levar? *kwang*·too *teng*·poo vai le·*vaar*

Bicycle

I'd like my bicycle repaired.	Queria consertar a minha bicicleta. ke·*ree*·aa kong·ser·*taar* a *mee*·nya bee·see·*kle*·ta

I'd like to buy a bicycle.	Queria comprar uma bicicleta. ke·*ree*·aa kong·*praar* oo·ma bee·see·*kle*·ta
I'd like to hire a bicycle.	Queria alugar uma bicicleta. ke·*ree*·aa a·loo·*gaar* oo·ma bee·see·*kle*·ta
I'd like a mountain bike.	Queria uma bicicleta de montanha. ke·*ree*·a oo·ma bee·see·*kle*·ta de mong·*taa*·nya
I'd like a racing bike.	Queria uma bicicleta de corrida. ke·*ree*·a oo·ma bee·see·*kle*·ta de koo·*rree*·da
I'd like a second-hand bike.	Queria uma bicicleta em segunda mão. ke·*ree*·a oo·ma bee·see·*kle*·ta eng se·*goong*·da mowng
How much is it per day/hour?	Quanto custa por dia/hora? *kwang*·too *koosh*·ta poor *dee*·a/o·ra
Do I need a helmet?	Preciso de usar capacete? pre·*see*·soo de oo·*zaar* ka·pa·*se*·te
Are there bicycle paths?	Há trilhos para bicicletas? aa *tree*·lyoosh *pa*·ra bee·see·*kle*·tash
I have a puncture.	Tenho um furo no pneu. *ta*·nyoo oong *foo*·roo noo pe·*ne*·oo

Border Crossing

KEY PHRASES

I'm here for ... days.	Vou ficar por ... dias.	voh fee·*kaar* poor ... *dee*·ash
I'm staying at ...	Estou no ...	shtoh noo ...
I have nothing to declare.	Não tenho nada a declarar.	nowng *ta*·nyoo *naa*·da a de·kla·*raar*

Passport Control

I'm in transit.	Estou em trânsito. shtoh eng *trang*·zee·too
I'm on business.	Estou em negócios. shtoh eng ne·*go*·syoosh
I'm on holiday.	Estou de férias. shtoh de *fe*·ree·ash
I'm here for (10) days.	Vou ficar por (dez) dias. voh fee·*kaar* poor (desh) *dee*·ash
I'm here for (three) weeks.	Vou ficar por (três) semanas. voh fee·*kaar* poor (tresh) se·*ma*·nash

◀)) LISTEN FOR

família f	fa·*mee*·lya	family
grupo m	*groo*·poo	group
passaporte m	paa·sa·*por*·te	passport
visto m	*veesh*·too	visa

🔍 LOOK FOR

Alfândega	aal·*fang*·de·ga	Customs
Controlo de Passaportes	kong·*tro*·loo de paa·sa·*por*·tesh	Passport Control
Imigração	ee·mee·gra·*sowng*	Immigration
Quarentena	kwa·reng·*te*·na	Quarantine

I'm here for (two) months.	Vou ficar por (dois) meses. voh fee·*kaar* poor (doysh) *me*·zesh
I'm going to (Elvas).	Vou para (Elvas). voh *pa*·ra (*el*·vash)
I'm staying at ...	Estou no ... shtoh noo ...

At Customs

I have nothing to declare.	Não tenho nada a declarar. nowng *ta*·nyoo *naa*·da a de·kla·*raar*
I have something to declare.	Tenho algo a declarar. *ta*·nyoo *al*·goo a de·kla·*raar*
That's (not) mine.	Isto (não) é meu. *eesh*·too (nowng) e *me*·oo
Do you have this form in (English)?	Tem este formulário em (inglês)? teng *esh*·te foor·moo·*laa*·ree·oo eng (eeng·*glesh*)
Could I please have an (English) interpreter?	Pode-me arranjar um intérprete de (inglês), por favor? *po*·de·me a·rrang·*zhaar* oong eeng·*ter*·pre·te de (eeng·*glesh*) poor fa·*vor*

Directions

KEY PHRASES

Where's ...?	Onde é ...?	*ong*·de e ...
What's the address?	Qual é o endereço?	kwaal e oo eng·de·re·soo
How far is it?	A que distância fica?	a ke deesh·*tang*·sya *fee*·ka

Q **Where's (the market)?**
Onde é (o mercado)?
ong·de e oo (mer·*kaa*·doo)

A **It's ...**
É ...
e ...

What's the address?
Qual é o endereço?
kwaal e oo eng·de·*re*·soo

What (street) is this?
Que (rua) é isto?
ke (*rroo*·a) e *eesh*·too

How far is it?
A que distância fica?
a ke deesh·*tang*·sya *fee*·ka

Can you show me (on the map)?
Pode-me mostrar (no mapa)?
po·de·me moosh·*traar* (noo *maa*·pa)

north
norte
nor·te

south
sul
sool

east
leste
lesh·te

west
oeste
o·*esh*·te

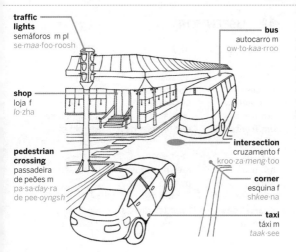

traffic lights
semáforos m pl
se·*maa*·foo·roosh

shop
loja f
lo·zha

pedestrian crossing
passadeira
de peões m
pa·sa·*day*·ra
de pee·*oyngsh*

bus
autocarro m
ow·to·*kaa*·rroo

intersection
cruzamento f
kroo·za·*meng*·too

corner
esquina f
shk*ee*·na

taxi
táxi m
taak·see

PRACTICAL
DIRECTIONS

How do I get there?	Como é que eu chego lá? *ko*·moo e ke e·oo s*he*·goo laa
by bus	de autocarro de ow·to·*kaa*·rroo
by taxi	de táxi de *taak*·see
by train	de comboio de kong·*boy*·oo
by tram	de tram de trang
on foot	a pé a pe

PRACTICAL DIRECTIONS

🔊 LISTEN FOR

ao lado de ...	ow *laa*·doo de ...	next to ...
aqui	a·*kee*	here
atrás de ...	a·*traash* de ...	behind ...
do lado oposto ...	doo *laa*·doo oo·*posh*·too ...	opposite ...
em frente	eng *freng*·te	straight ahead
em frente de ...	eng *freng*·te de ...	in front of ...
lá	laa	there
metros	*me*·troosh	metres
minutos	mee·*noo*·toosh	minutes
perto	*per*·too	close
perto de ...	*per*·too de ...	near ...
quarteirões	kwar·tay·*royngsh*	blocks
quilómetros	kee·*lo*·me·troosh	kilometres

Turn ...	Vire ... *vee*·re ...	
at the corner	na esquina	na *shkee*·na
at the traffic lights	nos semáforos	noosh se·*maa*·foo·roosh
left	à esquerda	aa *shker*·da
right	à direita	aa dee·*ray*·ta

For information on reading Portuguese addresses, see the box on page 132.

Accommodation

KEY PHRASES

Where's a hotel?	Onde é que há um hotel?	*ong*·de e ke aa oong o·*tel*
Do you have a double room?	Tem um quarto de casal?	teng oong *kwaar*·too de ka·*zaal*
How much is it per night?	Quanto custa por noite?	*kwang*·too *koosh*·ta poor *noy*·te
Is breakfast included?	Inclui o pequeno almoço?	eeng·*kloo*·ee oo pe·*ke*·noo aal·*mo*·soo
What time is checkout?	A que horas é a partida?	a ke o·*rash* e a par·*tee*·da

Finding Accommodation

Where's a ...?	Onde é que há ...?
	ong·de e ke aa ...

bed and breakfast	um turismo de habitação	oong too·*reezh*·moo de a·bee·ta·*sowng*
guesthouse	uma casa de hóspedes	*oo*·ma *kaa*·za de *osh*·pe·desh
hotel	um hotel	oong o·*tel*
inn	uma pousada	*oo*·ma poh·*zaa*·da
youth hostel	uma pousada de juventude	*oo*·ma poh·*zaa*·da de zhoo·veng·*too*·de

Can you recommend somewhere ...?	Pode recomendar algum lugar ...? *po·de rre·koo·meng·daar aal·goong loo·gaar ...*	
cheap	barato	ba·*raa*·too
clean	limpo	*leeng*·poo
nearby	perto daqui	*per*·too da·*kee*
safe for women travellers	seguro para viajantes do sexo feminino	se·*goo*·ro pa·ra vee·a·*zhang*·tesh doo sek·soo fe·me·*nee*·noo

I want something near the ...	Eu quero algo perto ... *e·oo ke·roo aal·goo per·too ...*	
beach	da praia	da *prai*·a
city centre	do centro da cidade	doo *sen*·troo da see·*daa*·de
shops	de lojas	de *lo*·zhash
train station	da estação do comboio	da shta·*sowng* doo kong·*boy*·oo

Booking Ahead & Checking In

I'd like to book a room, please.	Eu queria fazer uma reserva, por favor. *e·oo ke·ree·a fa·zer oo·ma rre·zer·va poor fa·vor*

✂ **Are there rooms?**   Tem vaga?   teng *va*·ga

Finding a Room

Do you have a ... room?
Tem um quarto ...?
teng oong kwaar·too ...

double
de casal
de ka·zaal

single
de solteiro
de sol·tay·roo

How much is it per ...?
Quanto custa por ...?
kwang·too koosh·ta poor ...

night
noite
noy·te

person
pessoa
pe·so·a

Is breakfast included?
Inclui o pequeno almoço?
eeng·kloo·ee oo pe·ke·noo aal·mo·soo

Can I see it?
Posso ver?
po·soo ver

I'll take it.
Fico com ele.
fee·koo kong e·le

No, thanks.
Não, obrigado/a. **m/f**
nowng o·bree·gaa·doo/da

I have a reservation.	Eu tenho uma reserva. *e·oo ta·nyoo oo·ma rre·zer·va*
For (three) nights/weeks.	Para (três) noites/ semanas. *pa·ra (tresh) noy·tesh/ se·ma·nash*
From (2 July) to (6 July).	De (dois de julho) até (seis de julho). *de (doysh de zhoo·lyoo) a·te (saysh de zhoo·lyoo)*
Do you have a double room?	Tem um quarto de casal? *teng oong kwaar·too de ka·zaal*
Do you have a single room?	Tem um quarto de solteiro? *teng oong kwaar·too de sol·tay·roo*
Do you have a twin room?	Tem um quarto duplo? *teng oong kwaar·too doo·ploo*
How much is it per night?	Quanto custa por noite? *kwang·too koosh·ta poor noy·te*
How much is it per person?	Quanto custa por pessoa? *kwang·too koosh·ta poor pe·so·a*

🔊 LISTEN FOR

Quantas noites?	*kwang·tash noy·tesh*	How many nights?
chave f	*shaa·ve*	key
identificação f	*ee·deng·tee·fee·ka·sowng*	identification
não há vaga	*nowng aa vaa·ga*	full/no vacancy
recepção f	*rre·se·sowng*	reception

How much is it per week?	Quanto custa por semana? *kwang·too koosh·ta poor se·ma·na*
Do I need to pay upfront?	Tenho que pagar adiantado? *ta·nyoo ke pa·gaar aa·dee·ang·taa·doo*
Can I see it?	Posso ver? *po·soo ver*
I'll take it.	Fico com ele. *fee·koo kong e·le*

Requests & Queries

Is breakfast included?	Inclui o pequeno almoço? *eeng·kloo·ee oo pe·ke·noo aal·mo·soo*
When/Where is breakfast served?	Quando/Onde é que servem o pequeno almoço? *kwang·doo/ong·de e ke ser·veng oo pe·ke·noo aal·mo·soo*
Is there hot water all day?	Há água quente todo o dia? *aa aa·gwa keng·te to·doo oo dee·a*
Please wake me at (seven).	Por favor acorde-me às (sete). *poor fa·vor aa·kor·de·me aash (se·te)*
Can I use the kitchen?	Posso usar a cozinha? *po·soo oo·zaar a koo·zee·nya*
Can I use the laundry?	Posso usar a lavandaria? *po·soo oo·zaar a la·vang·da·ree·a*
Can I use the telephone?	Posso usar o telefone? *po·soo oo·zaar oo te·le·fo·ne*

Do you have a/an ...?	**Tem ...?** teng ...

elevator	elevador	e·le·va·*dor*
laundry **service**	tratamento de roupas	tra·ta·*meng*·too de *rroh*·pash
message **board**	quadro de recados	*kwaa*·droo de rre·*kaa*·doosh
safe	cofre	*ko*·fre
swimming pool	piscina	pesh·*see*·na

Do you arrange tours here?	Organizam passeios aqui? or·ga·*nee*·zowng pa·*say*·oosh aa·*kee*
Do you change money here?	Trocam dinheiro aqui? *tro*·kowng dee·*nyay*·roo aa·*kee*
Could I have my key, please?	Pode-me dar a minha chave, por favor? *po*·de·me daar a *mee*·nya *shaa*·ve poor fa·*vor*
I'm locked out of my room.	Fiquei fechado/ fechada fora do quarto. m/f fee·*kay* fe·*shaa*·doo/ fe·*shaa*·da *fo*·ra doo *kwaar*·too
Is there a message for me?	Há algum recado para mim? aa aal·*goong* rre·*kaa*·doo *pa*·ra meeng
Can I leave a message for someone?	Posso deixar um recado para alguém? *po*·soo day·*shaar* oong rre·*kaa*·doo *pa*·ra aal·*geng*

TV
televisão f
te·le·vee·*zowng*

fan
ventoínha f
veng·too·ee·nya

air-conditioning
ar condicionado m
aar kong·dee·syoo·*naa*·doo

bed
cama f
kaa·ma

key
chave f
shaa·ve

toilet
sanita m
sa·*nee*·ta

bathroom
casa de banho f
kaa·za de ba·nyoo

Answering the Door

Who is it?	Quem é? keng e
Just a moment.	Um minuto. oong mee·*noo*·too
Come in.	Pode entrar. *po*·de eng·*traar*
Come back later, please.	Volte mais tarde, por favor. *vol*·te maish *taar*·de poor fa·*vor*

Complaints

It's too ...		É demasiado ... e de·ma·zee·*aa*·doo ...
bright	claro	*klaa*·roo
cold	frio	*free*·oo
dark	escuro	*shkoo*·roo
noisy	barulhento	ba·roo·*lyeng*·too
small	pequeno	pe·*ke*·noo

The air-conditioning doesn't work.	O ar condicionado não funciona. oo aar kong·dee·syoo·*naa*·doo nowng foong·see·o·na
The fan doesn't work.	A ventoínha não funciona. a veng·too·*ee*·na nowng foong·see·o·na
The toilet doesn't work.	A sanita não funciona. a sa·*nee*·ta nowng foong·see·o·na
Can I get another (blanket)?	Pode-me dar mais um (cobertor)? *po*·de·me daar maish oong (koo·ber·*tor*)
This (pillow) isn't clean.	Esta (almofada) está suja. *esh*·ta (aal·moo·*faa*·da) shtaa *soo*·zha
There's no hot water.	Não há água quente. nowng aa *aa*·gwa *keng*·te

Checking Out

What time is checkout?	A que horas é a partida? *a ke o·rash e a par·tee·da*
Can I have a late checkout?	Posso deixar o quarto mais tarde? *po·soo day·shaar oo kwaar·too maish taar·de*
Can you call a taxi for me (for 11am)?	Pode-me chamar um taxi (para as onze da manhã)? *po·de·me sha·maar oong taak·see (pa·ra ash ong·ze da ma·nyang)*
Can I leave my bags here?	Posso deixar as minhas malas aqui? *po·soo day·shaar ash mee·nyash maa·lash a·kee*

PRACTICAL ACCOMMODATION

Posso ficar na sua casa?
po·soo fee·kaar na soo·a kaa·za
Can I stay at your place?

I'm leaving now.	Vou sair agora. *voh sa·eer a·go·ra*
I had a great stay, thanks.	A estadia foi óptima, obrigado/obrigada. m/f *a shta·dee·a foy o·tee·ma* *o·bree·gaa·doo/o·bree·gaa·da*
Could I have my deposit, please?	Pode-me devolver o depósito, por favor? *po·de·me de·vol·ver oo* *de·po·zee·too poor fa·vor*
Could I have my passport, please?	Pode-me devolver o passaporte, por favor? *po·de·me de·vol·ver oo* *paa·sa·por·te poor fa·vor*
Could I have my valuables, please?	Pode-me devolver os objectos de valor, por favor? *po·de·me de·vol·ver oosh* *o·be·zhe·toosh de va·lor* *poor fa·vor*
I'll be back in (three) days.	Vou regressar em (três) dias. *voh rre·gre·saar eng (tresh)* *dee·ash*
I'll be back on (Tuesday).	Vou regressar na (terça-feira). *voh rre·gre·saar na* *(ter·sa fay·ra)*

Camping

Can I camp here?	Posso acampar aqui? *po·soo a·kang·paar a·kee*
Who do I ask to stay here?	A quem é que peço para ficar aqui? *a keng e ke pe·soo pa·ra* *fee·kaar a·kee*

Can I park next to my tent?	Posso estacionar ao lado da minha tenda?	po·soo shta·syoo·*naar* ow *laa*·doo da *mee*·nya *teng*·da
Do you have (a) ...?	Tem ...?	teng ...

campsite	um lugar para acampar	oong loo·*gaar* pa·ra a·kang·*paar*
electricity	eletricidade	ee·le·tree·see·*daa*·de
laundry	uma lavandaria	*oo*·ma la·vang·da·*ree*·a
shower facilities	chuveiro	shoo·*vay*·roo
tents for hire	tendas para alugar	*teng*·dash pa·ra a·loo·*gaar*

How much is it per ...?	Quanto custa por ...?	*kwang*·too *koosh*·ta poor ...

caravan	caravana	ka·ra·*va*·na
person	pessoa	pe·*so*·a
tent	tenda	*teng*·da
vehicle	veículo	ve·*ee*·koo·loo

Is the water drinkable?	A água é potável?	a *aa*·gwa e poo·*taa*·vel
Could I borrow (a lighter)?	Empresta-me (um isqueiro)?	eng·*presh*·ta·me (oong eesh·*kay*·roo)

Renting

Do you have a/an ... for rent?	Tem ... para alugar? teng ... pa·ra a·loo·gaar

apartment	um apartamento	oong a·par·ta·meng·too
cabin	uma cabana	oo·ma ka·ba·na
house	uma casa	oo·ma kaa·za
room	um quarto	oong kwaar·too

I'm here about the ... for rent.	Estou aqui por causa de ... para alugar. shtoh a·kee poor kow·za de ... pa·ra a·loo·gaar
furnished	mobilado/ mobilada **m/f** moo·bee·laa·doo/ moo·bee·laa·da
unfurnished	sem mobília seng moo·bee·lya
Is there a deposit?	Há depósito? aa de·po·zee·too
Are bills extra?	As contas são à parte? ash kong·tash sowng aa par·te

Staying with Locals

Can I stay at your place?	Posso ficar na sua casa? po·soo fee·kaar na soo·a kaa·za
Is there anything I can do to help?	Posso ajudar nalguma coisa? po·soo a·zhoo·daar naal·goo·ma koy·za

🔍 LOOK FOR

Casa de Banho	kaa·za de ba·nyoo	Bathroom
Há Vaga	aa vaa·ga	Vacancy
Lavandaria	la·vang·da·ree·a	Laundry
Não Há Vaga	nowng aa vaa·ga	No Vacancy

I have my own mattress.	Tenho o meu próprio colchão. ta·nyoo o me·oo pro·pree·oo kol·showng
I have my own sleeping bag.	Tenho o meu próprio saco cama. ta·nyoo o me·oo pro·pree·oo saa·koo kaa·ma
Can I ...?	Posso ...? po·soo ...

bring anything for the meal	trazer alguma coisa para a refeição	tra·zer aal·goo·ma koy·za pa·ra a rre·fay·sowng
do the dishes	lavar a loiça	la·vaar a loy·sa
set/clear the table	por/tirar a mesa	poor/tee·raar a me·za
take out the rubbish	deitar o lixo fora	day·taar oo lee·shoo fo·ra

Thanks for your hospitality.	Obrigado/ Obrigada pela hospitalidade. **m/f** o·bree·gaa·doo/ o·bree·gaa·da pe·la osh·pee·ta·lee·daa·de

To compliment your hosts' cooking, see **eating out** (p180).

PRACTICAL SHOPPING

Shopping

KEY PHRASES

I'd like to buy ...	Queria comprar ...	ke·*ree*·a kong·*praar* ...
Can I look at it?	Posso ver?	*po*·soo ver
Can I try it on?	Posso experimentar?	*po*·soo shpree·meng·*taar*
How much is this?	Quanto custa isto?	*kwang*·too *koosh*·ta *eesh*·too
That's too expensive.	Está muito caro.	shtaa *mweeng*·too *kaa*·roo

Looking For ...

What hours are the shops open?	Qual é o horário de abertura das lojas? kwaal e oo o·*raa*·ryoo de a·ber·*too*·ra dash *lo*·zhash
Where's (a convenience store)?	Onde fica (um mini-mercado)? *ong*·de *fee*·ka (oong *mee*·nee·mer·*kaa*·doo)
Where can I buy (a padlock)?	Onde é que posso comprar (um cadeado)? *ong*·de e ke *po*·soo kong·*praar* (oong ka·de·*aa*·doo)

For more items and shopping locations, see the **dictionary**.

Making a Purchase

I'm just looking.	Estou só a ver. shtoh so a ver
I'd like to buy (an adaptor plug).	Queria comprar (um adaptador). ke·ree·a kong·praar (oong a·da·pe·ta·dor)
How much is this?	Quanto custa isto? kwang·too koosh·ta eesh·too

%<	How much?	Quanto custa?	kwang·too koosh·ta

Can you write down the price?	Pode escrever o preço? po·de shkre·ver oo pre·soo
Do you have any others?	Tem outros? teng oh·troosh
Can I look at it?	Posso ver? po·soo ver
Do you accept credit cards?	Aceitam cartão de crédito? a·say·tang kar·towng de kre·dee·too
Do you accept debit cards?	Aceitam multi-banco? a·say·tang mool·tee·bang·koo
Do you accept travellers cheques?	Aceitam traveller cheques? a·say·tang tra·ve·ler she·kesh
Could I have a bag, please?	Pode-me dar um saco, por favor? po·de·me daar oong saa·koo poor fa·vor

PRACTICAL SHOPPING

| I don't need a bag, thanks. | Não preciso de saco, obrigado/obrigada. m/f
nowng pre·*see*·zoo de *saa*·koo o·bree·*gaa*·doo/o·bree·*gaa*·da |
| Could I have a receipt, please? | Pode-me dar um recibo, por favor?
po·de·me daar oong rre·*see*·boo poor fa·*vor* |

| ✂ | Receipt, please. | O recibo, por favor. | oo rre·*see*·boo poor fa·*vor* |

Could I have it wrapped?	Pode embrulhar? *po*·de eng·broo·*lyaar*
Does it have a guarantee?	Tem garantia? teng ga·rang·*tee*·a
It's faulty.	Tem defeito. teng de·*fay*·too
I'd like (a) ..., please.	Queria ..., por favor. ke·*ree*·a ... poor fa·*vor*

my change	o troco	oo *tro*·koo
receipt	um recibo	oong rre·*see*·boo
refund	ser reembolsado/ reembolsada m/f	ser rre·eng·bol·*saa*·doo/ rre·eng·bol·*saa*·da
to return this	devolver isto	de·vol·*ver* eesh·too

Bargaining

| That's too expensive. | Está muito caro.
shtaa *mweeng*·too *kaa*·roo |
| Can you lower the price? | Pode baixar o preço?
po·de bai·*shaar* oo *pre*·soo |

Making a Purchase

I'd like to buy ...
Queria comprar ...
ke·ree·a kong·praar ...

How much is it?
Quanto custa?
kwang·too koosh·ta

.... **OR** ....

Can you write down the price?
Pode escrever o preço?
po·de shkre·ver oo pre·soo

Do you accept credit cards?
Aceitam cartão de crédito?
a·say·tang kar·towng de kre·dee·too

Could I have a ..., please?
Pode-me dar um ..., por favor?
po·de·me daar oong ... poor fa·vor

 receipt
recibo
rre·see·boo

 bag
saco
saa·koo

🔊 LISTEN FOR

Posso ajudar?	po·soo a·zhoo·*daar*	Can I help you?
O que deseja?	oo ke de·*ze*·zha	What would you like?
Não, não temos.	nowng nowng *te*·moosh	No, we don't have any.
Mais alguma coisa?	maish al·*goo*·ma *koy*·za	Anything else?

Do you have something cheaper?	Tem algo mais barato? teng *aal*·goo maish ba·*raa*·too
I'll give you (five euros).	Dou-lhe (cinco euros). *doh*·lye (*seeng*·koo e·*oo*·roosh)

Books & Reading

Is there an English-language bookshop?	Há uma livraria de língua inglesa? aa *oo*·ma lee·vra·*ree*·a de *leeng*·gwa eeng·*gle*·za
Is there an English-language section?	Há uma secção de língua inglesa? aa oo·ma sek·*sowng* de *leeng*·gwa eeng·*gle*·za
Do you have a book (by Fernando Pessoa)?	Tem algum livro (do Fernando Pessoa)? teng aal·*goong* lee·vroo (doo fer·*nang*·doo pe·*so*·a)
Can you recommend a book for me?	Recomenda-me algum livro? rre·koo·*meng*·da·me aal·*goong* lee·vroo

| I'd like a dictionary. | Queria comprar um dicionário. |
| | ke·*ree*·a kong·*praar* oong dee·see·oo·*naa*·ryoo |

| I'd like a newspaper (in English). | Queria comprar um jornal (em inglês). |
| | ke·*ree*·a kong·*praar* oong zhor·*naal* (eng eeng·*glesh*) |

Clothes

| My size is ... | O meu número é ... |
| | oo *me*·oo *noo*·me·roo e ... |

(40)	(quarenta)	(kwa·*reng*·ta)
small	pequeno	pe·*ke*·noo
medium	médio	*me*·dyoo
large	grande	*grang*·de

| Can I try it on? | Posso experimentar? |
| | *po*·soo shpree·meng·*taar* |

| It doesn't fit. | Não serve. |
| | nowng *ser*·ve |

For different types of clothing and colours see the **dictionary**, and for sizes see **numbers & amounts** (p30).

Music & DVD

| I'd like a CD/DVD. | Queria comprar um CD/DVD. |
| | ke·*ree*·a kong·*praar* oong se·*de*/de·ve·*de* |

| I'd like a video. | Queria comprar um vídeo. |
| | ke·*ree*·a kong·*praar* oong *vee*·dee·oo |

> ### *Estou só a ver.*
> shtoh so a ver
> *I'm just looking.*

I'm looking for something by (Amália Rodrigues).	Estou à procura de qualquer coisa (da Amália Rodrigues). shtoh aa proo·*koo*·ra de kwaal·*ker koy*·za (da a·*maa*·lya rroo·*dree*·gesh)
What's his/her best recording?	Qual é o melhor disco dele/dela? m/f kwaal e oo me·*lyor deesh*·koo *de*·le/*de*·la
What region is this DVD for?	Qual é região deste DVD? kwaal e rre·zhee·*owng desh*·te de·ve·*de*
Is this for a PAL or NTSC system?	Que sistema é este, PAL ou NTSC? ke seesh·*te*·ma e *esh*·te paal oh *e*·ne te *e*·se se

Video & Photography

I need a cable to recharge this battery.	Preciso de um cabo para carregar esta pilha. pre·*see*·zoo de oong *kaa*·boo *pa*·ra ka·rre·*gaar esh*·ta *pee*·lya
I need a cable to connect my camera to a computer.	Preciso de um cabo para ligar a minha máquina a um computador. pre·*see*·zoo de oong *kaa*·boo *pa*·ra lee·*gaar* a *mee*·nya *maa*·kee·na a oong kong·poo·ta·*dor*
Do you have (a) ... for this camera?	Tem ... para esta máquina? teng ... *pa*·ra *esh*·ta *maa*·kee·na

batteries	pilhas	*pee*·lyash
(zoom) lens	lente (zoom)	*leng*·te (zoom)
memory cards	cartão de memória	kar·*towng* de me·*mo*·ree·a
video cassette	uma cassete de vídeo	*oo*·ma ka·se·te de *vee*·dee·oo

PRACTICAL
SHOPPING

CULTURE TIP

Souvenirs

Portugal's most famous export is *porto por·too* (port wine). If you want to support the Portuguese cork (*cortiça* koor·*tee*·sa) industry further, you can pick up cork handicrafts in most towns. The famous hand-painted tiles (*azulejos* a·zoo·*le·*zhoosh) are another distinctive option. For something a bit more utilitarian, consider a leather belt (*cinto de couro seeng*·too de *koh*·roo) or bag (*saco de couro sa*·koo de *koh*·roo), as leather products are of good quality in Portugal.

I need a/an ... film for this camera.	Preciso de filme ... para esta máquina. pre·*see*·zoo de *feel*·me ... *pa*·ra esh·ta maa·kee·na

(200) ASA	de (duzentos) ASA	de (doo·*zeng*·toosh) *aa*·za
B&W	a preto e branco	a *pre*·too e *brang*·koo
colour	a cores	a *ko*·resh
slide	de diapositivos	de dee·a·po·zee·*tee*·voosh

Can you ...?	Pode ...? *po*·de ...

develop digital photos	revelar fotos digitais	rre·ve·*laar* fo·toosh dee·zhee·*taysh*
develop this film	revelar este filme	rre·ve·*laar* esh·te *feel*·me
recharge the battery for my digital camera	carregar a pilha da minha máquina fotográfica digital	ka·rre·*gaar* a *pee*·lya da *mee*·nya *maa*·kee·na foo·too·*graa*·fee·ka dee·zhee·*tal*
transfer photos from my camera to CD	transferir as fotografias da minha máquina para um CD	trangsh·fe·*reer* ash foo·too·gra·*fee*·ash da *mee*·nya *maa*·kee·na *pa*·ra oong se·*de*

I need a passport photo taken.	Preciso de tirar fotos para o passaporte. pre·*see*·zoo de tee·*raar* fo·toosh *pa*·ra oo paa·sa·*por*·te

🔊 LISTEN FOR

pechincha f	pe·*sheeng*·sha	bargain
preço especial m	*pre*·soo es·pe·see·*al*	specials
roubo m	*rroh*·boo	rip-off
saldos m pl	*saal*·doosh	sale

I'm not happy with these photos.	Não gostei destas fotos. nowng gosh·*tay* desh·tash *fo*·toosh

Repairs

Can I have my ... repaired here?	Vocês consertam ...? vo·*sesh* kong·*ser*·tang ...
When will my ... be ready?	Quando é que ...? *kwang*·doo e ke ...

bag	o saco está pronto	oo *saa*·koo shtaa *prong*·too
camera	a câmera está pronta	*kaa*·me·ra shtaa *prong*·ta
(sun)glasses	os óculos (de sol) estão prontos	oosh *o*·koo·loosh (de sol) shtowng *prong*·toosh
shoes	os sapatos estão prontos	oosh sa·*paa*·toosh shtowng *prong*·toosh

Communications

KEY PHRASES

Where's the local internet cafe?	Onde fica um café da internet nas redondezas?	*ong*·de *fee*·ka oong ka·*fe* da eeng·ter·*net* nash rre·dong·*de*·zash
I'd like to check my email.	Queria ler o meu email.	ke·*ree*·a ler oo *me*·oo ee·*mayl*
I want to send a parcel.	Quero enviar uma encomenda.	*ke*·roo eng·vee·*aar* oo·ma eng·koo·*meng*·da
I want to make a call to ...	Quero fazer uma chamada para ...	*ke*·roo fa·*zer* oo·ma sha·*maa*·da *pa*·ra ...
I'd like a SIM card.	Queria um cartão SIM.	ke·*ree*·a oong kar·*towng* seeng

The Internet

Where's the local internet cafe?	Onde fica um café da internet nas redondezas? *ong*·de *fee*·ka oong ka·*fe* da eeng·ter·*net* nash rre·dong·*de*·zash
Do you have internet access here?	Você tem acesso à internet? vo·*se* teng a·*se*·soo a eeng·ter·*net*
Is there wireless internet access here?	Você tem conexão sem fio a internet? vo·*se* teng kon·nayk·*sowng* seng *fee*·o a eeng·ter·*net*

I'd like to ...	Queria ... ke·*ree*·a ...	
burn a CD	gravar um CD	gra·*vaar* oong se·*de*
check my email	ler o meu email	ler oo *me*·oo ee·*mayl*
download my photos	fazer o download das minhas fotos	fa·*zer* oo down·*lohd* dash *mee*·nyash fo·*toosh*
get internet access	ter acesso à internet	ter a·*se*·soo aa eeng·ter·*net*
use a printer	usar uma impressora	oo·*zaar* oo·ma eeng·pre·*so*·ra
use a scanner	usar um digitalizador	oo·*zaar* oong dee·zhee·ta·lee·za·*dor*
use Skype	usar o Skype	oo·*zaar* oo skaip

Can I connect my laptop here?

Posso conectar meu computador portátil?
po·soo ko·nek·*taar* me·oo kong·poo·ta·*dor* por·*taa*·teel

Do you have headphones (with a microphone)?

Você tem fone de ouvidos (com microfone)?
vo·*se* teng *fo*·ne de oo·*vee*·doosh (kong mee·kro·*fo*·ne)

Do you have PCs/Macs?

Tem PCs/Macs?
teng pe·*sesh*/maksh

Do you have a Zip drive?

Tem um zip drive?
teng oong zeep draiv

How much is it per hour/page?

Quanto custa por hora/página?
kwang·too *koosh*·ta poor o·ra/*paa*·zhee·na

Can I connect my ... to this computer?

Posso ligar a minha ...
a este computador?
*po·soo lee·gar a mee·nya ...
a esh·te kong·poo·ta·dor*

camera	máquina	*maa·kee·na*
media player	mp3	*e·me·pe·tresh*
portable hard drive	impulsor rígido portátil	*eeng·pool·sor rree·zhee·doo por·taa·tel*
USB flash drive	flash drive USB	*flash draiv oo·e·se·be*

How do I log on?	Como é que eu entro? *ko·moo e ke e·oo eng·troo*
Please change it to the English-language setting.	Mude o programa para inglês, por favor. *moo·de oo proo·gra·ma pa·ra eeng·glesh poor fa·vor*
It's crashed.	Desligou-se. *desh·lee·goh·se*
I've finished.	Acabei. *a·ka·bay*

Mobile/Cell Phone

What are the call rates?	Qual é o valor cobrado? *kwaal e oo va·lor koo·braa·doo*

🔊 LISTEN FOR

(Trinta cêntimos) por (trinta) segundos.	*(treeng·ta seng·tee·moosh) poor (treeng·ta) se·goong·doosh* (30c) per (30) seconds.

I'd like a ...	Queria ... ke·ree·a ...

battery for my phone	uma pilha para o meu telefone	oo·ma pee·lya pa·ra oo me·oo te·le·fo·ne
mobile/cell phone for hire	alugar um telemóvel	a·loo·gaar oong te·le·mo·vel
prepaid mobile/cell phone	um telemóvel pré-pago	oong te·le·mo·vel pre·paa·goo
SIM card for your network	um cartão SIM para a sua rede	oong kar·towng seeng pa·ra a soo·a rre·de

Phone

Q What's your phone number?	Qual é o seu número de telefone? kwaal e oo se·oo noo·me·roo de te·le·fo·ne
A The number is ...	O número é ... oo noo·me·roo e ...
Where's the nearest public phone?	Onde fica o telefone público mais perto? ong·de fee·ka o te·le·fo·ne poo·blee·koo maish per·too
Can I look at a phone book?	Posso usar a lista telefónica? po·soo oo·zaar a leesh·ta te·le·fo·nee·ka
Can I have some coins/ tokens?	Pode-me dar algumas moedas/fichas? po·de·me daar aal·goo·mash moo·e·dash/fee·shash

What's the code for (New Zealand)?	Qual é o indicativo para (a Nova Zelândia)?	kwaal e o eeng·dee·ka·tee·voo pa·ra (a no·va ze·lang·dee·a)
I want to ...	Quero ...	ke·roo ...

buy a phonecard	comprar um cartão telefónico	kong·praar oong kar·towng te·le·fo·nee·koo
call (Singapore)	telefonar (para Singapura)	te·le·foo·naar (pa·ra seeng·ga·poo·ra)
make a (local) call	fazer uma chamada (local)	fa·zer oo·ma sha·maa·da (loo·kaal)
reverse the charges	fazer uma chamada a cobrar	fa·zer oo·ma sha·maa·da a koo·braar
speak for (three) minutes	falar por (três) minutos	fa·laar poor (tresh) mee·noo·toosh

How much does a (three)-minute call cost?	Quanto custa uma ligação de (três) minutos? kwang·too koosh·ta oo·ma lee·ga·sowng de (tresh) mee·noo·toosh
How much does each extra minute cost?	Quanto custa cada minuto extra? kwang·too koosh·ta kaa·da mee·noo·too aysh·tra
It's engaged.	Está ocupado. shtaa o·koo·paa·doo

LANGUAGE TIP

Text-Message Shortcuts
Indulging in a little SMS or online flirting in Portugal can be difficult. Some letters tend to get dropped from Portuguese words in text messages – just like in English – so that a simple phrase such as 'Where do you want to meet?' (*Onde é que te queres encontrar comigo?* *ong*·de e ke te *ke*·resh eng·kong·*trar* koo·*mee*·goo) becomes the novice learner's nightmare: *Od é k t keres enctr cmg?*

I've been cut off.	Desligaram. desh·lee·*gaa*·rowng
The connection's bad.	A ligação está má. a lee·ga·*sowng* shtaa maa
Hello.	Está? shtaa
It's ...	Daqui fala ... da·*kee faa*·la ...
Can I speak to ...?	Queria falar com ...? ke·*ree*·a fa·*laar* kong ...
Can I leave a message?	Posso deixar um recado? *po*·soo day·*shaar* oong rre·*kaa*·doo
Please tell him/her I called.	Por favor diga-lhe que eu telefonei. poor fa·*vor dee*·ga·lye ke e·oo te·le·foo·*nay*
I don't have a contact number.	Eu não tenho um número de contacto. e·oo nowng *ta*·nyoo oong *noo*·me·roo de kong·*taak*·too
My number is ...	O meu número é ... oo *me*·oo *noo*·me·roo e ...

PRACTICAL COMMUNICATIONS

Quem fala?	keng *faa*·la Who's calling?
Com quem quer falar?	kong keng ker fa·*laar* Who do you want to speak to?
Só um minuto.	so oong mee·*noo*·too One moment.
Ele/Ela não está.	e·le/e·la nowng shtaa He/She isn't here.
Marcou o número errado.	mar·*koh* oo *noo*·me·roo ee·*rraa*·doo Wrong number.

I'll call back later.	Volto a telefonar mais tarde. *vol*·too a te·le·foo·*naar* maish *taar*·de
What time should I call?	A que horas devo telefonar? a ke o·rash *de*·voo te·le·foo·*naar*

Post Office

I want to buy a postcard/stamp.	Quero comprar um postal/selo. ke·roo kong·*praar* oong poosh·*taal*/se·loo
I want to send a letter/parcel.	Quero enviar uma carta/encomenda. *ke*·roo eng·vee·*aar* oo·ma *kaar*·ta/eng·koo·*meng*·da
It contains (souvenirs).	Contém (lembranças). kong·*teng* (leng·*brang*·sash)

Where's the poste restante section?	Onde é a secção de posta restante? *ong*·de e a sek·*sowng* de *posh*·ta rresh·*tang*·te
Is there any mail for me?	Há alguma correspondência para mim? aa aal·*goo*·ma koo·rresh·pong·*deng*·sya *pa*·ra meeng

PRACTICAL

COMMUNICATIONS

🔊 LISTEN FOR

código postal m	*ko*·dee·goo poosh·*taal*	postcode
correio azul m	koo·*rray*·oo a·*zool*	express mail
declaração f **de alfândega**	de·kla·ra·*sowng* de aal·*fang*·de·ga	customs declaration
doméstico	doo·*mesh*·tee·koo	domestic
envelope m **(almofadado)**	eng·ve·*lo*·pe (aal·moo·fa·*daa*·doo)	(padded) envelope
internacional	eeng·ter·na·syoo·*naal*	international
registada f	rre·zheesh·*taa*·da	registered
registado m	rre·zheesh·*taa*·doo	registered
selo m	*se*·loo	stamp
via aérea	*vee*·a a·e·ree·a	by air
via marítima	*vee*·a ma·*ree*·tee·ma	by sea
via terrestre	*vee*·a te·*rresh*·tre	by land

Money & Banking

KEY PHRASES

How much is it?	Quanto custa?	kwang·too koosh·ta
What's the exchange rate?	Qual é o câmbio do dia?	kwaal e oo kang·byoo doo dee·a
Where's an ATM?	Onde há um caixa automático?	ong·de aa oong kai·sha ow·too·maa·tee·koo
I'd like to change money.	Queria trocar dinheiro.	ke·ree·a troo·kaar dee·nyay·roo
I'd like to get change for this note.	Queria trocar esta nota.	ke·ree·a troo·kaar esh·ta no·ta

Paying the Bill

Do I have to pay?	Tenho de pagar? ta·nyoo de pa·gaar
Q How much is it?	Quanto custa? kwang·too koosh·ta
A It's (12) euros.	É (doze) euros. e (do·ze) e·oo·roosh
A It's free.	É gratuito. e gra·twee·too
Can you write down the price?	Pode escrever o preço? po·de shkre·ver oo pre·soo
Do you accept credit cards?	Aceitam cartão de crédito? a·say·tang kar·towng de kre·dee·too

Do you accept debit cards?	Aceitam multibanco? a·*say*·tang mool·tee·*bang*·koo
Do you accept travellers cheques?	Aceitam traveller cheques? a·*say*·tang *tra*·ve·ler *she*·kesh
I'd like my change, please.	Queria o troco, por favor. ke·*ree*·a oo *tro*·koo poor fa·*vor*
I'd like a receipt, please.	Queria um recibo, por favor. ke·*ree*·a oong rre·*see*·boo poor fa·*vor*
I'd like a refund, please.	Queria ser reembolsado/ reembolsada, por favor. m/f ke·*ree*·a ser rre·eng·bol·*saa*·doo/ rre·eng·bol·*saa*·da poor fa·*vor*
How much is it per ...?	Quanto é que é por ...? *kwang*·too e ke e poor ...

day	dia	*dee*·a
hour	hora	*o*·ra
night	noite	*noy*·te
week	semana	se·*ma*·na

Banking

What days is the bank open?	Em que dias é que abre o banco? eng ke *dee*·ash e ke *aa*·bre oo *bang*·koo
What times is the bank open?	A que horas é que abre o banco? a ke *o*·rash e ke *aa*·bre oo *bang*·koo

| **Where can I ...?** | | Onde é que posso ...? *ong*·de e ke *po*·soo ... |
| **I'd like to ...** | | Queria ... ke·*ree*·a ... |

cash a cheque	trocar um cheque	troo·*kaar* oong *she*·ke
change a travellers cheque	trocar traveller cheque	troo·*kaar tra*·ve·ler shek
change money	trocar dinheiro	troo·*kaar* dee·*nyay*·roo
get a cash advance	fazer um levantamento adiantado	fa·*zer* oong le·vang·ta·*meng*·too a·dee·ang·*taa*·doo
get change for this note	trocar esta nota	troo·*kaar* esh·ta *no*·ta
withdraw money	levantar dinheiro	le·vang·*taar* dee·*nyay*·roo

Where's an ATM?	Onde há um caixa automático? *ong*·de aa oong *kai*·sha ow·too·*maa*·tee·koo
Where's a foreign exchange office?	Onde é que há um câmbio? *ong*·de e ke aa oong *kang*·byoo
What's the charge for that?	Qual é a taxa aplicável? kwaal e a *taa*·sha a·plee·*kaa*·vel
What's the exchange rate?	Qual é o câmbio do dia? kwaal e oo *kang*·byoo doo *dee*·a

🔊 **LISTEN FOR**

identificação f	ee·deng·tee·fee·ka·*sowng* identification
Assine aqui.	a·*see*·ne a·*kee* Sign here.
Temos um problema.	*te*·moosh oong pro·*ble*·ma There's a problem.
Não tem mais fundos disponíveis.	nowng teng maish *foong*·doosh deesh·poo·*nee*·vaysh You have no funds left.
Não podemos fazer isso.	nowng poo·*de*·moosh fa·*zer* ee·soo We can't do that.

The ATM took my card.	O caixa automático ficou com o meu cartão. oo *kai*·sha ow·too·*maa*·tee·koo fee·*koh* kong oo *me*·oo kar·*towng*
I've forgotten my PIN.	Esqueci-me do código. shke·*see*·me doo *ko*·dee·goo
Can I use my credit card to withdraw money?	Posso utilizar o cartão de crédito para levantar dinheiro? *po*·soo oo·tee·lee·*zaar* oo kar·*towng* de *kre*·dee·too *pa*·ra le·vang·*taar* dee·*nyay*·roo
Has my money arrived yet?	O meu dinheiro já chegou? oo *me*·oo dee·*nyay*·roo zhaa she·*goh*
How long will it take to arrive?	Quanto tempo vai levar para chegar? *kwang*·too *teng*·poo vai le·*vaar pa*·ra she·*gaar*

Business

KEY PHRASES

I'm attending a conference.	Estou a participar numa conferência.	shtoh a par·tee·see·*paar* numa *noong*·ma kong·fe·*reng*·sya
I have an appointment with ...	Tenho uma reunião marcada com ...	*ta*·nyoo oo·ma rree·oo·*nyowng* mar·*kaa*·da kong ...
Can I have your business card?	Pode-me dar o seu cartão de visita?	*po*·de·me daar oo *se*·oo kar·*towng* de vee·*zee*·ta

Where's the business centre?	Onde é o centro de negócios? *ong*·de e oo *seng*·troo de ne·*go*·syoosh
Where's the conference?	Onde é a conferência? *ong*·de e a kong·fe·*reng*·sya
Where's the meeting?	Onde é a reunião? *ong*·de e a rree·oo·*nyowng*
I'm attending a ...	Estou a participar ... shtoh a par·tee·see·*paar* ...

conference	numa conferência	*noong*·ma kong·fe·*reng*·sya
course	num curso	noong *koor*·soo
meeting	numa reunião	noo·ma rree·oo·*nyowng*
trade fair	numa feira de comércio	noo·ma *fay*·ra de koo·*mer*·syoo

I'm here for (two) days.	Vou ficar aqui por (dois) dias. voh fee·*kaar* a·*kee* poor (doysh) *dee*·ash
I'm here for (three) weeks.	Vou ficar aqui por (três) semanas. voh fee·*kaar* a·*kee* poor (tresh) se·*ma*·nash
I'm with colleagues.	Estou com colegas de trabalho. shtoh kong koo·*le*·gash de tra·*baa*·lyoo
I'm with (two) others.	Estou com outros (dois). shtoh kong *oh*·troosh (doysh)
I'm alone.	Estou sozinho/ sozinha. **m/f** shtoh so·*zee*·nyoo/ so·*zee*·nya
I have an appointment with ...	Tenho uma reunião marcada com ... *ta*·nyoo oo·ma rree·oo·*nyowng* mar·*kaa*·da kong ...
I need ...	Preciso de ... pre·*see*·zoo de ...

a computer	um computador	oong kong·poo·ta·*dor*
an internet connection	ligação à internet	lee·ga·*sowng* aa eeng·ter·*net*
an interpreter	um intérprete	oong eeng·*ter*·pre·te
to send a fax	enviar um fax	eng·vee·*aar* oong faks

PRACTICAL BUSINESS

What's your ...?	Qual é o seu ...?	kwaal e oo se·oo ...
Here's my ...	Aqui está o meu ...	a·kee shtaa oo me·oo ...

(email) address	endereço (de email)	eng·de·re·soo (de ee·mayl)
mobile/cell number	número do telemóvel	noo·me·roo doo te·le·mo·vel
pager number	número do pager	noo·me·roo doo pay·zher
work number	número de telefone do trabalho	noo·me·roo de te·le·fo·ne doo tra·baa·lyoo

Can I have your business card?	Pode-me dar o seu cartão de visita? po·de·me daar oo se·oo kar·towng de vee·zee·ta
Thank you for your time.	Obrigado/Obrigada pela atenção. m/f o·bree·gaa·doo/o·bree·gaa·da pe·la a·teng·sowng
Shall we go for a drink?	Vocês gostariam de tomar alguma coisa? vo·sesh gosh·ta·ree·ang de too·maar aal·goo·ma koy·za
Shall we go for a meal?	Vocês gostariam de jantar? vo·sesh gosh·ta·ree·ang de zhang·taar
It's on me.	Eu pago. e·oo paa·goo

Sightseeing

KEY PHRASES

I'd like a guide.	Queria um guia.	ke·*ree*·a oong *gee*·a
Can I take a photo?	Posso tirar uma fotografia?	*po*·soo tee·*raar oo*·ma foo·too·gra·*fee*·a
When's the museum open?	Quando é que o museu está aberto?	*kwaang*·doo e ke oo moo·*ze*·oo shtaa a·*ber*·too
I'm interested in ...	Eu estou interessado/ interessada em ... m/f	*e*·oo shtoh eeng·te·re·*saa*·doo/ eeng·te·re·*saa*·da eng ...
When's the next tour?	Quando é a próxima excursão?	*kwang*·doo e a *pro*·see·ma shkoor·*sowng*

I'd like a/an ...   Queria ...
ke·*ree*·a ...

audio set	um aparelho de áudio	oong a·pa·re·lyoo de *ow*·dee·oo
catalogue	um catálogo	oong ka·*taa*·loo·goo
guide (person)	um guia	oong *gee*·a
(local) map	um mapa (local)	oong *maa*·pa (loo·*kaal*)

I'd like to see ...   Eu gostava de ver ...
e·oo goosh·*taa*·va de ver ...

Do you have information on cultural sights?	Tem informações sobre locais culturais? teng eeng·foor·ma·*soyngsh* so·bre loo·*kaish* kool·too·*raish*
Do you have information on historical sights?	Tem informações sobre locais históricos? teng eeng·foor·ma·*soyngsh* so·bre loo·*kaish* esh·*to*·ree·koosh
Do you have information on religious sights?	Tem informações sobre locais religiosos? teng eeng·foor·ma·*soyngsh* so·bre loo·*kaish* rre·lee·zhee·o·*zoosh*
What's that?	O que é aquilo? oo ke e a·*kee*·loo
Could you take a photo of me/us?	Pode-me/Pode-nos tirar uma fotografia? *po*·de·me/*po*·de·noosh tee·*raar* oo·ma foo·too·gra·*fee*·a
Can I take a photo (of you)?	Posso(-lhe) tirar uma fotografia? *po*·soo(·lye) tee·*raar* oo·ma foo·too·gra·*fee*·a
I'll send you the photo.	Eu envio-lhe a fotografia. e·oo eng·*vee*·o·lye a foo·too·gra·*fee*·a

Getting In

What time does it open/ close?	A que horas abre/fecha? a ke o·rash *aa*·bre/*fe*·sha
What's the admission charge?	Qual é o preço de entrada? kwaal e oo *pre*·soo de eng·*traa*·da

CULTURE TIP

Arts & Crafts

A number of regions in Portugal are well-known for specific arts and crafts. Types of ceramics include *porcelana da vista Alegre* poor·se·*la*·na da *veesh*·ta a·*le*·gre from Ílhavo, Barcelos roosters (*galo de Barcelos gaa*·loo de bar·*se*·loosh) and black ceramics from Bisalhães. Basketry (*cestaria* ses·ta·*ree*·a), bobbin lace (*renda de bilros rreng*·da de *beel*·rroosh) from the Peniche harbour region and embroidery (*bordados* boor·*daa*·doosh) from northern Portugal are also highly regarded.

Is there a discount for ...?	Tem desconto para ...? teng desh·*kong*·too *pa*·ra ...

children	crianças	kree·*ang*·sash
groups	grupos	*groo*·poosh
older people	terceira idade	ter·*say*·ra ee·*daa*·de
students	estudantes	shtoo·*dang*·tesh

Museums & Galleries

When's the museum open?	Quando é que o museu está aberto? *kwaang*·doo e ke oo moo·ze·oo shtaa a·*ber*·too
Q **What kind of art are you interested in?**	Qual é o tipo de arte que mais lhe interessa? kwaal e oo *tee*·poo de *aar*·te ke maish lye eeng·te·*re*·sa
A **I'm interested in ...**	Eu estou interessado/interessada em ... **m/f** e·oo shtoh eeng·te·re·*saa*·doo/eeng·te·re·*saa*·da eng ...

🔊 LISTEN FOR

arte gráfica f	*aar*·te *graa*·fee·ka	graphic art
arte manuelina f	*aar*·te man·wel·ee·na	Manueline art
arte moderna f	*aar*·te moo·*der*·na	modern art
arte mourisca f	*aar*·te moh·*reesh*·ka	Moorish art

Q What's in the collection?	Que obras há no museu? ke o·brash aa noo moo·ze·oo
A It's an exhibition of ...	É uma exposição de ... e *oo*·ma shpoo·zee·*sowng* de ...
What do you think of ...?	O que acha de ...? oo ke *aa*·sha de ...

Tours

Can you recommend (a tour)?	Pode recomendar (uma excursão)? *po*·de rre·koo·meng·*daar* (*oo*·ma shkoor·*sowng*)
When's the next boat trip?	Quando é a próxima viagem de barco? *kwang*·doo e a *pro*·see·ma vee·*aa*·zheng de *baar*·koo
When's the next day trip?	Quando é o próximo passeio? *kwang*·doo e oo *pro*·see·moo pa·*say*·oo
Is accommodation included?	Inclui hospedagem? eeng·*kloo*·ee osh·pe·*daa*·zheng

O que é aquilo?
oo ke e a·*kee*·loo

What's that?

Is food included?	Inclui comida? eeng·*kloo*·ee koo·*mee*·da
Is transport included?	Inclui transporte? eeng·*kloo*·ee trangsh·*por*·te
How long is the tour?	Quanto tempo dura a excursão? *kwang*·too *teng*·poo *doo*·ra a shkoor·*sowng*
What time should we be back?	A que hora é que devemos estar de volta? a ke o·ra e ke de·*ve*·moosh shtaar de *vol*·ta
I've lost my group.	Perdi o meu grupo. per·*dee* oo *me*·oo *groo*·poo

Senior & Disabled Travellers

KEY PHRASES

I need assistance.	Preciso de ajuda.	pre·*see*·zoo de a·*zhoo*·da
Is there wheelchair access?	Tem acesso para cadeira de rodas?	teng a·*se*·soo *pa*·ra ka·*day*·ra de *rro*·dash
Are there toilets for the disabled?	Tem casa de banho para deficientes físicos?	teng *kaa*·za de *ba*·nyoo *pa*·ra de·fee·see·*eng*·tesh *fee*·zee·koosh

I have a disability.	Eu tenho uma deficiência física. e·oo *ta*·nyoo *oo*·ma de·fee·see·*eng*·sya *fee*·zee·ka
I need assistance.	Preciso de ajuda. pre·*see*·zoo de a·*zhoo*·da
Are there toilets for the disabled?	Tem casa de banho para deficientes físicos? teng *kaa*·za de *ba*·nyoo *pa*·ra de·fee·see·*eng*·tesh *fee*·zee·koosh
Are there parking spaces for the disabled?	Tem estacionamento para deficientes físicos? teng shta·see·oo·na·*meng*·too *pa*·ra de·fee·see·*eng*·tesh *fee*·zee·koosh
Is there wheelchair access?	Tem acesso para cadeira de rodas? teng a·*se*·soo *pa*·ra ka·*day*·ra de *rro*·dash

Are guide dogs permitted?	É permitida a entrada de cães-guia? *e per·mee·tee·da a eng·traa·da de kaingsh·gee·a*
How many steps are there?	Quantos degraus há ai? *kwang·toosh de·growsh aa a·ee*
Is there an elevator?	Tem elevador? *teng e·le·va·dor*
Are there rails in the bathroom?	Tem corrimão na casa de banho? *teng koo·rree·mowng na kaa·za de ba·nyoo*
Could you call me a taxi for the disabled?	Pode-me chamar um táxi para deficientes físicos? *po·de·me sha·maar oong taak·see pa·ra de·fee·see·eng·tesh fee·zee·koosh*
Could you help me cross the street safely?	Pode-me ajudar a atravessar a rua com segurança? *po·de·me a·zhoo·daar a a·tra·ve·saar a rroo·a kong se·goo·rang·sa*
Is there somewhere I can sit down?	Há algum lugar onde me possa sentar? *aa aal·goong loo·gaar ong·de me po·sa seng·taar*
ramp	rampa f *rrang·pa*
walking frame	armação para andar f *ar·ma·sowng pa·ra ang·daar*
walking stick	bengala f *beng·gaa·la*
wheelchair	cadeira de rodas f *ka·day·ra de rro·dash*

Travel with Children

KEY PHRASES

Are children allowed?	É permitida a entrada a crianças?	e per·mee·*tee*·da a eng·*traa*·da a kree·*ang*·sash
Is there a discount for children?	Há desconto para crianças?	aa desh·*kong*·too *pa*·ra kree·*ang*·sash
Is there a baby change room?	Há uma sala reservada para bebés?	aa oo·ma *saa*·la rre·zer·*vaa*·da *pa*·ra be·*besh*

Is there a ...?

Há ...?
aa ...

baby change room	uma sala reservada para bebés	*oo*·ma *saa*·la rre·zer·*vaa*·da *pa*·ra be·*besh*
child-minding service	serviço de ama	ser·*vee*·soo de *a*·ma
children's menu	menu para crianças	me·*noo* pa·ra kree·*ang*·sash
crèche	creche	*kre*·she
discount for children	desconto para crianças	desh·*kong*·too *pa*·ra kree·*ang*·sash
family ticket	passagem de família	pa·*saa*·zheng de fa·*mee*·lya

Where can I change a nappy/diaper?	Onde posso mudar a fralda?
	ong·de *po*·soo moo·*daar* a *fraal*·da

I need a/an ...	Preciso de ...
	pre·*see*·zoo de ...

baby seat	um lugar para bebés	oong loo·*gaar* *pa*·ra be·*besh*
(English-speaking) babysitter	uma ama (que fale inglês)	*oo*·ma *a*·ma (ke *faa*·le eeng·*glesh*)
booster seat	assento de elevação	a·*seng*·too de ee·le·va·*sowng*
cot	cama de grades	*ka*·ma de *graa*·desh
highchair	uma cadeira para crianças	*oo*·ma ka·*day*·ra *pa*·ra kree·*ang*·sash
plastic bag	um saco de plástico	oong *saa*·koo de *plaash*·tee·koo
potty	um bacio	oong ba·*see*·oo
pram/stroller	um carrinho de bebé	oong ka·*rree*·nyoo de be·*be*

Do you sell ...?	Vendem ...?
	veng·deng ...

baby wipes	toalhinhas de bebé	twa·*lyee*·nyash de be·*be*
disposable nappies/diapers	fraldas descartáveis	*fraal*·dash desh·kar·*taa*·vaysh
painkillers for infants	analgésicos infantis	a·naal·*zhe*·zee·koosh eeng·*fang*·teesh
tissues	lenços de papel	*leng*·soosh de pa·*pel*

Where's the nearest ...?	Onde está ... mais próximo/próxima? **m/f** *ong*·de *shtaa* ... maish *pro*·see·moo/*pro*·see·ma	

park	o parque	oo *paar*·ke
playground	o parque infantil	oo *paar*·ke eeng·fang·*teel*
swimming pool	a piscina	a pesh·*see*·na
theme park	o parque de diversões	oo *paar*·ke de dee·ver·*zoyngs*h
toyshop	a loja de brinquedos	a *lo*·zha de breeng·*ke*·doosh

Could I have some paper and pencils, please?	Pode-me dar papel e lápis, por favor? *po*·de·me daar pa·*pel* ee *laa*·peesh poor fa·*vor*
Are children allowed?	É permitida a entrada a crianças? e per·mee·*tee*·da a eng·*traa*·da a kree·*ang*·sash
Is this suitable for ...-year-old children?	Isto é apropriado para crianças de ... anos de idade? *eesh*·too e a·proo·pree·*aa*·doo *pa*·ra kree·*ang*·sash de ... *a*·noosh de ee·*daa*·de
Do you mind if I breastfeed here?	Importa-se que eu amamente aqui? eeng·*por*·ta·se ke *e*·oo a·ma·*meng*·te a·*kee*
Do you know a doctor/ dentist who is good with children?	Conhece algum médico/ dentista bom para crianças? ko·*nye*·se aal·*goong* me·dee·koo/ deng·*teesh*·ta bong *pa*·ra kree·*ang*·sash

If your child is sick, see **health** (p161).

Social

Meeting People

KEY PHRASES

My name is ...	O meu nome é ...	oo *me*·oo *no*·me e ...
I'm from ...	Eu sou de ...	e·oo soh de ...
I work in ...	Trabalho em ...	tra·*baa*·lyoo eng ...
I'm ... years old.	Tenho ... anos.	*ta*·nyoo ... *a*·noosh
And you?	E você?	e vo·*se*

Basics

Yes.	Sim. seeng
No.	Não. nowng
Please.	Por favor. poor fa·*vor*
Thank you (very much).	(Muito) Obrigado. **m** (*mweeng*·too) o·bree·*gaa*·doo (Muito) Obrigada. **f** (*mweeng*·too) o·bree·*gaa*·da
You're welcome.	De nada. de *naa*·da
Excuse me. (to get attention)	Faz favor! faash fa·*vor*
Excuse me. (to get past)	Com licença. kong lee·*seng*·sa
Sorry.	Desculpe. desh·*kool*·pe

Greetings & Goodbyes

Hello./Hi.	Olá.	o·*laa*
Good morning/day.	Bom dia.	bong *dee*·a
Good afternoon.	Boa tarde.	bo·a *taar*·de
Good evening.	Boa noite.	bo·a *noy*·te
Q How are you?	Como está?	*ko*·moo shtaa
A Fine, and you?	Bem, e você?	beng e vo·*se*
Q What's your name?	Qual é o seu nome?	kwaal e oo *se*·oo *no*·me
A My name is …	O meu nome é …	oo *me*·oo *no*·me e …
I'd like to introduce you to …	Eu gostava de te apresentar ao/á … **m/f**	e·oo goosh·*taa*·va de te a·pre·zeng·*taar* ow/aa …
This is …	Isto é …	*eesh*·too e …
I'm pleased to meet you.	Prazer em conhecê-lo/conhecê-la. **m/f**	pra·*zer* eng koo·nye·*se*·lo/koo·nye·*se*·la
See you later.	Até logo.	a·*te* lo·goo
Goodbye.	Adeus.	a·*de*·oosh
Good night.	Boa noite.	bo·a *noy*·te

SOCIAL MEETING PEOPLE

Addressing People

Mr	Senhor se·*nyor*
Sir	Cavalheiro ka·va·*lyay*·roo
Mrs/Ms	Senhora se·*nyo*·ra
Miss	Menina me·*nee*·na
Madam	Senhora Dona se·*nyo*·ra *do*·na

Making Conversation

Nice/Awful weather!	Que tempo fantástico/terrível! ke *teng*·poo fang·*taash*·tee·koo/te·*rree*·vel
That's (beautiful), isn't it?	Isto é (lindo), não acha? *eesh*·too e (*leeng*·doo) nowng *aa*·sha
What's this called?	Como se chama isto? *ko*·moo se *sha*·ma *eesh*·too
Do you live here?	Mora aqui? *mo*·ra a·*kee*
Where are you going?	Onde vai? *ong*·de vai
What are you doing?	O que é que está a fazer? oo ke e ke shtaa a fa·*zer*
Q **Do you like it here?**	Gosta daqui? *goosh*·ta da·*kee*
A **I love it here.**	Eu adoro. e·oo a·*do*·roo

Q How long are you here for?	Quanto tempo vai cá ficar? *kwang·too teng·poo vai kaa fee·kaar*
A I'm here for (four) days/weeks.	Fico cá (quatro) dias/semanas. *fee·koo kaa (kwaa·troo) dee·ash/se·ma·nash*
Q Are you here on holiday?	Está aqui de férias? *shtaa a·kee de fe·ree·ash*
A I'm here for a holiday.	Estou aqui de férias. *shtoh a·kee de fe·ree·ash*
A I'm here on business.	Estou aqui em negócios. *shtoh a·kee eng ne·go·syoosh*
A I'm here to study.	Estou aqui a estudar. *shtoh a·kee a shtoo·daar*

SOCIAL MEETING PEOPLE

Eu adoro.
e·oo a·do·roo
I love it here.

Nationalities

Where are you from?	De onde é?	*dong·de e*
I'm from ...	Eu sou ...	*e·oo soh ...*

Australia	da Austrália	*da owsh·traa·lya*
Canada	do Canadá	*doo ka·na·da*
England	da Inglaterra	*da eeng·gla·te·rra*
the USA	dos Estados Unidos	*doosh shtaa·doosh oo·nee·doosh*

For more countries, see the **dictionary**.

Age

How old are you?	Quantos anos tem?	*kwang·toosh a·noosh teng*
I'm ... years old.	Tenho ... anos.	*ta·nyoo ... a·noosh*
How old is your daughter?	Quantos anos tem a sua filha?	*kwang·toosh a·noosh teng a soo·a fee·lya*
How old is your son?	Quantos anos tem o seu filho?	*kwang·toosh a·noosh teng oo se·oo fee·lyoo*
He/She is ... years old.	Ele/Ela tem ... anos.	*e·le/e·la teng ... a·noosh*
I'm younger than I look.	Sou mais novo/nova do que pareço. **m/f**	*soh maish no·voo/no·va doo ke pa·re·soo*

| I'm older than I look. | Sou mais velho/velha do que pareço. **m/f** soh maish *ve*·lyoo/*ve*·lya doo ke pa·*re*·soo |

For your age, see **numbers & amounts** (p30).

Occupations & Studies

Q What's your occupation?	Qual é a sua profissão? kwaal e a *soo*·a proo·fee·*sowng*
A I'm a (teacher).	Sou (professor/ professora). **m/f** soh (proo·fe·*sor*/ proo·fe·*so*·ra)
A I work in (health).	Trabalho em (saúde). tra·*baa*·lyoo eng (sa·oo·de)
A I'm retired.	Eu estou reformado/ reformada. **m/f** e·oo shtoh rre·for·*maa*·doo/ rre·for·*maa*·da
A I'm self-employed.	Eu sou empregado/ empregada por conta própria. **m/f** e·oo soh eng·pre·*gaa*·doo/ eng·pre·*gaa*·da poor *kong*·ta *pro*·pree·a
A I'm unemployed.	Eu estou desempregado/ desempregada. **m/f** e·oo shtoh de·zeng·pre·*gaa*·doo/ de·zeng·pre·*gaa*·da
Q What are you studying?	O que é que está a estudar? oo ke e ke shtaa a shtoo·*daar*
A I'm studying humanities.	Estudo humanísticas. *shtoo*·doo oo·ma·*neesh*·tee·kash

| 🅐 I'm studying science. | Estudo ciências.
shtoo·doo see·eng·see·ash |
| 🅐 I'm studying Portuguese. | Estudo português.
shtoo·do poor·too·gesh |

For more occupations, see the **dictionary**.

Family

| 🆀 Do you have a ...? | Tem ...?
teng ... |
| 🅐 I (don't) have a ... | Eu (não) tenho ...
e·oo (nowng) ta·nyoo ... |

brother	um irmão	*oong eer·mowng*
daughter	uma filha	*oo·ma fee·lya*
granddaughter	neta	*ne·ta*
grandson	neto	*ne·too*
husband	marido	*ma·ree·doo*
partner	companheiro m	*kong·pa·nyay·roo*
	companheira f	*kong·pa·nyay·ra*
sister	uma irmã	*oo·ma eer·mang*
son	um filho	*oong fee·lyoo*
wife	esposa	*shpo·za*

🆀 Are you married?	É casado/casada? m/f *e ka·zaa·doo/ka·zaa·da*
🅐 I'm married.	Eu sou casado/ casada. m/f *e·oo soh ka·zaa·doo/ ka·zaa·da*
🅐 I'm divorced.	Eu sou divorciado/ divorciada. m/f *e·oo soh dee·vor·see·aa·doo/ dee·vor·see·aa·da*

🅰 I'm single.	Eu sou solteiro/solteira. m/f e·oo soh sol·*tay*·roo/sol·*tay*·ra
🅰 I'm separated.	Eu estou separado/separada. m/f e·oo se·pa·*raa*·doo/se·pa·*raa*·da
🅰 I live with someone (a man).	Vivo com o meu namorado. m *vee*·voo kong oo *me*·oo na·moo·*raa*·doo
🅰 I live with someone (a woman).	Vivo com a minha namorada. f *vee*·voo kong a *mee*·nya na·moo·*raa*·da

Talking with Children

When's your birthday?	Quando é que fazes anos? *kwang*·doo e ke *faa*·zesh a·noosh
Do you go to school?	Vais à escola? vaish aa *shko*·la
What grade are you in?	Em que ano estás? eng ke a·noo shtaash
Do you like (sport)?	Gostas (de desporto)? *goosh*·tash (de desh·*por*·too)
What do you do after school?	O que é que fazes depois da escola? o ke e ke *faa*·zesh de·*poysh* da *shko*·la
Do you learn (English)?	Aprendes (inglês)? a·*preng*·desh (eeng·*glesh*)

Talking about Children

When's the baby due?	Para quando está previsto o nascimento do bebé? *pa·ra kwang·doo shtaa pre·veesh·too oo nash·see·meng·too doo be·be*
What are you going to call the baby?	Que nome vai dar ao bebé? *ke no·me vai daar ow be·be*
Is this your first child?	É o seu primeiro filho? *e oo se·oo pree·may·roo fee·lyoo*
How many children do you have?	Quantos filhos tem? *kwang·toosh fee·lyoosh teng*
What a beautiful child!	Que linda criança! *ke leeng·da kree·ang·sa*
Is it a boy or a girl?	É menino ou menina? *e me·nee·noo oh me·nee·na*
How old is he/she?	Quantos anos tem? *kwang·toosh a·noosh teng*
What's his/her name?	Como se chama? *ko·moo se sha·ma*
Does he/she go to school?	Vai à escola? *vai aa shko·la*

Farewells

Tomorrow is my last day here.	Amanhã é o meu último dia aqui. *aa·ma·nyang e oo me·oo ool·tee·moo dee·a a·kee*
It's been great meeting you.	Foi fantástico conhecê-lo/conhecê-la. **m/f** *foy fang·taash·tee·koo koo·nye·se·loo/koo·nye·se·la*

Keep in touch!	Mantenha-se em contacto! mang·*te*·nya·se eng kong·*taak*·too
If you come to (Scotland), you can stay with me.	Se vier à (Escócia) pode ficar em minha casa. se vee·*er* aa (*shko*·sya) po·de fee·*kar* eng *mee*·nya *kaa*·za
Q **What's your address/ email?**	Qual é o seu endereço/email? kwaal e oo *se*·oo eng·de·*re*·soo/ee·*mayl*
Q **What's your phone number?**	Qual é o seu número de telefone? kwaal e oo *se*·oo *noo*·me·roo de te·le·*fo*·ne
A **Here's my ...**	Aqui está o meu ... a·*kee* shtaa oo *me*·oo ...

Well-Wishing

Bless you!	Deus o abençoe! de·ooz oo a·beng·*so*·e
Congratulations!	Parabéns! pa·ra·*bengzh*
Good luck!	Boa sorte! bo·a *sor*·te
Bon voyage!	Boa viagem! bo·a vee·*aa*·zheng
Happy birthday!	Feliz aniversário! fe·*leesh* a·nee·ver·*saa*·ree·oo
Happy New Year!	Feliz Ano Novo! fe·*leesh* a·noo *no*·voo
Merry Christmas!	Feliz Natal! fe·*leesh* na·*taal*

Interests

KEY PHRASES

What do you do in your spare time?	O que faz nos seus tempos livres?	oo ke fazh noosh se·oosh *teng*·poosh *lee*·vresh
Do you like ...?	Gosta de ...?	*gosh*·ta de ...
I (don't) like ...	Eu (não) gosto de ...	e·oo (nowng) *gosh*·too de ...

Common Interests

What do you do in your spare time?	O que faz nos seus tempos livres? oo ke fazh noosh se·oosh *teng*·poosh *lee*·vresh
Q Do you like ...?	Gosta de ...? *gosh*·ta de ...
A I (don't) like ...	Eu (não) gosto de ... e·oo (nowng) *gosh*·too de ...

cooking	cozinhar	koo·zee·*nyaar*
gardening	jardinagem	zhar·dee·*naa*·zheng
hiking	caminhar	ka·mee·*nyaar*
photography	fazer fotografia	fa·*zer* foo·too·gra·*fee*·a
reading	ler	ler
shopping	ir às compras	eer aash *kong*·prash
travelling	viajar	vee·a·*zhaar*

For types of sports, see **sport** (p142), and the **dictionary**.

Music

Do you ...?		Costuma ...? koosh·*too*·ma ...
dance	ir dançar	eer dang·*saar*
go to concerts	ir a concertos	eer a kong·*ser*·toosh
listen to music	ouvir música	oh·*veer* moo·zee·ka
play an instrument	tocar algum instrumento	too·*kaar* aal·*goong* eeng·shtroo·*meng*·too
sing	cantar	kang·*taar*

Which bands do you like?	De que conjuntos gosta? de ke kong·*zhoong*·toosh *gosh*·ta
Which artists do you like?	De que artistas gosta? de ke ar·*teesh*·tash *gosh*·ta
What music do you like?	De que tipo de música gosta? de ke *tee*·poo de *moo*·zee·ka *gosh*·ta
... music	música f *moo*·zee·ka

classical	clássica	*klaa*·see·ka
electronic	electrónica	ee·le·*tro*·nee·ka
folk	popular	poo·poo·*laar*
traditional Portuguese	tradicional portuguesa	tra·dee·syoo·*naal* poor·too·*ge*·za
world	todo o mundo	*to*·doo oo *moong*·doo

Cinema & Theatre

I feel like going to a/an ...	Apetece-me ir ao/à ... m/f	a·pe·*te*·se·me eer ow/aa ...
Q Did you like the ...?	Gostou ...?	goosh·*toh* ...

ballet	do ballet	doo ba·*le*
film	do filme	doo *fil*·me
opera	da ópera	da *o*·pe·ra
play	da peça (de teatro)	da *pe*·sa (de tee·*aa*·troo)

A I thought it was boring.	Eu achei que era chato/chata. m/f	e·oo a·*shay* ke e·ra *shaa*·too/*shaa*·ta
A I thought it was excellent.	Eu achei que era excelente.	e·oo a·*shay* ke e·ra aysh·se·*leng*·te
A I thought it was OK.	Eu achei que era razoável.	e·oo a·*shay* ke e·ra rra·zoo·*aa*·vel
What's showing at the cinema/theatre tonight?	O que é que está no cinema/teatro hoje à noite?	oo ke e ke shtaa noo see·*ne*·ma/tee·*aa*·troo o·zhe aa *noy*·te
Is it in English?	É em inglês?	e eng eeng·*glesh*
Does it have English subtitles?	Tem legendas em inglês?	teng le·*zheng*·dash eng eeng·*glesh*
Is there a matinée show?	Há alguma matiné?	aa aal·*goo*·ma ma·tee·*ne*
Is this seat taken?	Este lugar está ocupado?	*esh*·te loo·*gaar* shtaa o·koo·*paa*·doo

SOCIAL INTERESTS

Tongue Twisters
Think you've got a bit of a handle on Portuguese? Amuse the locals by reciting one of these little beauties:

Um prato de trigo para três tigres tristes.
oong *praa*·too de *tree*·goo *pa*·ra tresh *tee*·gresh *treesh*·tesh
A plate of wheat for three sad tigers.

Se cá nevasse fazia-se cá esqui.
se kaa ne·*vaa*·se fa·*zee*·a·se kaa shkee
If it snowed here you could ski.

O rato roeu a rolha do garrafão do rei da Rússia.
oo *rraa*·too rroo·*e*·oo a *rro*·lya doo ga·rra·*fowng* doo rray da *rru*·sya
The mouse nibbled the cork of the large wickerwork bottle from the king of Russia.

Have you seen (José e Pilar)?	Já viu a *(José e Pilar)*? zha *vee*·oo a (zho·ze e pee·*laar*)
Q Who's in it?	Com quem é? kong keng e
A It stars (José Saramago).	É com o (José Saramago). e kong oo (zho·ze sa·ra·*maa*·goo)
Do you have tickets for ...?	Tem bilhetes para ...? teng bee·*lye*·tesh *pa*·ra ...
I'd like the best tickets.	Eu queria os melhores bilhetes. e·oo ke·*ree*·a oosh me·*lyor*·esh bee·*lye*·tesh
I'd like cheap tickets.	Eu queria bilhetes baratos. e·oo ke·*ree*·a bee·*lye*·tesh ba·*ra*·toosh

SOCIAL INTERESTS

I'd like ...	Eu queria ... *e·oo ke·ree·a ...*	
1st/2nd balcony seats	lugares no primeiro/ segundo balcão	loo·*gaa*·resh noo pree·*may*·roo/ se·*goong*·doo baal*kowng*
box seats	um camarote	oong ka·ma·ro·te
orchestra seats	lugares na plateia	loo·*gaa*·resh na pla·*tay*·a
wings seats	coxias	koo·*shee*·ash

action movies	filmes de acção m pl *feel*·mesh de a·*sowng*
animated films	desenhos animados m pl de·*ze*·nyoosh a·nee·*maa*·doosh
comedies	comédias f pl koo·*me*·dyash
drama	drama f *dra*·ma
documentaries	documentários m pl doo·koo·meng·*ta*·ryoosh
horror movies	filmes de terror m pl *feel*·mesh de te·*rror*
Portuguese cinema	cinema português m see·*ne*·ma poor·too·*gesh*
sci-fi	ficção científica f feek·*sowng* see·eng·*tee*·fee·ka
short films	curtas-metragens f pl *koor*·tash·me·*traa*·zhengsh
thrillers	filmes de suspense m pl *feel*·mesh de soosh·*pengs*
war movies	filmes de guerra m pl *feel*·mesh de ge·rra

Feelings & Opinions

KEY PHRASES

Are you ...?	Está ...?	shtaa ...
I'm (not) ...	(Não) Estou ...	(nowng) shtoh ...
What do you think of it?	O que é que acha disso?	oo ke e ke aa·sha dee·soo
I thought it was OK.	Eu achei que razoável.	e·oo a·shay ke rra·zoo·aa·vel
Did you hear about ...?	Ouviu falar de ...?	oh·vee·oo fa·laar de ...

Feelings

Q Are you ...?
Está ...?
shtaa ...

A I'm (not) ...
(Não) Estou ...
(nowng) shtoh ...

cold	com frio	kong free·oo
happy	feliz	fe·leesh
hot	com calor	kong ka·lor
hungry	com fome	kong fo·me
in a hurry	com pressa	kong pre·sa
sad	triste	treesh·te
thirsty	com sede	kong se·de
tired	cansado m	kang·saa·doo
	cansada f	kang·saa·da
well	bem	beng

What's wrong?	Qual é o problema? kwaal e oo proo·*ble*·ma
What happened?	O que aconteceu? oo ke aa·kong·te·se·oo
I'm a little (sad).	Estou um bocadinho (triste). shtoh oon boo·ka·*dee*·nyoo (*treesh*·te)
I feel very (lucky).	Sinto-me com muita (sorte). *seeng*·too·me kong *mweeng*·ta (*sor*·te)
I'm not at all (tired).	Não estou nada (cansado/cansada). **m/f** nowng shtoh *naa*·da (kang·*saa*·doo/kang·*saa*·da)

If you're not feeling well, see **health** (p161).

Opinions

Q Did you like it?	Gostou? *gosh*·toh
Q What do you think of it?	O que é que acha disso? oo ke e ke *aa*·sha dee·soo
A I thought it was ...	Eu achei que ... e·oo a·*shay* ke ...
A It's ...	É ... e ...

awful	horrível	o·*rree*·vel
beautiful	lindo/linda **m/f**	*leeng*·doo/*leeng*·da
boring	chato/chata **m/f**	*shaa*·too/*shaa*·ta
great	óptimo/óptima **m/f**	o·*tee*·moo/o·*tee*·ma
interesting	interessante	eeng·te·re·*sang*·te
OK	razoável	rra·zoo·*aa*·vel
strange	estranho **m**	*shtra*·nyoo
	estranha **f**	*shtra*·nya

Politics & Social Issues

Q Who do you vote for?	Em que partido vota? eng ke par·*tee*·da *vo*·ta
A I support the ... party.	Eu apoio o ... e·oo a·*poy*·oo oo ...
A I'm a member of the ... party.	Eu sou membro ... e·oo soh *meng*·broo ...
Did you hear about ...?	Ouviu falar de ...? oh·*vee*·oo fa·*laar* de ...
Q Do you agree with it?	Concorda? kong·*kor*·da
A I (don't) agree with ...	Eu (não) concordo com ... e·oo (nowng) kong·*kor*·doo kong ...
How do people feel about ...?	O que é que as pessoas pensam sobre ...? oo ke e ke ash pe·*so*·ash *peng*·sang *so*·bre ...
How can we protest against ...?	Como é que podemos protestar contra ...? ko·moo e ke poo·*de*·moosh pro·tesh·*taar* *kong*·tra ...
How can we support ...?	Como é que podemos apoiar ...? ko·moo e ke poo·*de*·moosh a·poy·*aar* ...
immigration	imigração f ee·mee·gra·*sowng*
the economy	a economia f a ee·ko·noo·*mee*·a
the environment	o ambiente m oo ang·bee·*eng*·te
the war in ...	a guerra em ... f a *ge*·rra eng ...

The Environment

Is there a ... problem here?	Há algum problema de ... aqui? aa aal·*goong* pro·*ble*·ma de ... a·*kee*
What should be done about ...?	O que é que deve ser feito em relação ...? oo ke e ke *de*·ve ser *fay*·too eng rre·la·*sowng* ...
pollution	poluição f poo·loo·ee·*sowng*
recycling programme	programas de reciclagem m pl proo·*gra*·mash de rre·see·*klaa*·zheng
Is this a protected forest/ species?	Esta floresta/espécie está protegida? *esh*·ta flo·*resh*·ta/*shpe*·sye shtaa proo·te·*zhee*·da
Is this a protected park?	Este parque está protegido? *esh*·te *par*·ke shtaa proo·te·*zhee*·doo

---

LANGUAGE TIP

Masculine & Feminine
In this book, many Portuguese words listed as stand-alone have different masculine and feminine forms, marked with m and f respectively. When an adjective is used with a noun, its form matches the gender of the noun, eg *parque protegido* *par*·ke proo·te·*zhee*·doo (masculine) vs *floresta protegida* flo·*resh*·ta proo·te·*zhee*·da (feminine). The same applies to saying 'thank you' – the form should match the speaker's gender: *Obrigado* m o·bree·*gaa*·doo or *Obrigada* f o·bree·*gaa*·da. See also **gender** in the **grammar** chapter (p18).

Going Out

KEY PHRASES

What's on tonight?	O que é que há hoje à noite?	oo ke e ke aa o·zhe aa noy·te
Where can I find clubs?	Onde é que há discotecas?	ong·de e ke aa deesh·koo·te·kash
Would you like to go for a coffee?	Gostava de ir a um café?	goosh·taa·va de eer a oong ka·fe
Where will we meet?	Onde é que nos encontramos?	ong·de e ke noosh eng·kong·traa·moosh
What time do you want to meet?	A que horas é que nos encontramos?	a ke o·rash e ke noosh eng·kong·traa·moosh

Where To Go

What's there to do in the evenings?	O que é que se pode fazer à noite? oo ke e ke se po·de fa·zer aa noy·te
What's on tonight?	O que é que há hoje à noite? oo ke e ke aa o·zhe aa noy·te
What's on this weekend?	O que é que há este fim-de-semana? oo ke e ke aa esh·te feeng·de·se·ma·na
Is there a local entertainment guide?	Há um guia local de entertenimento? aa oong gee·a loo·kaal de eng·ter·te·nee·meng·too

I feel like going to a ...

Está-me a apetecer
ir a ...
*shtaa·me a a·pe·te·ser
eer a ...*

bar	um bar	oong bar
bullfight	uma tourada	oo·ma toh·*raa*·da
cafe	um café	oong ka·*fe*
concert	um concerto	oong kong·*ser*·too
fado house	uma casa de fados	oo·ma *kaa*·za de *faa*·doosh
film	um filme	oong *feel*·me
nightclub	uma discoteca	oo·ma deesh·koo·*te*·ka
party	uma festa	oo·ma *fesh*·ta
play	uma peça de teatro	oo·ma *pe*·sa de tee·*aa*·troo
restaurant	um restaurante	oong rresh·tow·*rang*·te
street party	uma festa de rua	oo·ma *fesh*·ta de *rroo*·a

Where can I find ...?

Onde é que há ...?
ong·de e ke aa ...

bars	bares	*ba*·resh
clubs	discotecas	deesh·koo·*te*·kash
gay/lesbian venues	lugares de gays/ lésbicas	loo·*gaa*·resh de gaysh/ *lezh*·bee·kash
places to eat	sítios para comer	*see*·tyoosh *pa*·ra koo·*mer*

Invitations

What are you doing tonight?	O que é que vai fazer hoje à noite? oo ke e ke vai fa·*zer* o·zhe aa *noy*·te
What are you doing this weekend?	O que é que vai fazer este fim-de-semana? oo ke e ke vai fa·*zer esh*·te feeng·de·se·*ma*·na
Would you like to go (for a) ...?	Gostava de ir ...? goosh·*taa*·va de eer ...
I feel like going (for a) ...	Apetece-me ir ... a·pe·*te*·se·me eer ...

coffee	a um café	a oong ka·*fe*
dancing	dançar	dang·*saar*
drink	beber alguma coisa	be·*ber* aal·*goo*·ma *koy*·za
meal	comer	koo·*mer*
out	sair	sa·*eer*
walk	andar a pé	ang·*daar* a pe

Do you know a good restaurant?	Conhece um bom restaurante? kong·*nye*·se oong bong rresh·tow·*rang*·te
Do you want to come to the concert with me?	Quer vir ao concerto comigo? ker veer ow kong·*ser*·too koo·*mee*·goo
We're having a party.	Vamos dar uma festa. *vaa*·moosh daar *oo*·ma *fesh*·ta
You should come.	Devia vir. de·*vee*·a veer

SOCIAL GOING OUT

🔍 LOOK FOR

Street numbers follow the name of the street. Often apartments are indicated by floor number as well as by the side of the landing on which they're located — ie *direita* dee·*ray*·ta for right, *esquerda* shker·da for left. For example, *Rua do Rei, no. 15 – 3° drt.* could be translated as '15 King Street, 3rd floor, right side of the landing'.

avenida (av.) f	a·ve·*nee*·da	avenue/boulevard
beco m	*be*·koo	alley
estrada (estd.) f	esh·*traa*·da	road
rua (r.) f	*rroo*·a	street

Responding to Invitations

Yes, I'd love to.	Sim, adorava.
	seeng a·doo·*raa*·va
That's very kind of you.	É muito simpático
	da sua parte.
	e *mweeng*·too seeng·*paa*·tee·koo
	da *soo*·a *par*·te
Where shall we go?	Onde é que podemos ir?
	ong·de e ke poo·*de*·moosh eer
No, I'm afraid I can't.	Tenho muita pena,
	mas não posso.
	ta·nyoo *mweeng*·ta *pe*·na
	mash nowng *po*·soo
Sorry, I can't sing/dance.	Tenho muita pena, mas
	não sei cantar/dançar.
	ta·nyoo *mweeng*·ta *pe*·na mas
	nowng say kang·*taar*/dang·*saar*
What about tomorrow?	E que tal amanhã?
	ee ke taal aa·ma·*nyang*

Arranging to Meet

What time do you want to meet?	A que horas é que nos encontramos? a ke o·rash e ke noosh eng·kong·*traa*·moosh
Q Where will we meet?	Onde é que nos encontramos? *ong*·de e ke noosh eng·kong·*traa*·moosh
A Let's meet (at the entrance).	Encontramo-nos (à entrada). eng·kong·*traa*·moo·noosh (aa eng·*traa*·da)
I'll pick you up.	Eu vou buscá-lo/-la. m/f e·oo voh boosh·*kaa*·loo/la

> ### *Vai ser um prazer.*
> vai ser oong pra·*zer*
> ### *I'm looking forward to it.*

SOCIAL GOING OUT

I'll be coming later.	Eu vou mais tarde. e·oo voh maish *taar*·de
Where will you be?	Onde é que vais estar? *ong*·de e ke vaish shtaar
Q Are you ready?	Está pronto/pronta? **m/f** shtaa *prong*·too/*prong*·ta
A I'm ready.	Estou pronto/pronta. **m/f** shtoh *prong*·too/*prong*·ta
I'll see you then.	Até já. a·*te* zhaa
I'm looking forward to it.	Vai ser um prazer. vai ser oong pra·*zer*
Sorry I'm late.	Desculpe o atraso. desh·*kool*·pe oo a·*traa*·zoo

Drugs

Do you want to have a smoke?	Quer um cigarro? ker oong see·*gaa*·rroo
Do you have a light?	Tem lume? teng *loo*·me
I don't take drugs.	Eu não tomo drogas. e·oo nowng *to*·moo *dro*·gash

If the police are talking to you about drugs, see **police** (p158).

LANGUAGE TIP

Reading Portuguese

A vowel followed by *m* or *n*, or with a tilde (~) above it, is usually nasalised – eg *viagem* vee·*aa*·zheng, *avião* a·vee·*owng*.

The letter *o* is often pronounced oo, especially at the end of a word – eg *gato gaa*·too.

The letters *es* at the start of a word, and *s* at the end of a word, are almost always pronounced sh – eg *estômago shto*·ma·goo, *crianças* kree·*ang*·sash.

Romance

KEY PHRASES

Would you like to do something?	Queres fazer alguma coisa?	ke·resh fa·zer aal·goo·ma koy·za
I love you.	Amo-te.	a·moo·te
Leave me alone!	Deixa-me!	day·sha·me

Asking Someone Out

Where would you like to go (tonight)?	Onde é que queres ir (hoje à noite)? ong·de e ke ke·resh eer (o·zhe aa noy·te)
Q Would you like to do something (tomorrow)?	Queres fazer alguma coisa (amanhã)? ke·resh fa·zer aal·goo·ma koy·za (aa·ma·nyang)
A Yes, I'd love to.	Sim, adorava. seeng a·doo·raa·va
A Sorry, I can't.	Desculpa, mas não posso. desh·kool·pa mash nowng po·soo

Pick-up Lines

Would you like a drink?	Queres uma bebida? ke·resh oo·ma be·bee·da
You're a fantastic dancer.	Danças muito bem. daang·sash mweeng·too beng

Can I dance with you?	Posso dançar contigo? *po·soo dang·saar* kong·*tee*·goo
Can I sit here?	Posso sentar-me aqui? *po·soo seng·taar·me a·kee*

Rejections

No, thank you.	Não, obrigado/ obrigada. m/f nowng o·bree·*gaa*·doo/ o·bree·*gaa*·da
I'd rather not.	É melhor não. e me·*lyor* nowng
I'm here with my girlfriend.	Estou aqui com a minha namorada. shtoh a·*kee* kong a *mee*·nya na·moo·*raa*·da
I'm here with my boyfriend.	Estou aqui com o meu namorado. shtoh a·*kee* kong oo *me*·oo na·moo·*raa*·doo
Excuse me, I have to go now.	Desculpa, tenho de me ir embora. desh·*kool*·pa ta·nyoo de me eer eng·*bo*·ra
Leave me alone!	Deixa-me! *day*·sha·me
Get lost!	Desaparece! de·za·pa·*re*·se

Getting Closer

I really like you.	Eu gosto mesmo de ti. *e*·oo *gosh*·too *mezh*·moo de tee

You're great.	És fantástico/fantástica. **m/f** esh fang·*taash*·tee·koo/fang·*taash*·tee·ka
Can I kiss you?	Posso dar-te um beijo? *po*·soo *dar*·te oong *bay*·zhoo
Do you want to come inside for a while?	Queres entrar? *ke*·resh eng·*traar*
Would you like to stay over?	Queres passar a noite aqui? *ke*·resh pa·*saar* a *noy*·te a·*kee*
Can I stay over?	Posso passar a noite aqui? *po*·soo pa·*saar* a *noy*·te a·*kee*

Sex

Kiss me.	Dá-me um beijo. *daa*·me oong *bay*·zhoo
I want you.	Quero-te. *ke*·roo·te
Touch me here.	Toca-me aqui. *to*·ka·me a·*kee*
🇶 **Do you like this?**	Gostas disto? *gosh*·tash *deesh*·too
🇦 **I (don't) like that.**	Eu (não) gosto disso. *e*·oo (nowng) *gosh*·too *dee*·soo

---

LANGUAGE TIP

Multiple Meanings

There's no specific word for 'date' in Portuguese – the Portuguese use the word *encontro* eng·*kong*·troo, which is just a general word for 'meeting'. Be sure you know what kind of meeting you're going to before you turn up with chocolates or flowers!

I think we should stop now.	Acho que é melhor pararmos. *aa*·shoo ke e me·*lyor* pa·*raar*·moosh
Let's go to bed.	Vamos para a cama. *vaa*·moosh pa·ra a *kaa*·ma
Do you have a (condom)?	Tens (um preservativo)? tengsh (oong pre·zer·va·*tee*·voo)
Let's use a (condom).	Vamos usar (um preservativo). *vaa*·moosh oo·*zaar* (oong pre·zer·va·*tee*·voo)
I won't do it without protection.	Eu não faço isso sem protecção. e·oo nowng *faa*·soo ee·soo seng proo·te·*sowng*
It's my first time.	É a minha primeira vez. e a *mee*·nya pree·*may*·ra vezh
That's great.	Fantástico! fang·*taash*·tee·koo
That was amazing.	Foi extraordinário. foy shtra·or·dee·*naa*·ree·oo
That was romantic.	Foi romântico. foy rroo·*mang*·tee·koo
That was wild.	Foi selvagem. foy sel·*vaa*·zheng

Love

I think we're good together.	Eu acho que nós estamos bem juntos. e·oo *aa*·shoo ke nosh *shta*·moosh beng *zhoong*·toosh

🔊 LISTEN FOR

fofa	*fo*·fa	sweetie
meu amor	*me*·oo a·*mor*	my love
querida f	ke·*ree*·da	dear
querido m	ke·*ree*·doo	dear

I love you.	Amo-te.
	a·moo·te
Will you go out with me?	Queres sair comigo?
	ke·resh sa·*eer* koo·*mee*·goo
Will you meet my parents?	Queres conhecer os meus pais?
	ke·resh koo·nye·*ser* oosh *me*·oosh paish
Will you marry me?	Queres casar comigo?
	ke·resh ka·*zaar* koo·*mee*·goo

Leaving

I have to leave (tomorrow).	Vou ter que me ir embora (amanhã).
	voh ter ke me eer eng·*bo*·ra (aa·ma·*nyang*)
I'll keep in touch.	Eu vou manter-me em contacto.
	e·oo voh mang·*ter*·me eng kong·*taak*·too
I'll miss you.	Eu vou ter saudades tuas.
	e·oo voh ter sow·*daa*·desh *too*·ash
I'll visit you.	Eu vou visitar-te.
	e·oo voh vee·zee·*taar*·te

SOCIAL · ROMANCE

Beliefs & Culture

KEY PHRASES

What's your religion?	Qual é a sua religião?	kwaal e a *soo*·a rre·lee·zhee·*owng*
I'm ...	Eu sou ...	e·oo soh ...
I'm sorry, it's against my beliefs.	Desculpe, mas é contra a minha crença.	desh·*kool*·pe mash e *kong*·tra a *mee*·nya *kreng*·sa

Religion

Q What's your religion?

Qual é a sua religião?
kwaal e a *soo*·a rre·lee·zhee·*owng*

A I'm not religious.

Não sou religioso/religiosa. m/f
nowng soh
rre·lee·zhee·o·*zoo*/
rre·lee·zhee·o·*za*

A I'm ...

Eu sou ...
e·oo soh ...

Buddhist	budista	boo·*deesh*·ta
Christian	cristão m	kreesh·*towng*
	cristã f	kreesh·*tang*
Hindu	hindu	eeng·*doo*
Jewish	judeu m	zhoo·*de*·oo
	judia f	zhoo·*dee*·a
Muslim	muçulmano m	moo·sool·*maa*·noo
	muçulmana f	moo·sool·*maa*·na

I (don't) believe in God.	Eu (não) acredito em Deus.
	e·oo (nowng) a·kre·*dee*·too eng *de*·oosh
Where can I attend a service?	Onde posso assistir a oong serviço religioso?
	ong·de po·soo a·seesh·*teer* a oong ser·*vee*·soo rre·lee·zhee·o·zoo
Can I pray here?	Posso rezar aqui?
	po·soo rre·*zaar* a·*kee*

Cultural Differences

Is this a local custom?	Este é um costume local?
	esh·te e oong koosh·*too*·me loo·*kaal*
I don't want to offend you.	Não quero ofendê-lo/ ofendê-la. **m/f**
	nowng *ke*·roo oo·feng·*de*·lo/ oo·feng·*de*·la
I'm not used to this.	Não estou acostumado/ acostumada a isso. **m/f**
	nowng shtoh a·koosh·too·*maa*·doo/ a·koosh·too·*maa*·da a *ee*·soo
I'll try it.	Vou experimentar.
	voh shpree·meng·*taar*
I'd rather not join in.	Prefiro não tomar parte.
	pre·*fee*·roo nowng too·*maar* *paar*·te
I didn't mean to do/ say anything wrong.	Não tive intenção de fazer/dizer nada de mal.
	nowng *tee*·ve eeng·teng·*sowng* de fa·*zer*/dee·*zeer* *naa*·da de maal
I'm sorry, it's against my beliefs.	Desculpe, mas é contra a minha crença.
	desh·*kool*·pe mash e *kong*·tra a *mee*·nya *kreng*·sa

Sports

KEY PHRASES

Which sport do you play?	Que desporto é que pratica?	ke desh·*por*·too e ke pra·*tee*·ka
Who's your favourite team?	Qual é a sua equipa favorita?	kwaal e a *soo*·a e·*kee*·pa fa·voo·*ree*·ta
What's the score?	Qual é o resultado?	kwaal e oo rre·zool·*taa*·doo

Sporting Interests

Q Which sport do you play?	Que desporto é que pratica? ke desh·*por*·too e ke pra·*tee*·ka
Q Which sport do you follow?	Que desporto é que segue? ke desh·*por*·too e ke *se*·ge
A I play/do ...	Eu faço/pratico ... e·oo *faa*·soo/pra·*tee*·koo ...
A I follow ...	Eu sigo ... e·oo *see*·goo ...

athletics	atletismo	at·le·*teezh*·moo
basketball	basquetebol	bash·ke·te·*bol*
football (soccer)	futebol	foo·te·*bol*
roller-blading hockey	hóquei em patins	o·kay eng pa·*teengsh*
scuba diving	mergulho	mer·*goo*·lyoo
volleyball	voleibol	*vo*·lay·bol

I cycle.	Eu faço ciclismo. *e·oo faa·soo see·kleesh·moo*
I run.	Eu corro. *e·oo ko·rroo*
Who's your favourite sportsperson?	Qual é o seu atleta favorito? *kwaal e oo se·oo at·le·ta fa·voo·ree·too*
Who's your favourite team?	Qual é a sua equipa favorita? *kwaal e a soo·a e·kee·pa fa·voo·ree·ta*
🇶 **Do you like (football)?**	Gosta de (futebol)? *gosh·ta de (foo·te·bol)*
🇦 **Yes, very much.**	Sim, gosto muito. *seeng gosh·too mweeng·too*
🇦 **Not really.**	Nem por isso. *neng poor ee·soo*
🇦 **I like watching it.**	Eu gosto de ver. *e·oo gosh·too de ver*

Going to a Game

Would you like to go to a game?	Quer ir a um jogo? *ker eer a oong zho·goo*
Who are you supporting?	Por quem está? *poor keng shtaa*
Who's playing?	Quem está a jogar? *keng shtaa a zhoo·gaar*
Who's winning?	Quem está a ganhar? *keng shtaa a ga·nyaar*
What's the score?	Qual é o resultado? *kwaal e oo rre·zool·taa·doo*

> **CULTURE TIP**
>
> **Bullfighting**
> The ancient rite of bullfighting (*tourada* toh·*raa*·da) remains one of Portugal's most popular spectator sports. It's a bit different from the Spanish version. The bull (*touro* toh·roo) first faces a horseman (*cavaleiro* ka·va·*lay*·roo), who must plant a number of barbs into the bull's neck muscle. The bull's horns are cut (so as not to have sharp points) and padded with leather. A crew of foot soldiers (*forcados* foor·*kaa*·doosh) then enters the ring, taunts the bull into charging forcefully, and eventually wrestles him to a standstill. The bull doesn't die in the ring but is almost always killed just afterwards by a butcher.

That was a bad game!	Foi um mau jogo! foy oong mow *zho*·goo
That was a great game!	Foi um jogo óptimo! foy oong *zho*·goo o·tee·moo
That was a boring game!	Foi um jogo chato! foy oong *zho*·goo *shaa*·too

Playing Sport

Some of the phrases in this section are in the informal form, as people tend to be casual in the middle of a game. See **grammar** (p20), for more details on polite and informal forms.

Q	**Can I join in?**	Posso entrar? po·soo eng·*traar*
Q	**Do you want to play?**	Quer jogar? ker zhoo·*gaar*
A	**That would be great.**	Isso era óptimo. ee·soo e·ra o·tee·moo
A	**I can't.**	Não posso. nowng po·soo

🔊 LISTEN FOR

bola de partida	*bo*·la de par·*tee*·da	match-point
empate	eng·*paa*·te	draw/even
nada	*naa*·da	love (zero)
zero	*ze*·roo	nil (zero)

SOCIAL SPORTS

🅰 I have an injury.	Estou lesado/lesada. m/f shtoh le·*zaa*·doo/le·*zaa*·da
Your/My point.	O ponto é teu/meu. oo *pong*·too e te·oo/me·oo
Kick/Pass it to me!	Passa! *paa*·sa
You're a good player.	És um bom jogador. m esh oong bong zhoo·ga·*dor* És uma boa jogadora. f esh oo·ma *bo*·a zhoo·ga·*do*·ra
Thanks for the game.	Obrigado/Obrigada pelo jogo. m/f o·bree·*gaa*·doo/o·bree·*gaa*·da pe·loo *zho*·goo
Where's the nearest golf course/tennis court?	Onde é que é o campo de golfe/ténis mais próximo? *ong*·de e ke e oo *kang*·poo de *gol*·fe/*te*·neesh maish *pro*·see·moo
Where's the nearest gym?	Onde é que é o ginásio mais próximo? *ong*·de e ke e oo zhee·*naa*·zyoo maish *pro*·see·moo

Where's the nearest swimming pool?		Onde é que é a piscina mais próxima? *ong·de e ke e a pesh·see·na maish pro·see·ma*
What's the charge per ...?		Quanto se paga por ...? *kwang·too se paa·ga poor ...*

day	dia	*dee·a*
game	jogo	*zho·goo*
hour	hora	*o·ra*
visit	visita	*vee·zee·ta*

Can I hire a ...?		Pode-se alugar ...? *po·de·se a·loo·gaar ...*

ball	uma bola	*oo·ma bo·la*
bicycle	uma bicicleta	*oo·ma bee·see·kle·ta*
court	um campo	*oong kang·poo*
racquet	uma raquete	*oo·ma rra·ke·te*

Where's a good place to ...?		Onde é que há um bom lugar para ...? *ong·de e ke aa oong bong loo·gaar pa·ra ...*

fish	pescar	*pesh·kaar*
go horseriding	andar a cavalo	*ang·daar a ka·vaa·loo*
run	correr	*koo·rrer*
ski	esquiar	*shkee·aar*
snorkel	fazer snorkel	*fa·zer snor·kel*
surf	fazer surf	*fa·zer sarf*

Do I have to be a member to attend?	Tenho de ser membro para entrar? *ta*·nyoo de ser *meng*·broo *pa*·ra eng·*traar*
Is there a women-only session?	Há alguma sessão só para mulheres? aa aal·*goo*·ma se·*sowng* so *pa*·ra moo·*lye*·resh
Where are the changing rooms?	Onde são os balneários? *ong*·de sowng oosh bal·nee·*aa*·ree·oosh

Football/Soccer

Who plays for (Porto)?	Quem joga no (Porto)? keng *zho*·ga noo (*por*·too)
He's a great (player).	Ele é um grande (jogador). *e*·le e oong *grang*·de (zhoo·ga·*dor*)
He played brilliantly in the match against (Italy).	Ele jogou muito bem contra (a Itália). *e*·le zho·*goh mweeng*·too beng *kong*·tra (a ee·*taa*·lya)
Which team is at the top of the league?	Qual é a equipa que vai à frente no campeonato? kwaal e a e·*kee*·pa ke vai aa *freng*·te noo kang·pee·oo·*naa*·too
What a great/terrible team!	Que equipa fantástica/ horrível! ke e·*kee*·pa fang·*taash*·tee·ka/ o·*rree*·vel

SOCIAL SPORTS

🔊 LISTEN FOR

árbitro m	*ar·bee·troo*	referee
atacante m	*a·ta·kang·te*	striker
baliza f	*ba·lee·za*	goal (structure)
bola f	*bo·la*	ball
canto m	*kang·too*	corner (kick)
cartão m amarelo	*kar·towng a·ma·re·loo*	yellow card
cartão m vermelho	*kar·towng ver·me·lyoo*	red card
falta f	*faal·ta*	foul
fora-de-jogo	*fo·ra·de·zho·goo*	offside
grande f penalidade	*grang·de pe·na·lee·daa·de*	penalty
guarda-redes m	*gwaar·da·rre·desh*	goalkeeper
jogador m	*zhoo·ga·dor*	player
lançamento m lateral	*lang·sa·meng·too la·te·raal*	throw-in
livre m	*lee·vre*	free kick
treinador m	*tray·na·dor*	coach

What a ...!		Que ...! ke ...
goal	golo	*go·loo*
hit	pancada	*pang·kaa·da*
kick	pontapé	*pong·ta·pe*
pass	passe	*paa·se*
performance	actuação	*a·too·a·sowng*

Off to see a match? Check out **buying tickets** (p42), and **going to a game** (p143).

Outdoors

KEY PHRASES

Where can I buy supplies?	Onde é que posso comprar mantimentos?	*ong*·de e ke *po*·soo kong·*praar* mang·tee·*meng*·toosh
Do we need a guide?	Precisamos de um guia?	pre·see·*za*·moosh de oong *gee*·a
Is it safe?	É seguro?	e se·*goo*·roo
I'm lost.	Estou perdido/ perdida. m/f	shtoh per·*dee*·doo/ per·*dee*·da
What's the weather like?	Como está o tempo?	*ko*·moo shtaa oo *teng*·poo

Hiking

Where can I ...?   Onde é que posso ...?
ong·de e ke *po*·soo ...

buy supplies	comprar mantimentos	kong·*praar* mang·tee·*meng*·toosh
find someone who knows this area	encontrar alguém que conheça esta área	eng·kong·*traar* aal·*geng* ke koo·*nye*·sa *esh*·ta *aa*·re·a
get a map	arranjar um mapa	a·rrang·*zhaar* oong *maa*·pa
hire hiking gear	alugar equipamento de caminhada	a·loo·*gaar* e·kee·pa·*meng*·too de ka·mee·*nyaa*·da

How high is the climb?	Qual é a altura da escalada? kwaal e a aal·*too*·ra da shka·*laa*·da
How long is the trail?	Qual é o comprimento do atalho? kwaal e oo kong·pree·*meng*·too doo a·*taa*·lyoo
Is it safe?	É seguro? e se·*goo*·roo
Are there guided treks?	Há caminhadas com guia? aa ka·mee·*nyaa*·dash kong *gee*·a
Do we need a guide?	Precisamos de um guia? pre·see·*za*·moosh de oong *gee*·a
Do we need to take food/water?	Precisamos de levar comida/água? pre·see·*za*·moosh de le·*vaar* koo·*mee*·da/*aa*·gwa
Is the track (well-) marked?	O trilho está (bem) sinalizado? oo *tree*·lyoo shtaa (beng) see·na·lee·*zaa*·doo
Is the track open?	O trilho está aberto? oo *tree*·lyoo shtaa a·*ber*·too
Which is the easiest/ shortest route?	Qual é a rota mais fácil/curta? kwaal e a *rro*·ta maish *faa*·seel/*koor*·ta
Does this path go to ...?	Este caminho leva a ...? *esh*·te ka·*mee*·nyoo *le*·va a ...
Can I go through here?	Posso ir por aqui? *po*·soo eer poor a·*kee*
I'm lost.	Estou perdido/perdida. m/f shtoh per·*dee*·doo/per·*dee*·da

Where can I find the ...? Onde ...?
ong·de ...

campsite	é o parque de campismo	e oo *par*·ke de kang·*peesh*·moo
nearest village	é a aldeia mais próxima	e a aal·*day*·a maish *pro*·see·ma
showers	são os chuveiros	sowng oosh shoo·*vay*·roosh
toilets	são as casas de banho	sowng ash *kaa*·zash de *ba*·nyoo

When does it get dark? A que horas fica escuro?
a ke o·rash *fee*·ka *shkoo*·roo

Is there a hut? Há alguma cabana?
aa aal·*goo*·ma ka·*ba*·na

SOCIAL OUTDOORS

Onde é que é a melhor praia?
ong·de e ke e a me·lyor prai·a
Where's the best beach?

Do we need to take a sleeping bag?	Precisamos de levar saco-cama?	pre·see·*za*·moosh de le·*vaar saa*·koo·*kaa*·ma
Is the water OK to drink?	Pode-se beber esta água?	*po*·de·se be·*ber* esh·ta *aa*·gwa

Beach

Where's the ... beach?	Onde é que é a ...?	*ong*·de e ke e a ...

best	melhor praia	me·*lyor prai*·a
nearest	praia mais próxima	*prai*·a maish *pro*·see·ma
nudist	praia de nudismo	*prai*·a de noo·*deesh*·moo
public	praia pública	*prai*·a *poo*·blee·ka

Is it safe to dive/swim here?	É seguro mergulhar/nadar aqui?	e se·*goo*·roo mer·goo·*lyaar*/na·*daar* a·*kee*
What time is high/low tide?	A que horas é a maré alta/baixa?	a ke *o*·rash e a ma·*re aal*·ta/*bai*·sha

🔊 LISTEN FOR

Cuidado com a corrente!	kwee·*daa*·doo kong a koo·*rreng*·te Be careful of the undertow!
É perigoso!	e pree·*go*·zoo It's dangerous!

LOOK FOR

Não Mergulhar	nowng mer·goo·lyaar	No Diving
Não Nadar	nowng na·daar	No Swimming

How much to rent a ...?
Quanto custa para alugar ...?
kwang·too koosh·ta pa·ra
a·loo·gaar ...

chair	uma cadeira	oo·ma ka·day·ra
hut	uma cabana	oo·ma ka·ba·na
sun umbrella	um guarda-sol	oong gwaar·da·sol
wind stopper	um pára-vento	oong paa·ra·veng·too

Weather

What's the weather like?	Como está o tempo? ko·moo shtaa oo teng·poo
What will the weather be like tomorrow?	Como vai estar o tempo amanhã? ko·moo vai shtaar oo teng·poo aa·ma·nyang
It's ...	Está ... shtaa ...

cloudy	enublado	e·noo·blaa·doo
(very) cold	(muito) frio	(mweeng·too) free·oo
raining	a chover	a shoo·ver
snowing	a nevar	a ne·vaar
sunny	sol	sol
warm	quente	keng·te
windy	ventoso	veng·to·zoo

SOCIAL   OUTDOORS

Where can I buy a rain jacket?	Onde é que posso comprar uma gabardina?
	ong·de e ke po·soo kong·praar oo·ma ga·baar·dee·na
Where can I buy an umbrella?	Onde é que posso comprar um guarda-chuva?
	ong·de e ke po·soo kong·praar oong gwaar·da·shoo·va

Flora & Fauna

| What ... is that? | Que ...? |
| | *ke ...* |

animal	animal é aquele	*aa·nee·maal e a·ke·le*
flower	flor é aquela	*flor e a·ke·la*
plant	planta é aquela	*plang·ta e a·ke·la*
tree	árvore é aquela	*aar·vo·re e a·ke·la*

Is it dangerous?	É perigoso/perigosa? m/f
	e pree·go·zoo/pree·go·za
Is it poisonous?	É venenoso/venenosa? m/f
	e ve·ne·no·zoo/ve·ne·no·za
Is it protected?	É protegido/protegida? m/f
	e proo·te·zhee·doo/proo·te·zhee·da
What's it used for?	Para que é que é usado/usada? m/f
	pa·ra ke e ke e oo·zaa·doo/oo·zaa·da
Can you eat the fruit?	Pode-se comer esta fruta?
	po·de·se koo·mer esh·ta froo·ta

For names of plants and animals, see the **dictionary**.

Safe Travel

Emergencies

KEY PHRASES

Help!	Socorro!	*soo·ko·*rroo
There's been an accident.	Houve um acidente.	*oh*·ve oong a·see·*deng·*te
It's an emergency.	É uma emergência.	e *oo·*ma ee·mer·*zheng·*sya

Help!	Socorro! soo·*ko·*rroo
Stop!	Stop! stop
Go away!	Vá-se embora! *vaa*·se eng·*bo·*ra
Thief!	Ladrão! la·*drowng*
Fire!	Fogo! *fo·*goo
Watch out!	Cuidado! kwee·*daa·*doo
Call a doctor.	Chame um médico. *shaa·*me oong *me·*dee·koo
Call an ambulance.	Chame uma ambulância. *shaa·*me oo·ma ang·boo·*lang·*sya
Call the police.	Chame a polícia. *shaa·*me a poo·*lee·*sya
It's an emergency.	É uma emergência. e *oo·*ma ee·mer·*zheng·*sya

🔍 LOOK FOR

Esquadra da Polícia	*shkwaa*·dra da poo·*lee*·sya	Police Station
Hospital	osh·pee·*taal*	Hospital
Polícia	poo·*lee*·sya	Police
Urgências	oor·*zheng*·syash	Emergency Department

There's been an accident.	Houve um acidente. *oh*·ve oong a·see·*deng*·te
Could you please help?	Pode ajudar, por favor? *po*·de a·zhoo·*daar* poor fa·*vor*
Can I use your phone?	Posso usar o seu telefone? *po*·soo oo·*zaar* oo se·oo te·le·*fo*·ne
I'm lost.	Estou perdido/ perdida. **m/f** shtoh per·*dee*·doo/ per·*dee*·da
Where are the toilets?	Onde é a casa de banho? *ong*·de e a *kaa*·za de *ba*·nyoo
Is it safe ...?	É seguro ...? e se·*goo*·roo ...

at night	à noite	aa *noy*·te
for gay people	para gays	*pa*·ra gaysh
for travellers	para turistas	*pa*·ra too·*reesh*·tash
for women	para mulheres	*pa*·ra moo·*lye*·resh
on your own	ir sozinho/ sozinha **m/f**	eer so·*zee*·nyoo/ so·*zee*·nya

Police

KEY PHRASES

Where's the police station?	Onde é a esquadra da polícia?	*ong*·de e a *shkwaa*·dra da poo·*lee*·sya
I want to contact my embassy.	Eu quero contactar com a minha embaixada.	*e*·oo *ke*·roo kong·tak·*taar* kong a *mee*·nya eng·bai·*shaa*·da
My bag was stolen.	Roubaram o meu saco.	rroh·*baa*·rang oo *me*·oo *saa*·koo

Where's the police station?	Onde é a esquadra da polícia? *ong*·de e a *shkwaa*·dra da poo·*lee*·sya
I want to report an offence.	Eu quero denunciar um crime. *e*·oo *ke*·roo de·noong·see·*aar* oong *kree*·me
It was him/her.	Foi ele/ela. foy *e*·le/*e*·la
I've been (assaulted).	Eu fui (agredido/ agredida). m/f *e*·oo fwee (a·gre·*dee*·doo/ a·gre·*dee*·da)
He/She has been (raped).	Ele/Ela foi (violado/ violada). m/f *e*·le/*e*·la foy (vee·oo·*laa*·doo/ vee·oo·*laa*·da)

My ... was/were stolen.	Roubaram ... rroh·*baa*·rang ...
I've lost my ...	Eu perdi ... e·oo per·*dee* ...

backpack	a minha mochila	a *mee*·nya mo·*shee*·la
bag	o meu saco	oo *me*·oo *saa*·koo
handbag	a minha bolsa	a *mee*·nya *bol*·sa
jewellery	as minhas jóias	ash *mee*·nyash *zhoy*·ash
money	o meu dinheiro	oo *me*·oo dee·*nyay*·roo
papers	os meus papeís	oosh *me*·oosh pa·*paysh*
passport	o meu passaporte	oo *me*·oo paa·sa·*por*·te
wallet	a minha carteira	a *mee*·nya kar·*tay*·ra

I didn't realise I was doing anything wrong.	Eu não percebi que estava a fazer algo errado. e·oo nowng per·se·*bee* ke *shtaa*·va a fa·*zer* *aal*·goo e·*rraa*·doo
I didn't do it.	Eu não fiz isso. e·oo nowng feez ee·soo
What am I accused of?	De que sou acusado/ acusada? m/f de ke soh a·koo·*zaa*·doo/ a·koo·*zaa*·da
I want to contact my embassy.	Eu quero contactar com a minha embaixada. e·oo *ke*·roo kong·tak·*taar* kong a *mee*·nya eng·bai·*shaa*·da
Can I make a phone call?	Posso fazer um telefonema? *po*·soo fa·*zer* oong te·le·foo·*ne*·ma

🔊 LISTEN FOR

agressão	a·gre·*sowng* assault
distúrbio da ordem pública	deesh·*toor*·byoo da or·*deng* *poo*·blee·ka disturbing the peace
excesso de velocidade	aysh·*se*·soo de ve·loo·see·*daa*·de speeding
multa de estacionamento	*mool*·ta de shta·syoo·na·*meng*·too parking fine
não ter um visto legal	nowng ter oong *veesh*·too le·*gaal* not having a visa
pequeno furto	pe·ke·noo *foor*·too shoplifting
posse (de substâncias ilegais)	*po*·se (de su·be·*shtang*·syash ee·le·*gaish*) possession (of illegal substances)
roubo	*rroh*·boo theft
ter visto expirado	ter *veesh*·too aysh·pee·*raa*·doo overstaying a visa

Can I have a lawyer (who speaks English)?	Posso ter acesso a um advogado (que fale inglês)? *po*·soo ter a·*se*·soo a oong a·de·voo·*gaa*·doo (que *faa*·le eeng·*glesh*)
I have insurance.	Eu estou coberto/ coberta pelo seguro. **m/f** *e*·oo shtoh koo·*ber*·too/ koo·*ber*·ta pe·loo se·*goo*·roo
I have a prescription for this drug.	Eu tenho uma receita para esta droga. *e*·oo *ta*·nyoo *oo*·ma rre·*say*·ta *pa*·ra esh·ta *dro*·ga

Health

KEY PHRASES

Where's the nearest hospital?	Qual é o hospital mais perto?	kwaal e oo osh·pee·*taal* maish *per*·too
I'm sick.	Estou doente.	shtoh doo·*eng*·te
I need a doctor.	Eu preciso de um médico.	e·oo pre·*see*·zoo de oong *me*·dee·koo
I'm on medication for ...	Eu estou a tomar medicamentos para ...	e·oo shtoh a too·*maar* me·dee·ka·*meng*·toosh *pa*·ra ...
I'm allergic to ...	Eu sou alérgico/ alérgica a ... m/f	e·oo soh a·*ler*·zhee·koo/ a·*ler*·zhee·ka a ...

Doctor

Address doctors and dentists as *Senhor Doutor* se·*nyor* doh·*tor* (men) or *Senhora Doutora* se·*nyo*·ra doh·*to*·ra (women).

Where's the nearest ...?   Qual é ... mais perto/perta?
                             kwaal e ... maish *per*·too/*per*·ta

dentist	o dentista	oo deng·*teesh*·ta
doctor	o médico m	oo *me*·dee·koo
	a médica f	a *me*·dee·ka
hospital	o hospital	oo osh·pee·*taal*
optometrist	o oculista	oo o·koo·*leesh*·ta
(night) pharmacist	a farmácia (de serviço)	a far·*maa*·sya (de ser·*vee*·soo)

I need a doctor (who speaks English).	Eu preciso de um médico (que fale inglês). e·oo pre·*see*·zoo de oong *me*·dee·koo (que *faa*·le eeng·*glesh*)
Could I see a female doctor?	Posso ser visto/vista por uma médica? **m/f** *po*·soo ser *veesh*·too/*veesh*·ta poor *oo*·ma me·dee·ka
I've run out of my medication.	Os meus medicamentos acabaram. oosh *me*·oosh me·dee·ka·*meng*·toosh a·ka·*baa*·rowng
My prescription is ...	A minha receita é ... a *meeng*·nya rre·*say*·ta e ...
What's the correct dosage?	Qual é a dose correcta? kwaal e a *do*·ze koo·*rre*·ta
I don't want a blood transfusion.	Eu não quero uma transfusão sanguinea. e·oo nowng *ke*·roo *oo*·ma trangsh·foo·*zowng* sang·*gwee*·nee·a
Please use a new syringe.	Por favor use uma seringa nova. poor fa·*vor* *oo*·ze *oo*·ma se·*reeng*·ga *no*·va
I've been vaccinated against (hepatitis A/B/C).	Eu tenho as vacinas de (hepatite A/B/C). e·oo *ta*·nyoo ash va·*see*·nash de (e·pa·*tee*·te a/be/se)
He has been vaccinated against (tetanus).	Ele foi vacinado contra (tétano). *e*·la foy va·see·*naa*·da kong·tra (*te*·ta·noo)

🔊 LISTEN FOR

Onde é que dói?	*ong*·de e ke doy Where does it hurt?
Tem febre?	teng *fe*·bre Do you have a temperature?
É alérgico/alérgica a alguma coisa? m/f	e a·*ler*·zhee·koo/ a·*ler*·zhee·ka a aal·*goo*·ma *koy*·za Are you allergic to anything?
Está a tomar alguma coisa?	shtaa a too·*maar* aal·*goo*·ma *koy*·za Are you on medication?
Há quanto tempo tem estes sintomas?	aa *kwang*·too *teng*·poo teng *esh*·tesh seeng·*to*·mash How long have you been like this?

She has been vaccinated against (typhoid).	Ela foi vacinada contra (febre tifóide). *e*·la foy va·see·*naa*·da *kong*·tra (*fe*·bre tee·*foy*·de)
I need new contact lenses.	Eu preciso de lentes de contacto novas. *e*·oo pre·*see*·zoo de *leng*·tesh de kong·*taak*·too *no*·vash
I need new glasses.	Eu preciso de óculos novos. *e*·oo pre·*see*·zoo de *o*·koo·loosh *no*·voosh

Symptoms & Conditions

I'm sick.	Estou doente. shtoh doo·*eng*·te

I've been (vomiting).	Eu tenho estado (a vomitar).	e·oo ta·nyoo shtaa·doo (a voo·mee·taar)
He/She has been (injured).	Ele/Ela tem estado (magoado/magoada). m/f	e·le/e·la teng shtaa·doo (ma·goo·aa·doo/ ma·goo·aa·da)
I feel ...	Eu sinto-me ...	e·oo seeng·too·me ...

dizzy	tonto/tonta m/f	tong·too/tong·ta
hot and cold	com suores frios	kong soo·o·resh free·oosh
nauseous	enjoado m enjoada f	eng·zhoo·aa·doo eng·zhoo·aa·da
shivery	a tremer	a tre·mer
weak	fraco/fraca m/f	fraa·koo/fraa·ka

It hurts here.	Dói-me aqui.	doy·me a·kee
I'm dehydrated.	Estou desidratado/ desidratada. m/f	shtoh de·zee·dra·taa·doo/ de·zee·dra·taa·da
I can't sleep.	Não consigo dormir.	nowng kong·see·goo dor·meer
I'm on medication for ...	Eu estou a tomar medicamentos para ...	e·oo shtoh a too·maar me·dee·ka·meng·toosh pa·ra ...
I have (a/an) ...	Eu tenho ...	e·oo ta·nyoo ...

🔊 LISTEN FOR

Bebe?	*be*·be
	Do you drink?
Fuma?	*foo*·ma
	Do you smoke?
Toma drogas?	*to*·ma *dro*·gash
	Do you take drugs?
É sexualmente activo/activa? m/f	e sek·soo·al·*meng*·te a·*tee*·voo/a·*tee*·va
	Are you sexually active?
Alguma vez praticou sexo sem protecção?	aal·*goo*·ma vezh pra·tee·*koh* sek·soo seng proo·te·*sowng*
	Have you had unprotected sex?

food poisoning	intoxicação alimentar f eeng·tok·see·ka·*sowng* a·lee·meng·*taar*
sore throat	dores de garganta f pl *do*·resh de gar·*gang*·ta

Women's Health

(I think) I'm pregnant.	(Eu acho que) estou grávida. (*e*·oo *aa*·shoo ke) shtoh *graa*·vee·da
I haven't had my period for (six) weeks.	Eu já não tenho o período há (seis) semanas. *e*·oo zha nowng *ta*·nyoo oo pe·*ree*·o·doo aa (saysh) se·*ma*·nash
I've noticed a lump here.	Notei um alto aqui. no·*tay* oong *aal*·too a·*kee*

🔊 LISTEN FOR

Está com o período?	shtaa kong oo pe·*ree*·o·doo Are you menstruating?
Quando foi a última vez que teve o período?	*kwang*·doo foy a *ool*·tee·ma vezh ke *te*·ve oo pe·*ree*·oo·doo When did you last have your period?
Usa contraceptivos?	oo·za kong·tra·se·*tee*·voosh Are you using contraception?
Está grávida?	shtaa *graa*·vee·da Are you pregnant?
Está grávida.	shtaa *graa*·vee·da You're pregnant.

I'm on the Pill.	Eu tomo a pílula. *e*·oo *to*·moo a *pee*·loo·la
I need contraception.	Eu preciso de contraceptivos. *e*·oo pre·*see*·zoo de kong·tra·se·*tee*·voosh
I need the morning-after pill.	Eu preciso da pílula do dia seguinte. *e*·oo pre·*see*·zoo da *pee*·loo·la doo *dee*·a se·*geeng*·te
I need a pregnancy test.	Eu preciso de um teste de gravidez. *e*·oo pre·*see*·zoo de oong *tesh*·te de gra·vee·*desh*
period pain	dores do período f pl *do*·resh doo pe·*ree*·o·doo
yeast infection	infecção vaginal f eeng·fe·*sowng* va·zhee·*naal*

Parts of the Body

My ... hurts.	O meu ... está a doer-me. m
	oo *me*·oo ... shtaa a doo·*er*·me
	A minha ... está a doer-me. f
	a *meeng*·nya ... shtaa a doo·*er*·me
I can't move my ...	Eu não consigo mexer o meu ... m
	e·oo nowng kong·*see*·goo me·*sher*
	oo *me*·oo ...
	Eu não consigo mexer a minha ... f
	e·oo nowng kong·*see*·goo me·*sher*
	a *meeng*·nya ...

eye
olho m
o·lyoo

ear
orelha f
o·re·lya

arm
braço m
braa·soo

hand
mão f
mowng

bum
rabo m
rra·boo

foot
pé m
pe

head
cabeça f
ka·be·sa

nose
nariz m
na·*reesh*

mouth
boca f
bo·ka

chest
peito m
pay·too

stomach
estómago m
shto·ma·goo

leg
perna f
per·na

I have a cramp in my ...	Eu tenho uma cãibra no meu ... m e·oo ta·nyoo oo·ma ka·*eeng*·bra noo *me*·oo ... Eu tenho uma cãibra na minha ... f e·oo ta·nyoo oo·ma ka·*eeng*·bra na *meeng*·nya ...
My ... is swollen.	O meu ... está inchado. m oo *me*·oo ... shtaa eeng·*shaa*·doo A minha ... está inchada. f a *meeng*·nya ... shtaa eeng·*shaa*·da

Allergies

I have a skin allergy.	Eu tenho uma alergia da pele. e·oo ta·nyoo oo·ma a·ler·*zhee*·a da *pe*·le
I'm allergic to ...	Eu sou alérgico/ alérgica a ... m/f e·oo soh a·*ler*·zhee·koo/ a·*ler*·zhee·ka a ...
He/She is allergic to ...	Ele/Ela é alérgico/ alérgica a ... m/f e·le/e·la e a·*ler*·zhee·koo/ a·*ler*·zhee·ka a ...
anti-inflammatories	anti-inflamatórios m pl ang·tee·eeng·fla·ma·*to*·ryoosh
codeine	codeína f ko·de·*ee*·na
penicillin	penicilina f pe·nee·see·*lee*·na
sulphur-based drugs	medicamentos à base de enxofre m pl me·dee·ka·*meng*·toosh aa *baa*·ze de eng·*sho*·fre

For food-related allergies, see **special diets & allergies** (p192).

Pharmacist

I need something for (a headache).	Eu preciso de alguma coisa para (as dores de cabeça). e·oo pre·*see*·zoo de aal·*goo*·ma *koy*·za pa·ra (ash *do*·resh de ka·*be*·sa)
Do I need a prescription for (antihistamines)?	Necessito de uma receita para (antihistamínicos)? ne·se·*see*·too de *oo*·ma rre·*say*·ta pa·ra (ang·tee·eesh·ta·*mee*·nee·koosh)
I have a prescription.	Eu tenho uma receita. e·oo *ta*·nyoo *oo*·ma rre·*say*·ta
How many times a day?	Quantas vezes por dia? *kwang*·tash ve·zesh poor *dee*·a
Will it make me drowsy?	Vou ficar sonolento/ sonolenta? **m/f** voh fee·*kaar* soo·noo·*leng*·too/ soo·noo·*leng*·ta
This is my usual medicine.	Estes são os meus medicamentos habituais. *esh*·tesh sowng oosh *me*·oosh me·dee·ka·*meng*·toosh a·bee·too·*aish*

SAFE TRAVEL

HEALTH

🔊 LISTEN FOR

Antes/Depois de comer.	*ang*·tesh/de·*poysh* de koo·*mer* Before/After food.
Já tomou isto alguma vez?	zhaa to·*moh* eesh·too aal·*goo*·ma vezh Have you taken this before?
Tem que levar o tratamento até ao fim.	teng ke le·*vaar* oo tra·ta·*meng*·too a·te ow feeng You must complete the course.

🔊 LISTEN FOR

Abra bem a boca.	*aa*·bra beng a *bo*·ka	Open wide.
Morda isto.	*mor*·da *eesh*·too	Bite down on this.
Bocheche.	boo·*she*·she	Rinse.

Dentist

I have a broken tooth.	Eu tenho um dente partido. e·oo *ta*·nyoo oong *deng*·te par·*tee*·doo
I have a cavity.	Eu tenho uma cárie. e·oo *ta*·nyoo oo·ma *kaa*·ree·e
I have a toothache.	Eu tenho uma dor de dentes. e·oo *ta*·nyoo oong oo·ma dor de *deng*·tesh
I need a filling.	Eu preciso de um chumbo. e·oo pre·*see*·zoo de oong *shoong*·boo
My dentures are broken.	A minha dentadura está partida. a *mee*·nya deng·ta·*doo*·ra shtaa par·*tee*·da
My gums hurt.	As minhas gengivas doem-me. aash *meeng*·nyash zheng·*zhee*·vash do·*eng*·me
I don't want it extracted.	Eu não quero extrair o dente. e·oo nowng *ke*·roo aysh·tra·*eer* oo *deng*·te
I need an anaesthetic.	Eu preciso de anestesia. e·oo pre·*see*·zoo de a·nesh·te·*zee*·a

Food

Eating Out

KEY PHRASES

Can you recommend a restaurant?	Pode-me recomendar um restaurante?	*po·de·me rre·koo·meng·daar oong rresh·tow·rang·te*
A table for two, please.	Uma mesa para dois, por favor.	*oo·ma me·za pa·ra doysh poor fa·vor*
I'd like the menu, please.	Queria um menu, por favor.	*ke·ree·a oong me·noo poor fa·vor*
I'd like a beer, please.	Eu queria uma cerveja, por favor.	*e·oo ke·ree·a oo·ma ser·ve·zha poor fa·vor*
Please bring the bill.	Pode-me trazer a conta.	*po·de·me tra·zer a kong·ta*

Basics

Breakfast is a quick affair in Portugal, usually consisting of a coffee with toast or a pastry. Lunch (usually taken around 1pm) is the main meal of the day, and generally includes meat or fish, vegetables, and rice or potatoes – plus wine, cheese, olives and bread. Dinner is generally lighter and is eaten around 8 or 9pm – even later on weekends.

breakfast	pequeno almoço m *pe·ke·noo aal·mo·soo*
lunch	almoço m *aal·mo·soo*
dinner	jantar m *zhang·taar*
snack	lanche m *lang·she*

eat v	comer koo·*mer*
drink v	beber be·*ber*
I'd like ...	Eu queria ... e·oo ke·*ree*·a ...
I'm starving!	Estou esfomeado/ esfomeada! **m/f** shtoh shfo·mee·*aa*·doo/ shfo·mee·*aa*·da

Finding a Place to Eat

Can you recommend a ...?	Pode-me recomendar ...? *po*·de·me rre·koo·meng·*daar* ...

bar	um bar	oong bar
beer house	uma cervejaria	*oo*·ma ser·ve·zha·*ree*·a
cafe	um café	oong ka·*fe*
grill restaurant	uma churrasqueira	*oo*·ma shoo·rraash·*kay*·ra
neighbourhood restaurant	uma tasca	*oo*·ma *taash*·ka
pastry shop	uma pastelaria	*oo*·ma pash·te·la·*ree*·a
restaurant	um restaurante	oong rresh·tow·*rang*·te
tavern	uma taberna	*oo*·ma ta·*ber*·na
tea house	uma casa de chá	*oo*·ma *kaa*·za de shaa

FOOD EATING OUT

Where would you go for a celebration?	Onde é que iria para festejar? *ong·de e ke ee·ree·a pa·ra fesh·te·zhaar*
Where would you go for a cheap meal?	Onde é que iria para uma refeição barata? *ong·de e ke ee·ree·a pa·ra oo·ma rre·fay·sowng ba·raa·ta*
Where would you go for local specialities?	Onde é que iria para especialidades locais? *ong·de e ke ee·ree·a pa·ra shpe·see·a·lee·daa·desh lo·kaish*
I'd like to reserve a table for (five) people.	Eu queria reservar uma mesa para (cinco) pessoas. *e·oo ke·ree·a rre·zer·vaar oo·ma me·za pa·ra (seeng·ko) pe·so·ash*
I'd like to reserve a table for (8pm).	Eu queria reservar uma mesa para as (oito da noite). *e·oo ke·ree·a rre·zer·vaar oo·ma me·za pa·ra ash (oy·too da noy·te)*

CULTURE TIP

Bacalhau

It's famed as being in so many recipes that you could eat it a different way every day for a year. It's white, hard as a rock and it smells decidedly fishy ... Yes, it's *bacalhau* ba·ka·*lyow*, considered by many to be the Portuguese national food. The word is often translated as simply 'cod', but if that conjures up images involving five minutes with a frypan and a slice of lemon, you'll have to leave them behind – this is salted and dried fish, and needs serious soaking.

🔊 **LISTEN FOR**

Estamos fechados.	*shta*·moosh fe·*shaa*·doosh	We're closed.
Estamos cheios.	*shta*·moosh *shay*·oosh	We're full.
Um momento.	oong moo·*meng*·too	One moment.

Are you still serving food?	Ainda servem comida? a·*eeng*·da *ser*·veng koo·*mee*·da
How long is the wait?	Quanto tempo é que se tem de estar à espera? *kwang*·too *teng*·poo e ke se teng de shtaar aa *shpe*·ra

At the Restaurant

In Portugal restaurants usually have what is called *couvert* koo·*ver* – bread, butter, paté, olives and sometimes prosciutto at the tables. If you eat them you'll be charged a (normally small) fee.

I'd like a (non)smoking table, please.	Queria uma mesa de (não) fumador, por favor. ke·*ree*·a oo·ma *me*·za de (nowng) foo·ma·*dor* poor fa·*vor*
I'd like a table for (two), please.	Queria uma mesa para (dois), por favor. ke·*ree*·a oo·ma *me*·za pa·ra (doysh) poor fa·*vor*

✂	**For two, please.**	Para dois, por favor.	*pa*·ra doysh poor fa·*vor*

🔊 LISTEN FOR

Onde é que se quer/ querem sentar? sg/pl	*ong·*de e ke se ker/ *ke·*reng seng·*taar* Where would you like to sit?
Já decidiram?	zha de·see·*dee·*rowng What can I get for you?
Gosta/Gostam de ...? sg/pl	*goosh·*ta/*goosh·*towng de ... Do you like ...?
Eu aconselho ...	*e·*oo a·kong·*sa·*lyoo ... I suggest the ...
Bem passado ou mal passado?	beng pa·*saa·*doo oh mal pa·*saa·*doo How would you like that cooked?
Aqui está!	a·*kee* shtaa Here you go!
Bom apetite.	bong a·pe·*tee·*te Enjoy your meal.

What would you recommend?	O que é que recomenda? oo ke e ke rre·koo·*meng·*da
What's in that dish?	Quais são os ingredientes daquele prato? kwaish sowng oosh eeng·gre·dee·*eng·*tesh da·*ke·*le *praa·*too
What's that called?	Como é que se chama aquilo? ko·moo e ke se *shaa·*ma a·*kee·*loo
I'll have that.	Eu quero aquilo. eu *ke·*roo a·*kee·*loo
Does it take long to prepare?	Demora muito tempo a preparar? de·*mo·*ra *mweeng·*too *teng·*poo a pre·pa·*raar*

Eating Out

Can I see the menu, please?

Posso ver o menu, por favor?
po·soo ver oo me·noo poor fa·vor

What would you recommend for ...?

O que você recomenda para ...?
oo ke vo·se rre·koo·meng·da pa·ra ...

 the main meal
o prato principal
oo praa·too preeeng·see·paal

 dessert
sobremesa
soo·bre·me·za

drinks
bebidas
be·bee·dash

Can you bring me some ..., please?

Pode-me trazer ...
po·de·me tra·zer ...

I'd like the bill, please.

Queria a conta, por favor.
ke·ree·a a kong·ta poor fa·vor

| **Can you recommend a good local wine?** | Pode-me recomendar um bom vinho daqui da zona? *po·de·me rre·koo·meng·daar oong bong vee·*nyoo* da·kee daa zo·*na |
| **I'd like (a/the) ..., please.** | Queria ..., por favor. *ke·ree·*a ... poor fa·*vor* |

children's menu	o menu das crianças	oo me·*noo* dash kree·*ang*·sash
drink list	a lista das bebidas	a *leesh*·ta dash be·*bee*·dash
local speciality	uma especialidade local	*oo·*ma shpe·see·a·lee·*daa*·de loo·*kaal*
menu (in English)	um menu (em inglês)	oong me·*noo* (eng eeng·*lesh*)
wine list	uma lista dos vinhos	*oo·*ma *leesh*·ta doosh *vee·*nyoosh

 | **Menu, please.** | O menu, por favor. | oong me·*noo* poor fa·*vor* |

Requests

| **Please bring (a/the) ...** | Pode-me trazer ... *po·de·me tra·zer* ... |

cutlery	os talheres	oosh ta·*lye*·resh
(wine)glass	um copo (de vinho)	oong *ko*·poo (de *vee·*nyoo)
napkin	o guardanapo	oo gwar·da·*naa*·poo
tablecloth	a toalha de mesa	a *twaa*·lya de *me*·za

I'd like it ...	Eu queria ...	
	e·oo ke·ree·a ...	
I don't want it ...	Eu não quero ...	
	e·oo nowng ke·roo ...	

boiled	cozido m	koo·zee·doo
	cozida f	koo·zee·da
broiled/grilled	grelhado m	gre·lyaa·doo
	grelhada f	gre·lyaa·da
(deep-)fried	frito m	*free·too*
	frita f	*free·ta*
mashed	esmagado m	shma·gaa·doo
	esmagada f	shma·gaa·da
medium	nem bem nem	neng beng neng
	mal-passado/	maal·pa·saa·doo/
	mal-passada m/f	maal·pa·saa·da
rare	mal-passado m	maal·pa·saa·doo
	mal-passada f	maal·pa·saa·da
reheated	reaquecido m	rre·a·ke·see·doo
	reaquecida f	rre·a·ke·see·da
steamed	cozido/	koo·zee·doo/
	cozida a	koo·zee·da a
	vapor m/f	va·*por*
well-done	bem-passado m	beng·pa·saa·doo
	bem-passada f	beng·pa·saa·da
with the dressing on the side	o molho da salada à parte	oo mo·lyoo da sa·laa·da aa paar·te
without ...	sem ...	seng ...

I'd like it with/without ...	Eu queria com/sem ...
	e·oo ke·ree·a kong/seng ...

cheese	queijo	*kay·zhoo*
chilli	píri-píri	*pee·ree·pee·ree*
garlic	alho	*aa·lyoo*
nuts	oleaginosas	*o·lee·a·zhe·no·zash*
pepper	pimenta	*pee·meng·ta*
salt	sal	*saal*
tomato sauce	molho de tomate	*mo·lyoo de too·maa·te*

For other specific meal requests, see **vegetarian & special meals** (p192).

Compliments & Complaints

I love this dish.	Eu adoro este prato. *e·oo a·do·roo esh·te praa·too*
I love the local cuisine.	Eu adoro a comida local. *e·oo a·do·roo a koo·mee·da loo·kaal*
That was delicious!	Isto estava delicioso! *eesh·too shtaa·va de·lee·see·o·zoo*
This is hitting the spot.	Está a saber-me mesmo bem. *shtaa a sa·ber·me mesh·moo beng*
My compliments to the chef.	Os meus parabéns ao cozinheiro chefe. *oosh me·oosh pa·ra·bengzh ow koo·zee·nyay·roo she·fe*
I'm full.	Estou cheio/cheia. **m/f** *shtoh shay·oo/shay·a*

🔍 LOOK FOR

Petiscos	pe·*teesh*·koosh	Appetisers
Sopas	so·pash	Soups
Entradas	eng·*traa*·dash	Entrées
Saladas	sa·*laa*·dash	Salads
Pratos Principais	*praa*·toosh preeng·see·*paish*	Main Courses
Extras	*aysh*·trash	Side Dishes
Sobremesa	soo·bre·*me*·za	Desserts
Bebidas	be·*bee*·dash	Drinks
Aperitivos	a·pe·ree·*tee*·voosh	Apéritifs
Espirituosos	shpee·ree·too·o·zoosh	Spirits
Cerveja	ser·*ve*·zha	Beers
Refrigerantes	rre·free·zhee·*rang*·tesh	Soft Drinks
Vinhos Espumantes	*vee*·nyoosh shpoo·*mang*·tesh	Sparkling Wines
Vinhos Brancos	*vee*·nyoosh *brang*·koosh	White Wines
Vinhos Tintos	*vee*·nyoosh teeng·toosh	Red Wines
Digestivos	dee·zhesh·*tee*·voosh	Digestifs

See also the **menu decoder** (p194).

FOOD EATING OUT

This is ...		Isto está ... *eesh*·too shtaa ...
burnt	queimado	kay·*maa*·doo
cold	frio	*free*·oo
(too) spicy	(demasiado) picante	(de·ma·zee·*aa*·doo) pee·*kang*·te
stale	duro	*doo*·roo
superb	magnífico	maag·*nee*·fee·koo

spoon
colher f
koo·lyer

wineglass
copo de vinho m
ko·poo de vee·nyoo

glass
copo m
ko·poo

fork
garfo m
gar·foo

plate
prato m
praa·too

table
mesa f
me·za

knife
faca f
faa·ka

Paying the Bill

Please bring the bill.	Pode-me trazer a conta.
	po·de·me tra·zer a kong·ta

✂	**Bill, please.**	A conta, por favor.	a *kong*·ta poor fa·*vor*

There's a mistake in the bill.	Há um erro na conta.
	aa oong e·rroo na kong·ta

Nonalcoholic Drinks

coffee	café m
	ka·fe

orange juice	sumo de laranja natural m
	soo·moo de la·rang·zha na·too·raal

soft drink	refrigerante m
	rre·free·zhe·rang·te

sparkling mineral water	água mineral com gás f *aa·gwa mee·ne·raal kong gaash*	

still mineral water	água mineral sem gás f *aa·gwa mee·ne·raal seng gaash*	

CULTURE TIP

Coffee

The Portuguese make pretty decent coffee. As in Italy, if you just order a *café* ka·*fe* what you'll get is an espresso or short black – strong black coffee in a demitasse (small cup). The variations on the basic espresso are numerous, but the main terms are listed below. Just beware, if you ask for decaffeinated coffee (*café sem cafeína* ka·*fe* seng ka·fe·*ee*·na), a sachet of instant coffee will usually arrive with a pot of hot water for you to make yourself.

um café/ cimbalino/ expresso	oong ka·*fe*/ seeng·ba·*lee*·noo/ *shpre*·soo	an espresso
um café com leite	oong ka·*fe* kong *lay*·te	half espresso, half milk in a large cup (caffe latte)
um café duplo	oong ka·*fe* *doo*·ploo	a double espresso
um carioca	oong ka·ree·o·ka	a weak espresso
um galão	oong ga·*lowng*	an espresso with hot milk served in a tall glass
um garoto	oong ga·*ro*·too	an espresso with a dash of milk
uma bica	*oo*·ma *bee*·ka	an espresso
uma bica dupla	*oo*·ma *bee*·ka *doo*·pla	a double espresso

tea	chá m *shaa*
(hot) water	água (quente) f *aa·gwa (keng·te)*
with (milk)	com (leite) *kong (lay·te)*
without (sugar)	sem (açúcar) *seng (a·soo·kar)*

Alcoholic Drinks

beer	cerveja f *ser·ve·zha*
a shot of ...	um copinho de ... *oong koo·pee·nyoo de ...*

firewater	água-ardente	*aa·gwaar·deng·te*
gin	gin	*zheeng*
rum	rum	*rroong*
whisky	uísque	*oo·eesh·kee*

a bottle of ... wine	uma garrafa de vinho ... *oo·ma ga·rraa·fa de vee·nyoo ...*
a glass of ... wine	um copo de vinho ... *oong ko·poo de vee·nyoo ...*

dessert	de sobremesa	*de soo·bre·me·za*
red	tinto	*teeng·too*
rosé	rosé	*rro·ze*
sparkling	espumante	*shpoo·mang·te*
white	branco	*brang·koo*
young (green)	verde	*ver·de*

🔊 LISTEN FOR

à pressão	aa pre·*sowng*	draft
um fino	oong *fee*·noo	small (20cl) draft beer (in the centre and north of Portugal)
um jarro	oong *zhaa*·roo	a jug of beer
um quartilho	oong kwar·*tee*·lyoo	a pint of beer
uma caneca	oo·ma ka·*ne*·ka	larger (33cl) draft beer
uma garrafa de cerveja	oo·ma ga·*rraa*·fa de ser·*ve*·zha	large bottle of beer
uma imperial	oo·ma eeng·pree·*aal*	small (20cl) draft beer (in the south, including Lisbon)
uma mini	oo·ma *mee*·nee	small bottle of beer

For additional items, see the **menu decoder** (p194), and the **dictionary**.

In the Bar

Excuse me!	Desculpe! desh·*kool*·pe
I'm next.	Eu sou a seguir. e·oo soh a se·*geer*
🇶 **What would you like?**	O que é que quer? oo ke e ke ker
🇦 **I'll have (a beer).**	Eu queria (uma cerveja). e·oo ke·*ree*·a (oo·na ser·*ve*·zha)

🔊 LISTEN FOR

O que é que vão comer/ tomar?	oo ke e ke vowng koo·mer/ too·maar What are you having to eat/ drink?
Eu acho que já bebeu demais.	e·oo aa·shoo ke zhaa be·be·oo de·maish I think you've had enough.
Últimos pedidos.	ool·tee·moosh pe·dee·doosh Last orders.

Same again, please.	O mesmo, por favor. oo mezh·moo poor fa·vor
No ice, thanks.	Sem gelo, por favor. seng zhe·loo poor fa·vor
I'll buy you a drink.	Eu pago-lhe uma bebida. e·oo paa·goo·lye oo·ma be·bee·da
I don't drink alcohol.	Eu não bebo álcool. e·oo nowng be·boo aal·koo·ol
It's my round.	É a minha rodada. e a mee·nya rroo·daa·da
Do you serve meals here?	Vocês servem refeições aqui? vo·sesh ser·veng rre·fay·soyngsh a·kee
Are these complimentary?	Isto é gratuito? eesh·too e gra·twee·too

Drinking Up

Cheers!	À nossa! aa no·sa

I feel fantastic!	Estou a sentir-me mesmo bem. *shtoh a seng·teer·me mesh·moo beng*
I think I've had one too many.	Acho que bebi demais. *aa·shoo ke be·bee de·maish*
I'm feeling drunk.	Estou a sentir-me bêbado/bêbada. **m/f** *shtoh a seng·teer·me be·ba·doo/be·ba·da*
I'm pissed.	Estou completamente bêbado/bêbada. **m/f** *shtoh kong·ple·ta·meng·te be·ba·doo/be·ba·da*
I feel ill.	Sinto-me mal. *seeng·too·me maal*
Where's the toilet?	Onde é a casa de banho? *ong·de e a kaa·za de ba·nyoo*
I'm tired, I'd better go home.	Estou cansado/cansada, é melhor ir para casa. **m/f** *shtoh kang·saa·doo/kang·saa·da e me·lyoor eer pa·ra kaa·za*
Can you call a taxi for me?	Pode chamar-me um táxi? *po·de sha·maar·me oong taak·see*
I don't think you should drive.	Eu acho que não devia conduzir. *e·oo aa·shoo ke nowng de·vee·a kong·doo·zeer*

Self-Catering

KEY PHRASES

What's the local speciality?	Qual é a especialidade local?	kwaal e a shpe·see·a·lee·*daa*·de loo·*kaal*
Where can I find the ... section?	Onde é que é a secção de ...?	*ong*·de e ke e a sek·*sowng* de ...
I'd like some ...	Eu queria uns/ umas ... m/f	*e*·oo ke·*ree*·a oongsh/ *oo*·mash ...

Buying Food

What's the local speciality?	Qual é a especialidade local? kwaal e a shpe·see·a·lee·*daa*·de loo·*kaal*
What's that?	O que é aquilo? oo ke e a·*kee*·loo
Do you have other kinds?	Há de outros tipos? aa de *oh*·troosh *tee*·poosh
Can I taste it?	Posso provar? *po*·soo proo·*vaar*
Can I have a bag, please?	Pode-me dar um saco, por favor? *po*·de·me daar oong *saa*·koo poor fa·*vor*
How much is (a kilo of cheese)?	Quanto é (um quilo de queijo)? *kwang*·too e (oong *kee*·loo de *kay*·zhoo)

I'd like ...

Eu queria ...
e·oo ke·*ree*·a ...

(200) grams	(duzentos) gramas	(doo·*zeng*·toosh) *graa*·mash
half a dozen	meia dúzia	*may*·a doo·zya
a dozen	uma dúzia	oo·ma doo·zya
half a kilo	meio quilo	*may*·oo *kee*·loo
a kilo	um quilo	oong *kee*·loo
(two) kilos	(dois) quilos	(doysh) *kee*·loosh
a bottle	uma garrafa	oo·ma ga·*rraa*·fa
a jar	um frasco	oong *fraash*·koo
a packet	um pacote	oong pa·*ko*·te
a piece	uma peça	oo·ma *pe*·sa
(three) pieces	(três) peças	(tresh) *pe*·sash
a slice	uma fatia	oo·ma fa·*tee*·a
(six) slices	(seis) fatias	(saysh) fa·*tee*·ash
a tin (can)	uma lata	oo·ma *laa*·ta
some	uns/umas m/f	oongsh/*oo*·mash
that one	aquele m aquela f	a·*ke*·le a·*ke*·la
this one	este/esta m/f	*esh*·te/*esh*·ta

Less.	Menos. *me*·noosh
A bit more.	Um pouco mais. oong *poh*·koo maish
Enough.	Chega. *she*·ga
Do you have anything cheaper?	Há alguma coisa mais barata? aa aal·*goo*·ma *koy*·za maish ba·*raa*·ta

Where can I find the ... section?		Onde é que é ...? *ong*·de e ke e ...

dairy	a secção de produtos lácteos	a sek·*sowng* de proo·*doo*·toosh *laak*·tee·oosh
fish	a peixaria	a pay·sha·*ree*·a
frozen goods	os congelados	oosh kong·zhe·*laa*·doosh
fruit and vegetable	a fruta e vegetais	a *froo*·ta e ve·zhe·*taish*
meat	a carne	a *kaar*·ne

Cooking

Could I please borrow a ...?		Podia-me emprestar ...? poo·*dee*·a·me eng·presh·*taar* ...

I need a ...		Preciso de uma pre·*see*·zoo de *oo*·ma ...

chopping board	tábua para cortar	*taa*·boo·a *pa*·ra kor·*taar*
frying pan	frigideira	free·gee·*day*·ra
knife	faca	*faa*·ka
saucepan	caçarola	ka·sa·*ro*·la

cooked	cozinhado/cozinhada m/f koo·zee·*nyaa*·doo/koo·zee·*nyaa*·da
cured	curado/curada m/f koo·*raa*·doo/koo·*raa*·da
dried	seco/seca m/f *se*·koo/*se*·ka

Há de outros tipos?
aa de *oh*·troosh *tee*·poosh
Do you have other kinds?

fresh	fresco/fresca m/f *fresh*·koo/*fresh*·kaa
frozen	congelado/ congelada m/f kong·zhe·*laa*·doo/ kong·zhe·*laa*·da
raw	cru/crua m/f kroo/*kroo*·a
smoked	fumado/fumada m/f foo·*maa*·doo/foo·*maa*·da

For more cooking implements, see the **dictionary**.

Vegetarian & Special Meals

KEY PHRASES

Do you have vegetarian food?	Tem comida vegetariana?	teng koo·*mee*·da ve·zhe·ta·ree·*a*·na
Could you prepare a meal without ...?	Pode preparar sem ...?	*po*·de pre·pa·*raar* seng ...
I'm allergic to ...	Eu sou alérgico/ alérgica a ... m/f	e·oo soh a·*ler*·zhee·koo/ a·*ler*·zhee·ka a ...

Special Diets & Allergies

Is there a (vegetarian) restaurant near here?	Há algum restaurante (vegetariana) perto daqui? aa aal·*goong* rresh·tow·*rang*·te (ve·zhe·ta·ree·*aa*·na) per·too da·*kee*
I'm on a special diet.	Eu tenho uma dieta especial. e·oo *ta*·nyoo *oo*·ma dee·e·ta shpe·see·*aal*
I don't eat ...	Eu não como ... e·oo nowng *ko*·moo ...
I'm a vegan.	Eu sou vegan. e·oo soh vee·gang
I'm a vegetarian.	Eu sou vegetariano/ vegetariana. m/f e·oo soh ve·zhe·ta·ree·*a*·noo/ ve·zhe·ta·ree·*a*·na

I'm allergic to ...	Eu sou alérgico/ alérgica a ... m/f
	e·oo soh a·ler·zhee·koo/ a·ler·zhee·ka a ...

dairy produce	produtos lácteos	pro·doo·toosh laak·tee·oosh
eggs	ovos	o·voosh
honey	mel	mel
nuts	oleaginosas	o·lee·a·zhee·no·zash
peanuts	amendoins	a·meng·doo·eengsh
seafood	marisco	ma·reesh·koo
shellfish	crustáceos	kroosh·taa·se·oosh

Ordering Food

Do you have halal/ kosher food?	Tem comida halal/kosher? teng koo·mee·da a·laal/ko·sher
Do you have vegetarian food?	Tem comida vegetariana? teng koo·mee·da ve·zhe·ta·ree·a·na
Is it cooked with ...?	Leva ...? le·va ...
Could you prepare a meal without ...?	Pode preparar sem ...? po·de pre·pa·raar seng ...

butter	manteiga	mang·tay·ga
fish	peixe	pay·she
(red) meat	carne (vermelha)	kaar·ne (ver·me·lya)
oil	óleo	o·lee·oo
pork	carne de porco	kaar·ne de por·koo
poultry	aves	aa·vesh

FOOD

VEGETARIAN & SPECIAL MEALS

Menu
~ DECODER ~
livro de culinária

This miniguide to Portuguese cuisine is designed to help you navigate menus and get the most out of your gastronomic experience in Portugal. Portuguese nouns, and adjectives affected by gender, have their gender indicated by Ⓜ and/or Ⓕ. If it's a plural noun, you'll also see pl.

~ A ~

abacate Ⓜ a·ba·*kaa*·te avocado

abóbora Ⓕ a·bo·*boo*·ra pumpkin

abobrinha Ⓕ a·boo·*bree*·nya zucchini

açafrão Ⓜ a·sa·*frowng* saffron

acepipes Ⓜ pl a·se·*pee*·pesh delicacies • hors d'oeuvres • titbits

achigã Ⓜ a·shee·*gang* black bass

ácido/ácida Ⓜ/Ⓕ aa·see·doo/ aa·see·da sour

açorda Ⓕ a·*sor*·da bread-based thick soup, often flavoured with garlic, coriander & olive oil
— de bacalhau de ba·ka·*lyow* **açorda** with shredded salt cod
— de gambas de *gang*·bash **açorda** containing prawns
— de marisco de ma·*reesh*·koo **açorda** with prawns, mussels & cockles
— de sável de *saa*·vel spicy **açorda** flavoured with shad (fish) broth

açúcar Ⓜ a·*soo*·kar sugar
— amarelo a·ma·re·loo brown sugar
— granulado gra·noo·*laa*·doo granulated or refined sugar

agriões Ⓜ pl a·gree·*oyngsh* watercress

água-ardente Ⓕ aa·gwaar·*deng*·te brandy-like spirit
— de cana de *ka*·na sugar-cane spirit
— de figo de fee·goo fig brandy
— de medronho de me·*dro*·nyoo brandy made from arbutus berry
— velha ve·lya fine brandy

aipo Ⓜ ai·poo celery

alcachofra Ⓕ aal·ka·*sho*·fra artichoke

alecrim Ⓜ a·le·*kreeng* rosemary

Alentejana, à a·leng·te·*zha*·na, a Alentejo style – dish made with garlic, olive oil, paprika, usually pork & small cockles

alface Ⓕ aal·*faa*·se lettuce

alheiras Ⓕ pl a·*lyay*·rash sausage of bread, garlic, chilli & meats

alho Ⓜ aa·lyoo garlic
— francês frang·*sesh* leek
— porro po·rroo leek

almôndegas Ⓕ pl aal·*mong*·de·gash beef or pork meatballs

alperce Ⓜ aal·*per*·se apricot

amanteigado Ⓜ a·mang·tay·*gaa*·doo 'buttery' – describes creamy cheeses

A

amarguinha ① a·mar·*gee*·nya almond-flavoured liqueur

amêijoas ① pl a·may·*zhoo*·ash cockles

— à Bulhão Pato aa boo·*lyowng* paa·too broth of small cockles in coriander, white wine & garlic sauce

— ao natural ow na·too·*raal* steamed cockles

— na cataplana na ka·ta·*pla*·na small cockles cooked with onion, chopped **chouriço**, ham and red & green capsicum

ameixa ① a·*may*·sha plum

ameixas de Elvas ① pl a·may·shash de el·*vash* 'plums of Elvas' – sweet dessert plums preserved in sugar

ameixa seca ① a·*may*·sha se·ka prune

amêndoa ① a·*meng*·doo·a almond

amendoim ⓜ a·meng·doo·*eeng* peanut

amora ① a·*mo*·ra blackberry

ananás ⓜ a·na·*naash* pineapple

anho ⓜ a·*nyoo* lamb (see also **borrego**)

anis ⓜ a·*neesh* aniseed

anona ① a·*no*·na custard apple

areias ① pl a·*ray*·ash sweet biscuit flavoured with lemon

arenque ⓜ a·*reng*·ke herring

arjamolho ⓜ ar·zha·mo·*lyoo* Algarve name for **gaspacho**

arrepiadas ① pl a·rre·pee·*aa*·dash sliced almonds, held together with meringue

arroz ⓜ a·*rrosh* rice

— árabe aa·ra·be rice with raisins, nuts & sometimes chopped dried fruit

— à valenciana aa va·leng·see·a·na a saffron-flavoured rice dish similar to paella

— cozido koo·*zee*·doo boiled rice

— de bacalhau de ba·ka·*lyow* tomato-flavoured rice with shredded salt cod

— de berbigão de ber·bee·*gowng* rice with cockles, seasoned with coriander

— de bucho de *boo*·shoo creamy rice cooked in pork broth

— de cabidela de ka·bee·*de*·la chicken & rice casserole with fresh chicken blood

— de ervilhas de er·*vee*·lyash rice with peas

— de espigos de *shpee*·goosh rice with cabbage

— de feijão de fay·*zhowng* rice with red beans

— de forno de *for*·noo baked rice with onion & prosciutto or **salpicão**

— de grelos de *gre*·loosh rice with cabbage

— de lampreia de lang·*pray*·a lamprey & rice stew with onion, parsley, white wine, **chouriço** & lamprey blood

— de langueirão de lang·gay·*rowng* rice with razor clams & onion, seasoned with garlic & parsley

— de lapas de *laa*·pash rice with limpets

— de marisco de ma·*reesh*·koo casserole of seafood & rice in tomato sauce

— de pato de *paa*·too baked or braised casserole of rice with shredded duck & sausage slices

— de polvo de *pol*·voo chunks of octopus & onion in a tomato-rice stew

— de sarrabulho de sa·rra·*boo*·lyoo stew with rice, pork, beef, chicken & sauce made of onion & pig's blood

— de tamboril de tang·boo·*reel* tomato-rice stew with frog-fish chunks

— de tomate de too·*maa*·te rice cooked in a tomato broth, often served with fried fish

— doce *do*·se creamy rice sprinkled with cinnamon

— integral eeng·te·*graal* brown rice

arrufadas de Coimbra ① pl
a·rroo·*faa*·dash de *koyng*·bra dome-
shaped, cinnamon-flavoured bread

asa ① *aa*·za wing

— de frango de *frang*·goo chicken
wing

— de perú de pe·*roo* turkey wing

assado/assada ⓜ/① a·*saa*·doo/
a·*saa*·da roast

assado de peixe ⓜ a·*saa*·doo de
pay·she mixture of different roasted
or baked fish

atum ⓜ a·*toong* tuna

— de escabeche de shka·be·she raw
tuna 'pickled' or 'cooked' in vinegar

avelã ① a·ve·*lang* hazelnut

aves ① pl *aa*·vesh poultry

avestruz ⓜ&① a·vesh·*troosh*
ostrich

azeite ⓜ a·*zay*·te olive oil

azeitonas ① pl a·zay·*to*·nash olives

— pretas *pre*·tash black olives

— recheadas rre·shee·*aa*·dash
stuffed olives

— sem caroço song ka·ro·soo pitted
olives

— verdes *ver*·desh green olives

azevias ① pl a·ze·*vee*·ash fried puff
pastry with a sweet chickpea filling

~ **B** ~

baba de camelo ① *baa*·ba de
ka·*me*·loo 'camel drool' – caramel
mousse made with condensed milk

bacalhau ⓜ ba·ka·*lyow* dried salt cod

— à Assis aa a·*sees* crumbled salt
cod cooked in olive oil with vegetables,
mixed with eggs & parsley, then baked

— à Brás aa braas flaked cod fried
with egg, potato & olives

— à cozinha velha aa koo·*zee*·nya
ve·lya chopped salt cod, onions &
carrots fried in olive oil & cooked in
a white sauce, covered with bread-
crumbs, then baked

— à Gomes de Sá aa go·mes de
saa flaked salt cod soaked in milk &
browned in the oven with vegetables &
eggs

— albardado aal·bar·*daa*·doo salt
cod fried in a doughy batter

— assado com batatas a murro
a·*saa*·doo kong ba·*taa*·tash a *moo*·rroo
baked or roasted salt cod with smashed
baked potatoes, garlic & olive oil

— assado com pão de centeio
a·*saa*·doo kong powng de seng·*tay*·oo
baked salt cod steak sprinkled with
garlic, olive oil & crumbled rye bread

— com todos kong *to*·doosh boiled
salt cod served with boiled egg &
vegetables

— cozido koo·*zee*·doo boiled salt cod

— cru desfiado kroo desh·fee·*aa*·doo
shredded raw salt cod in an olive oil &
vinegar dressing

— desfiado desh·fee·*aa*·doo fine
strips of raw salt cod served with
chopped onion & garlic

— guisado gee·*zaa*·doo stewed salt
cod steaks with olive oil, tomatoes,
onion, potatoes, butter, herbs & spices

— no borralho noo boo·*rraa*·lyoo salt
cod steak in cabbage leaves & bacon,
cooked in burning embers

— no forno noo *for*·noo baked salt
cod, often smothered in an onion &
olive oil sauce

— roupa-velha rroh·pa·*ve*·lya mixture
of cabbage, salt cod & potatoes,
sautéed in olive oil & garlic

bagaço ⓜ ba·*gaa*·soo **água-ardente**,
often drunk with an espresso coffee

banha ① *baa*·nya lard

barriga-de-freira ①
ba·*rree*·ga·de·*fray*·ra sponge cake or
bread covered in a sugary syrup with
eggs & a hint of lemon

barrinhas de pescada ① pl
ba·*rree*·nyash de pesh·*kaa*·da fish
sticks

batata doce ① ba·*taa*·ta *do*·se sweet potato

batatas ① pl ba·*taa*·tash potatoes

— **a murro** a *moo*·rroo baked potatoes with the skin on, smashed & seasoned with olive oil & garlic

— **cozidas** koo·*zee*·dash boiled potatoes

— **fritas** *free*·tash potato chips/crisps

batido ⓜ ba·*tee*·doo milk/fruit shake

baunilha ① bow·*nee*·lya vanilla

bebida ① be·*bee*·da beverage

— **(não) alcoólica** (nowng) aal·koo·*o*·lee·ka (non)alcoholic drink

— **espirituosa** shpee·ree·too·o·za spirit

— **fria** *free*·a cold beverage

— **quente** *keng*·te hot beverage

berbigão ⓜ ber·bee·*gowng* cockle

beringela ① be·reeng·*zhe*·la aubergine • eggplant

besugo ⓜ be·*zoo*·goo sea bream

beterraba ① be·te·*rraa*·ba beetroot

bica ① *bee*·ka espresso coffee

— **cheia** *shay*·a espresso topped with hot water

— **com uma pinga** kong oo·ma *peeng*·ga espresso topped with **água-ardente** (drunk as a digestive)

bifana no pão ① bee·*fa*·na noo powng thin pork steak sandwich

bifana no prato ① bee·*fa*·na noo *praa*·too thin pork steak

bife ⓜ *bee*·fe fillet • steak of beef, other meats, poultry or fish

— **à café** aa ka·*fe* thick rump steak served with sauce of milk, lemon juice & mustard

— **à casa** aa *kaa*·za thin, pan-fried steak with a fried egg on top

— **à cerveja** aa ser·*ve*·zha steak with beer-based, buttery sauce

— **alto** *aal*·too thick steak

— **à Marrare** aa ma·*rraa*·re thick rump steak served with cream sauce & pepper

— **à pimenta** aa pee·*meng*·ta steak with whole peppercorns

— **bem passado** beng pa·*saa*·doo well-done steak

— **com ovo a cavalo** kong o·voo a ka·*vaa*·loo fried steak marinated with fresh garlic, served with a fried egg on top

— **da alcatra** da aal·*kaa*·tra rump steak

— **de atum** de a·*toong* tuna steak

— **do vazio** doo va·*zee*·oo sirloin steak

— **mal passado** maal pa·*saa*·doo rare steak

bifinho ⓜ bee·*fee*·nyoo thin, boneless slices of meat

biscoitos ⓜ pl beesh·*koy*·toosh biscuits • cookies

— **de Alcanena** de aal·ka·*ne*·na light, airy biscuit made with olive oil

— **de azeite** de a·*zay*·te light, airy biscuit made with olive oil

bitoque ⓜ bee·*to*·ke small steak or fillet usually served with a fried egg on top

bola ① *bo*·la breadroll

— **de Berlim com/sem creme** de ber·*leeng* kong/seng *kre*·me plain doughnut with/without custard filling

— **de carne** de *kaar*·ne baked meat pie with bread dough pastry

— **de presunto** de pre·*zoong*·too **bola de carne** with a layer of prosciutto

— **de sardinhas** de sar·*dee*·nyash **bola** with a layer of sardines

bolachas ① pl boo·*laa*·shash biscuits • cookies • crackers

bolachos ⓜ pl boo·*laa*·shoosh pig's blood made into a dumpling, served with the fatty cooking juices of **rojões**

boleima ① boo·*lay*·ma small cakes made of bread dough filled with apple slices or chopped walnuts

bolinhos ⓜ pl boo·lee·nyoosh biscuits
— de amêndoa de a·meng·doo·a almond marzipan moulded in many shapes: animals, fruit, vegetables
— de Jerimu de zhe·ree·moo pumpkin cakes flavoured with cinnamon
— de pinhão de pee·nyowng pine nut cakes
bolo ⓜ bo·loo pastry • sweet cake
— de arroz de a·rrosh cake made with rice & wheat flour topped with sugar
— de bolacha de boo·laa·sha biscuits layered with sweetened butter-cream frosting to form a cake
— de caco de kaa·koo griddle bread (bread toasted on an iron sheet on the stove or over coals) served hot with garlic butter, sometimes cooked with a spicy **chouriço** inside
— de coco de ko·koo coconut custard-filled pastry tart • coconut macaroon
— de Dom Rodrigo de dong rroo·dree·goo candy-like, soft confection made of real eggs, **ovos moles** & ground almonds
— de laranja de la·rang·zha orange cake
— de mel de mel rich molasses & spice cake with candied fruit & almonds
— de noz de nosh walnut cake
— de sertã de ser·tang corn biscuits cooked in a frying-pan
— do caco doo kaa·koo flat bread-rolls baked on a stone or cement slab
— lêvedo le·ve·doo light scone cooked in a frying-pan
— real rree·aal dense cake made with lots of eggs, grated almonds, pumpkin jam, cinnamon & lemon
— rei rray Christmas bread in the shape of a ring, studded with walnuts & pine nuts, with a gift and a broad bean inside
bonito ⓜ boo·nee·too bonito (fish)

borrachões ⓜ pl boo·rra·shoyngsh fried ring-shaped biscuits flavoured with brandy or white wine & cinnamon
borrachos ⓜ pl boo·rraa·shoosh breadcrumb fritters in a syrup of white **vinho verde**, lemon & cinnamon
borrego ⓜ boo·rre·goo lamb
— assado a·saa·doo roast lamb
broa ⓕ bro·a sweet potato & almond cakes
— de milho de mee·lyoo corn bread
— serrana se·rra·na highland bread (corn or rye bread)
broas de mel ⓕ pl bro·ash de mel soft biscuit made of honey & flour
brócolos ⓜ pl bro·koo·loosh broccoli
broínhas (de Natal) ⓕ pl bro·eeng·nyash (de na·taal) muffin-like pastry with raisins, pine nuts & walnuts
bucho de porco ⓜ boo·shoo de por·koo pig stomach
bucho recheado ⓜ boo·shoo rre·shee·aa·doo pig's belly stuffed with pork, bread or rice & cloves or cumin – served sliced
burras ⓕ pl boo·rrash roast pig cheeks

~ C ~

cabeça de xara ⓕ ka·be·sa de shaa·ra pig's head cooked with garlic, herbs & white wine, served sliced
de cabidela de ka·bee·de·la any dish made with blood
cabrito ⓜ ka·bree·too kid (goat)
caça ⓕ kaa·sa game
cacau ⓜ ka·kow cocoa
cacholeira ⓕ ka·shoo·lay·ra pork liver sausage
café ⓜ ka·fe coffee • espresso coffee
— em grão eng growng coffee beans
— instantâneo eeng·shtang·taa·nee·oo instant coffee
— moído moo·ee·doo ground coffee

— torrado too·rraa·doo roast coffee
cajú ⓜ ka·zhoo cashew
calda (de açúcar) ⓕ kaal·da (de a·soo·kar) syrup
caldeirada ⓕ kaal·day·raa·da soup-like stew, usually with fish
caldo ⓜ kaal·doo broth • soup • stock
camarão ⓜ ka·ma·rowng shrimp
canela ⓕ ka·ne·la cinnamon
canja/caldo de galinha ⓕ kaang·zha/kaal·doo de ga·lee·nya chicken broth
canja/sopa de conquilhas ⓕ kaang·zha/so·pa de kong·kee·lyash cockle soup
caracóis ⓜ pl ka·ra·koysh snails
caracol ⓜ ka·ra·kol similar to a Danish pastry but with raisins or candied fruit
caril ⓜ ka·reel curry (powder)
carne ⓕ kaar·ne meat
— assada a·saa·da roast meat
— de cavalo de ka·vaa·loo horse meat
— de porco de por·koo pork
— de porco à Portuguesa de por·koo aa poor·too·ge·za pork Alentejo-style without fava cockles
— de vaca de vaa·ka beef
— do alguidar doo aal·gee·daar chunks of cooked pork preserved in pork lard, served as an appetiser
— picada/passada pee·kaa·da/pa·saa·da ground meat (mince)
carneiro ⓜ kar·nay·roo lamb • mutton
carnes frias ⓕ pl kaar·nesh free·ash cold meats
castanhas ⓕ pl kash·taa·nyash chestnuts
cavacas ⓕ pl ka·vaa·kash sweet biscuit with white sugar icing
cavalas ⓕ pl ka·vaa·lash mackerel
cebola ⓕ se·bo·la onion
cenoura ⓕ se·noh·ra carrot
cereja ⓕ se·re·zha cherry
cerveja ⓕ ser·ve·zha beer
— à pressão aa pre·sowng beer on tap

— loura loh·ra 'blonde beer' – regular beer, as opposed to stout
— preta pre·ta dark beer • stout
chá ⓜ shaa tea
— de ervas de er·vash herbal tea
— de limão de lee·mowng glass or cup of boiling water with lemon rind
champanhe ⓜ shang·pa·nye champagne
chanfana ⓕ shang·fa·na hearty stew with goat or mutton in heavy red wine sauce
charros alimados ⓜ pl shaa·rroosh a·lee·maa·doosh skinned mackerel in olive oil & vinegar (or lemon) dressing, served with sliced onion, garlic & parsley
chila ⓕ shee·la spaghetti squash
chispe com feijão branco ⓜ sheesh·pe kong fay·zhowng brang·koo trotters with white beans, **chouriço**, pig's ear, kale & potatoes
chouriço ⓜ shoh·ree·soo garlicky pork sausage flavoured with red pepper paste
— assado a·saa·doo grilled sausage
— de sangue de sang·ge blood sausage
churrasco ⓜ shoo·rraash·koo barbecued • grilled on a spit or skewer
cidra ⓕ see·dra cider
coco ⓜ ko·koo coconut
codorniz ⓕ koo·door·nees quail
coelho ⓜ koo·e·lyoo rabbit
— à caçador aa ka·sa·dor rabbit stewed with wine & tomato
— em vinha d'alho eng vee·nya daa·lyoo baked rabbit with slices of fried bread & onion, drizzled with port or white wine
coentrada ⓕ kweng·traa·da sauce with abundant amounts of coriander
coentros ⓜ pl kweng·troosh coriander
cogumelos ⓜ pl koo·goo·me·loosh mushrooms

D

colorau ⓜ koo·loo·*row* sweet paprika
cominhos ⓜ pl koo·*mee*·nyoosh cumin
com todos kong *to*·doosh 'with everything' – a dish with the lot
conquilha ① kong·*kee*·lya cockle
cordeiro ⓜ cor·*day*·roo lamb
coscurões ⓜ pl koosh·koo·*royngsh* orange- & brandy-flavoured biscuit
costeleta ① koosh·te·*le*·ta chop
couve ① *koh*·ve cabbage
— de Bruxelas de broo·*she*·lash Brussels sprout
— flor flor cauliflower
coxa de galinha ① *ko*·sha de ga·*lee*·nya fried, savoury chicken thigh
cozido/cozida ⓜ/① koo·*zee*·doo/koo·*zee*·da boiled
cozido à Portuguesa ① koo·*zee*·doo aa poor·too·ge·za hearty meal made with chunks of different meats & sausages, vegetables, beans & rice
creme (de pasteleiro) ① *kre*·me (de pash·te·*lay*·roo) egg, flour, water & sugar paste used to fill cakes

~ D ~

delícia de batata ① de·*lee*·sya de ba·*taa*·ta little cakes of mashed potato mixed with almonds & cinnamon
dobrada ① doo·*braa*·da tripe with white beans & rice
doce ⓜ *do*·se dessert • jam • sweet
— de amêndoa de a·*meng*·doo·a marzipan sweets
duchesse ① doo·*shes* puff pastry filled with whipped cream & topped with fruit or thin threads of sugar & egg paste

~ E ~

empada ① eng·*paa*·da miniature pot pie
empadão ⓜ eng·pa·*downg* dish similar to shepherd's pie

encharcada ① eng·shar·*kaa*·da cooked egg yolks in a sugary syrup, decorated with cinnamon
enchido ⓜ eng·*shee*·doo any variety of sausage
engarrafado por ⓜ eng·ga·rra·*faa*·doo poor bottled by (winery name)
enguia ① eng·*gee*·a eel
ensopado ⓜ eng·soo·*paa*·doo stew served on toasted or deep-fried bread
entrecosto ⓜ eng·tre·*kosh*·too pork ribs
ervilhas ① pl er·*vee*·lyash peas
— com ovos escalfados kong o·voosh shkal·*faa*·doosh peas & sliced **chouriço** cooked with lard, olive oil, onions & parsley, served with poached eggs
— de vagem ① de *vaa*·zheng snow peas
escabeche ⓜ shka·*be*·she raw meat or fish pickled in olive oil, vinegar, garlic & bay leaf
escalfado/escalfada ⓜ/① shkaal·*faa*·doo/shkaal·*faa*·da poached
escalopes ⓜ pl shka·*lo*·pesh medallion-shaped cuts of boneless meat
espanhola, à shpa·*nyo*·la, aa dish in tomato & onion sauce
espargos ⓜ pl shpar·*goosh* asparagus
esparguete ⓜ shpar·*ge*·te spaghetti
espetada ① shpe·*taa*·da kebab
espinafres ⓜ pl shpee·*naa*·fresh spinach
estopeta de atum ① shtoo·*pe*·ta de a·*toong* tuna, onion, tomatoes & green capsicum in an olive oil & vinegar dressing

~ F ~

faisão ⓜ fai·*zowng* pheasant
farinha ① fa·*ree*·nya flour

farinheira ⓕ fa·ree·*nyay*·ra sausage stuffed with spiced, flour-based mix

farófias ⓕ pl fa·ro·fee·ash dessert of beaten egg whites in a custard sauce

farripas de laranja ⓕ pl fa·*rree*·pash de la·*rang*·zha chocolate-covered strips of orange peel

farturas ⓕ pl far·*too*·rash deep-fried dough swirls rolled in sugar & cinnamon, usually found at fairs

fataça na telha ⓕ fa·*taa*·sa na te·lya mullet seasoned with chopped onion, parsley, paprika & bacon, cooked between two clay roof tiles buried in embers

fatias ⓕ pl fa·tee·ash slices

— **da China/Tomar** da shee·na/ too·*maar* steam-cooked loaf made of whipped egg yolks & sugar

— **douradas** doh·*raa*·dash slices of bread soaked in milk & eggs, fried, smothered in sugar & topped with cinnamon

favada à Portuguesa ⓕ fa·vaa·da aa poor·too·*ge*·za stew of fava beans, sausage & sometimes poached eggs

fava-rica ⓕ fa·va·*rree*·ka fava bean soup with garlic & vinegar

favas ⓕ faa·vash broad bean

— **à Algarvia** ⓕ pl faa·vash aa aal·gar·vee·a fava beans cooked with blood sausage, bacon, sometimes **chouriço** & mint

febras ⓕ pl fe·brash pork cutlets

feijão ⓜ fay·*zhowng* bean

feijoada ⓕ fay·*zhwaa*·da bean stew with sausages or other meat

ferraduras ⓕ pl fe·rra·*doo*·rash horseshoe-shaped pastry, sometimes layered with candied fruit

fiambre ⓜ fee·*ang*·bre cold meat • ham

fígado ⓜ fee·ga·doo liver

figo ⓜ fee·goo fig

focinho de porco ⓜ foo·see·nyoo de por·koo pig's snout

folar ⓜ foo·*laar* brioche dough baked with chicken, spicy sausages & **presunto**, eaten at Easter

folhado ⓜ foo·*lyaa*·doo puff pastry

formigos ⓜ pl for·mee·goosh sweetmeats – thick paste of soaked hard bread or biscuit with egg yolks, sugar, honey, milk, cinnamon & wine, cooked slowly over low heat

framboesa ⓕ frang·bwe·za raspberry

francesinha ⓕ frang·se·zee·nya ham, sausage & cheese in a tomato-cream sauce, on slices of bread

frango ⓜ frang·goo chicken

frito/frita ⓜ/ⓕ free·too/free·ta fried

fruta ⓕ froo·ta fruit

frutas secas ⓕ pl froo·tash se·kash dried fruit

~ **G** ~

galão ⓜ ga·lowng an espresso with hot milk served in a tall glass

galinha ⓕ ga·lee·nya hen

— **do campo** doo *kaang*·poo free-range chicken

gambas ⓕ pl *gang*·bash prawns

garoto ⓜ ga·ro·too ready-made filter coffee topped with warm or hot milk

gaspacho ⓜ gash·*paa*·shoo chilled tomato & garlic bread soup flavoured with olive oil, vinegar & oregano

gelado ⓜ zhe·*laa*·doo ice cream

geleia ⓕ zhe·*lay*·a jelly

gengibre ⓜ zheng·*zhee*·bre ginger

gila ⓕ *zhee*·la spaghetti squash

ginja ⓕ *zheeng*·zha sour cherry

goiaba ⓕ goy·*aa*·ba guava

grão (de bico) ⓜ growng (de bee·koo) chickpeas • garbanzo beans

guardanapo ⓜ gwar·da·*naa*·poo a jelly roll cake cut into squares & folded in half, filled with **creme de pasteleiro**

guisado/guisada ⓜ/ⓕ gee·za·doo/ gee·za·da stewed

H

~ H ~

hortaliça ① or·ta·*lee*·sa vegetables
hortelã ① or·te·*lang* mint

~ I ~

iogurte ⓜ yo·*goor*·te yogurt
iscas ① pl *eesh*·kash pork liver

~ J ~

jaquinzinhos ⓜ pl
zha·keeng·*zee*·nyoosh small fried
horse-mackerel
jardineira ① zhar·dee·*nay*·ra hearty
beef & vegetable stew
jardineira, à zhar·dee·*nay*·ra, aa a
type of beef & vegetable stew
javali ⓜ zha·va·*lee* wild boar
jesuítas ⓜ pl zhe·zoo·ee·tash puff
pastry with baked meringue icing

~ L ~

lagosta ① la·*gosh*·ta lobster
lagostim ⓜ la·goosh·*teeng* crayfish
laranja ① la·*rang*·zha orange
lebre ① *le*·bre hare
— com feijão branco kong fay·*zhowng*
brang·koo hare & white bean stew
legumes ⓜ pl le·*goo*·mesh
vegetables
leitão ⓜ lay·*towng* roasted suckling
pig
leite ⓜ *lay*·te milk
— condensado kong·deng·*saa*·doo
condensed milk
— gordo *gor*·doo whole milk
— magro *maa*·groo skim milk
lentilha ① leng·*tee*·lya lentil
licor ⓜ lee·*kor* liqueur
lima ① *lee*·ma lime
limão ⓜ lee·*mowng* lemon
limonada ① lee·moo·*naa*·da lemonade
língua ① *leeng*·gwa tongue
— de gato de *gaa*·too very small,
hard vanilla biscuit

linguiça ① leeng·*gwee*·sa thin, long
garlicky sausage
lombinhos de porco ⓜ pl
long·*bee*·nyoosh de *por*·koo thinly
sliced pork tenderloin
lombo de porco assado ⓜ *long*·boo
de *por*·koo a·*saa*·doo roast pork loin
lulas ① pl *loo*·lash squid
— à Sevilhana aa se·vee·*lya*·na fried
squid rings served with mayonnaise
— recheadas rre·shee·*aa*·dash small
squid stuffed with a mixture of rice,
tomatoes, **presunto** & parsley

~ M ~

maçã ① ma·*sang* apple
Madeirense, à ma·day·*reng*·se, aa
Madeira-style – a dish cooked with
tomatoes, onion & garlic (and sometimes bananas or Madeira wine)
malagueta ① ma·la·ge·ta red hot
chilli peppers, also called **piripiri**
mal cozido/cozida ⓜ/① maal
koo·*zee*·doo/koo·*zee*·da soft-boiled
manga ① *mang*·ga mango
manjar branco ⓜ mang·*zhaar*
brang·koo coconut-milk pudding
with prunes, with syrup poured over
the top
manteiga ① mang·*tay*·ga butter
mão de vaca guisada ⓜ mowng de
vaa·ka gee·*zaa*·da stew of cow's feet,
chickpeas, tomatoes, onion, garlic
chouriço, parsley & white wine
maracujá ⓜ ma·ra·koo·*zhaa*
passionfruit
maranhos ma·ra·nyoosh pork belly
stuffed with lamb, **presunto**,
chouriço, wine & rice
marisco ⓜ ma·*reesh*·koo shellfish
marmelada ① mar·me·*laa*·da
quince paste
massas ① pl *maa*·sash noodles •
pasta
mel ⓜ mel honey

melancia ① me·lang·*see*·a watermelon

melão ⓜ me·*lowng* (honeydew) melon

— com presunto kong pre·*zoong*·too slices of honeydew melon topped with slices of **presunto**

meloa ① me·*lo*·a cantaloupe • rockmelon

melosa ① me·*lo*·za mixed drink of brandy & honey

merengue ⓜ me·*reng*·ge meringue

mexido/mexida ⓜ/① me·*shee*·doo/ me·*shee*·da scrambled

mexilhões ⓜ pl me·shee·*lyoyngsh* mussels

migas ① pl *mee*·gash a side dish, usually made of bread flavoured with olive oil, garlic & spices & fried

— de bacalhau de ba·ka·*lyow* migas made with bread, salt cod, onion, tomatoes, garlic, red capsicum paste & coriander, served with grilled eels

— de batata de ba·*taa*·ta side dish of mashed potatoes flavoured with bacon, sausage & garlic, shaped into round balls

mil folhas ⓜ pl meel *fo*·lyash layers of flaky pastry with custard filling

milho ⓜ *mee*·lyoo corn

— frito ⓜ *free*·too cubes of fried white cornmeal served with skewers of grilled meat or poultry

miolos (de porco) ⓜ pl mee·o·*loosh* (de *por*·koo) (pork) brains

miudezas ① pl myoo·de·*zash* giblets

moelas ① pl mo·e·*lash* chicken gizzards

molho ⓜ *mo*·lyoo dressing • gravy • sauce

morangos ⓜ pl moo·*rang*·goosh strawberries

morcela ① moor·*se*·la blood sausage

morgados ⓜ pl mor·*gaa*·doosh sweetmeats made with almonds & figs

moscatel ⓜ moosh·ka·*tel* topaz-coloured, sweet dessert wine

mostarda ① moosh·*taar*·da mustard

~ N ~

nabiça ① na·*bee*·sa turnip greens

nabo ⓜ *naa*·boo turnip

na púcara ① na poo·*ka*·ra chicken or duck cooked in a clay pot with **presunto**, tomatoes, onion, port, brandy, white wine, bay leaves & garlic

natas ① pl *naa*·tash cream (from milk)

negro ⓜ *ne*·groo type of sausage made from blood rather than meat

nêspera ① *nesh*·pe·ra loquat

novilho ⓜ noo·*vee*·lyoo veal

noz ① nos walnut

~ O ~

oleaginosa ① o·lee·a·zhee·*no*·za nut

óleo ⓜ *o*·lee·oo oil

orelha de porco de coentrada ① o·*re*·lya de *por*·koo de kweng·*traa*·da sliced pig's ear seasoned with garlic & coriander, in olive oil & vinegar dressing, served cold

ostra ① *osh*·tra oyster

ovo ⓜ *o*·voo egg

— cozido koo·*zee*·doo boiled egg

— de chocolate de shoo·koo·*laa*·te chocolate Easter egg

— escalfado shkal·*faa*·doo poached egg

— estrelado shtre·*laa*·doo fried egg

— mexido me·*shee*·doo scrambled egg

ovos moles ⓜ pl o·voosh *mo*·lesh sweetened egg yolks

ovos verdes ⓜ pl o·voosh *ver*·desh boiled eggs stuffed with a mixture of egg yolks, butter & parsley, coated in flour & fried

~ P ~

pá ① *paa* front leg of an animal

paio ⓜ *pai·oo* smoked pork tenderloin sausage

panado ⓜ *pa·naa·doo* breaded pork cutlet

pão ⓜ *powng* bread
— **de centeio** *de seng·tay·oo* light rye bread
— **de leite** *de lay·te* sweet roll made with wheat flour, eggs & milk
— **de milho** *de mee·lyoo* corn bread
— **integral** *eeng·te·graal* wholegrain bread

papas ① pl *paa·pash* gruel • porridge

papos-de-anjo ⓜ pl *paa·poosh·de·ang·zhoo* little egg-based puffs in a sugar syrup

papo-seco ⓜ *paa·poo·se·koo* most common type of bread roll

passas ① pl *paa·sash* raisins • sultanas

pastéis ⓜ pl *pash·taysh* pastries
— **de bacalhau** *do ba·ka·lyow* deep fried savouries made of mashed potato, onion, parsley & salt cod
— **de feijão** *de fay·zhowng* rich lima bean & almond mixture in flaky pastry shells
— **de massa tenra** *de ma·sa teng·ra* meat-filled fried pastries
— **de nata/Belém** *de na·ta/be·leng* egg custard tarts with flaky pastry shell
— **de Tentúgal** *de teng·too·gaal* flaky pastries with a filling of creamy egg yolk & sugar paste

pastel ⓜ *pash·tel* pastry

pataniscas de bacalhau ① pl *pa·ta·neesh·kash de ba·ka·lyow* seasoned salt cod fritters

paté ⓜ *paa·te* paté

pato ⓜ *paa·too* duck

peito de frango ⓜ *pay·too de frang·goo* chicken breast

peixe ⓜ *pay·she* fish

pepino ⓜ *pe·pee·noo* cucumber

pêra ① *pe·ra* pear

perdiz ① *per·deez* partridge

pernil no forno ⓜ *per·neel noo for·noo* roast leg of pork

peru ⓜ *pe·roo* turkey

pescadinhas de rabo na boca ① pl *pesh·ka·dee·nyash de rra·boo na bo·ka* small whiting fried with their tails in their mouths

pêssego ⓜ *pe·se·goo* peach

petingas ① pl *pe·teeng·gash* small sardines

pezinhos de porco *pe·zee·nyoosh de por·koo* pig's feet flavoured with coriander, garlic & onion

picante ⓜ&① *pee·kang·te* spicy/hot

pimenta ① *pee·meng·ta* pepper

pimento ⓜ *pee·meng·too* capsicum

pipis ⓜ pl *pee·peesh* stewed chicken giblets, flavoured with garlic, onion, paprika, white wine & chilli

piri piri *pee·ree pee·ree* red hot chilli peppers (also called **malagueta**) • sauce made from red hot chilli peppers

pito de Santa Luzia ⓜ *pee·too de sang·ta loo·zee·a* a sweet made from yeast dough filled with sugar, cinnamon & pumpkin

polvo ⓜ *pol·voo* octopus

porco ⓜ *por·koo* pork

posta ① *posh·ta* steak slice

prato de grão ⓜ *praa·too de growng* chickpea stew flavoured with tomato, garlic, bay leaf & cumin

pratos completos ⓜ pl *praa·toosh kong·ple·toosh* a dish with all the elements that would constitute a meal in itself

prego no pão ⓜ *pre·goo noo powng* small steak sandwich

presunto ⓜ pre-*zoong*-too
prosciutto • smoked ham
pudim ⓜ poo-*deeng* pudding
— de café de ka-*fe* coffee-flavoured
pudding
— de leite de *lay*-te custard-like
pudding with lemon-flavoured
caramel sauce
— de ovos de o-*voosh* very eggy,
baked custard-like pudding
— do Abade de Priscos doo
a-*baa*-de de *preesh*-koosh pudding
made of egg yolks, sliced smoked
bacon, port, lemon & cinnamon
— flan flang caramel custard
— molotov mo-lo-*tov* poached
meringue with caramel sauce
puré de batata ⓜ poo-*re* de
ba-*taa*-ta mashed potatoes

~ Q ~

queijada ⓕ kay-*zhaa*-da small tarts
with sweet, dense filling
queijo ⓜ *kay*-zhoo cheese
— da Serra/Estrela da se-rra/
shtre-la popular creamy cheese
made from sheep's milk
— de Azeitão de a-zay-*towng* soft,
creamy cheese made from sheep's
milk near the town of Azeitão
— de cabra de *kaa*-bra goat's milk
cheese
— de ovelha de oo-*ve*-lya sheep's
milk cheese
— de vaca de *vaa*-ka cow's milk
cheese
— saloio sa-*loy*-oo firm cow's milk
cheese
— seco se-*koo* dry cheese similar in
texture to parmesan
queimado/queimada ⓜ/ⓕ
kay-*maa*-doo/kay-*maa*-da burnt
queque ke-*ke* plain yellow cupcake
quivi kee-*vee* kiwi(fruit)

~ R ~

rabanadas ⓕ pl rra-ba-*naa*-dash see
fatias douradas
rabanete ⓜ rra-ba-*ne*-te radish
rancho ⓜ *rrang*-shoo hearty stew
of chickpeas, onion, potatoes,
macaroni, veal trotters, pork belly,
chouriço & beef
rebento de feijão ⓕ rre-*beng*-too de
fay-*zhwng* bean sprout
regueifas ⓕ pl rre-*gay*-fash
cinnamon- & saffron-flavoured
biscuit rings
rendinhas ⓕ pl rreng-*dee*-nyash
almond nougat which resembles lace
repolho ⓜ rre-*po*-lyoo cabbage
requeijada ⓕ rre-kay-*zhaa*-da tart
made with **requeijão**
requeijão ⓜ rre-kay-*zhowng* fresh,
ricotta-style cheese
rim ⓜ rreeng kidney • kidney-
shaped eclair
rissol ⓜ rree-*sol* fried pastry •
rissole
robalo ⓜ rroo-*baa*-loo rock bass
rocha ⓕ *rro*-sha large, soft spice
biscuit
rojões ⓜ pl rroo-*zhoyngsh* spiced &
marinated chunks of fried pork
rolo de carne ⓜ *rro*-loo de *kaar*-ne
meatloaf
rosbife ⓜ rrosh-*bee*-fe roast beef

~ S ~

safio ⓜ sa-*fee*-oo conger eel • sea eel
sal ⓜ saal salt
— fino *fee*-noo refined salt
— grosso *gro*-soo rock salt
salada ⓕ sa-*laa*-da salad
— de alface de aal-*fa*-se lettuce salad
— de atum de a-*toong* salad of tuna,
potato, peas, carrots & boiled eggs in
an olive oil & vinegar dressing

T

— de bacalhau com feijão frade de ba·ka·*lyow* kong fay·*zhowng fraa*·de salad of uncooked salt cod & black-eyed beans in olive oil & vinegar dressing

— de feijão frade de fay·*zhowng fraa*·de black-eyed bean salad flavoured with onion, garlic, olive oil & vinegar, sprinkled with chopped boiled egg & parsley

— de frutas de *froo*·tash fruit salad

— de tomate de too·*maa*·te tomato & onion salad, often flavoured with oregano

— mista *meesh*·ta tomato, lettuce & onion salad

— russa *rroo*·sa potato salad with peas, carrots & mayonnaise

salame de chocolate ⓜ sa·*la*·me de shoo·koo·*laa*·te dense chocolate fudge roll studded with bits of biscuits, served sliced

salgadinho ⓜ saal·ga·*dee*·nyoo small savoury pastry

salgado/salgada ⓜ/ⓕ saal·*gaa*·doo/saal·*gaa*·da salty • small savoury pastry

salmão ⓜ saal·*mowng* salmon

— fumado foo·*maa*·doo smoked salmon

salmonete ⓜ saal·moo·*ne*·te red mullet

salpicão ⓜ saal·pee·*kowng* smoked pork sausage flavoured with garlic, bay leaf & sometimes wine

salsa ⓕ *saal*·sa flat-leaf parsley • parsley

salsicha ⓕ saal·*see*·sha sausage

— fresca *fresh*·ka fresh pork sausage

salteado/salteada ⓜ/ⓕ saal·tee·*aa*·doo/saal·tee·*aa*·da sautéed

sálvia ⓕ *saal*·vee·a sage

sandes ⓕ *sang*·desh sandwich

sanduíche ⓕ sang·*dwee*·she sandwich (see also **sandes**)

sardinha ⓕ sar·*dee*·nya sardine

sarrabulho ⓜ sa·rra·*boo*·lyoo variety of meats cooked in pig's blood

sável ⓜ *saa*·vel shad (fish)

— na telha na *te*·lya fataça na telha made with shad

sericá/sericaia ⓕ se·ree·*ka*/ se·ree·*kay*·a soft cake with an almost creamy texture served with a stewed plum in syrup

simples ⓜ&ⓕ *seeng*·plesh plain • with no ccompaniments, filling or icing

sobremesa ⓕ soo·bre·*me*·za dessert • jam • sweet

sonhos ⓜ pl *so*·nyoosh sweet fried dough, sprinkled with sugar & cinnamon

sopa ⓕ *so*·pa soup

— de pedra de *pe*·dra vegetable soup with red beans, onions, potatoes, pig's ear, bacon & sausages

— do dia doo *dee*·a soup of the day

sumo ⓜ *soo*·moo juice

— de laranja natural de la *rang* zha na·too·*raal* freshly squeezed orange juice

~ T ~

tâmara ⓕ *taa*·ma·ra date (fruit)

tangerina ⓕ tang·zhe·*ree*·na mandarin

tarte ⓕ *tar*·te pie

tecolameco ⓜ te·koo·la·*me*·koo rich & sweet orange & almond cake, well loved around Portalegre

tigelada ⓕ tee·zhe·*laa*·da firm egg custard flavoured with vanilla, lemon or cinnamon

tomate ⓜ too·*maa*·te tomato

tomilho ⓜ too·*mee*·lyoo thyme

toranja ⓕ to·*rang*·zha grapefruit

tornedó ⓜ tor·ne·*do* thick, tender steak

torrada ⓕ too·*rraa*·da toast

torresmos ⓜ pl too·*rrezh*·moosh pork cracklings served as a snack

torta ⓕ *tor*·ta tart with filling

— de laranja de la·*rang*·zha rolled orange-flavoured tart made with lots of eggs & little flour

— de Viana de vee·*aa*·na tart filled with jam • tart with egg yolk icing

tortulhos ⓜ pl tor·*too*·lyoosh sheep's tripe stuffed with more sheep's tripe

tosta ⓕ *tosh*·ta pieces of toast

— mista *meesh*·ta toasted ham & cheese sandwich

toucinho ⓜ toh·*see*·nyoo uncured bacon

— rançoso rrang·*so*·zoo cake made with almonds & egg yolks, sprinkled with sugar & cinnamon

— salgado saal·*gaa*·doo salt-cured bacon

trança ⓕ *trang*·sa type of pastry topped with coconut mixture & chopped nuts

Transmontana, à aa trangsh·mong·*ta*·na, aa Trás-os-Montes style – hearty dish usually flavoured with sausages & other meat, garlic & onion

tremoços ⓜ pl tre·*mo*·soosh salted, preserved yellow lupins eaten as a snack

tripas ⓕ pl *tree*·pash tripe

— à moda do Porto aa *mo*·da doo *por*·too slow-cooked dried beans, trotters, tripe, chicken, vegetables, sausages & cumin

trouxas de ovos ⓕ pl *troh*·shash de o·*voosh* beaten egg poached in sugar syrup

truta ⓕ *troo*·ta trout

— de escabeche de shka·*be*·she trout prepared **escabeche**, fried &

prepared with a garlic, onion & parsley dressing, served cold with boiled potatoes

túberas com ovos ⓜ pl *too*·be·rash kong o·*voosh* sliced mushrooms fried with onion, bay leaf & eggs

~ U ~

uvas ⓕ pl *oo*·vash grapes

~ V ~

veado ⓜ vee·*aa*·doo venison

velhoses ⓕ pl ve·*lyo*·zesh orange- & brandy-flavoured pumpkin fritters

verde ⓜ&ⓕ *ver*·de unripe (fruit)

vinagre ⓜ vee·*naa*·gre vinegar

vinha d'alhos ⓕ *vee*·nya *daa*·lyoosh meat marinated in wine or vinegar, olive oil, garlic & bay leaf

vinho ⓜ *vee*·nyoo wine

— branco *brang*·koo white wine

— da casa da *kaa*·za house wine

— da região da rre·zhee·*owng* local wine

— do Porto doo *por*·too port

— do Porto branco doo *por*·too *brang*·koo dry white port

— espumante shpoo·*mang*·te sparkling wine

— rosé rro·ze rosé wine

— tinto *teeng*·too red wine

— verde *ver*·de young wine – light sparkling red, white or rosé wine

vitela (assada) ⓕ vee·*te*·la (a·*saa*·da) (roast) veal

~ X ~

xerém ⓜ she·*reng* cornmeal porridge, served with shellfish, **chouriço**, pork or other meat

A

Dictionary

ENGLISH *to* PORTUGUESE

inglês – português

Portuguese nouns have their gender indicated with ⓜ (masculine) and ⓕ (feminine). Where adjectives or nouns have separate masculine and feminine forms, these are divided by a slash and marked ⓜ/ⓕ. You'll also see words marked as v (verb), n (noun), a (adjective), pl (plural), sg (singular), inf (informal) and pol (polite) where necessary. Verbs are given in the infinitive – for details on how to change verbs for use in a sentence, see **grammar** (p25). For food and drink terms, see the **menu decoder** (p194).

A

aboard a bordo a *bor*·doo
abortion aborto ⓜ a·*bor*·too
about cerca de *ser*·ka de
above por cima de poor *see*·ma de
abroad no estrangeiro noo shtrang·*zhay*·roo
accident acidente ⓜ a·see·*deng*·te
accommodation hospedagem ⓕ osh·pe·*daa*·zheng
account (bill) conta ⓕ *kong*·ta
across através a·tra·*vesh*
activist activista ⓜ&ⓕ aa·tee·*veesh*·ta
actor actor/actriz ⓜ/ⓕ aa·*tor*/aa·*treesh*
adaptor adaptador ⓜ a·da·pe·ta·*dor*
addiction vício ⓜ *vee*·syoo
address endereço ⓜ eng·de·*re*·soo
administration administração ⓕ a·de·mee·neesh·tra·*sowng*
admission entrada ⓕ eng·*traa*·da
admit v admitir a·de·mee·*teer*

adult n&a adulto/adulta ⓜ/ⓕ a·*dool*·too/a·*dool*·ta
advertisement anúncio ⓜ a·*noong*·syoo
advice conselho ⓜ kong·*se*·lyoo
after depois de·*poysh*
afternoon tarde ⓕ *taar*·de
again novamente no·va·*meng*·te
age idade ⓕ ee·*daa*·de
agree concordar kong·koor·*daar*
agriculture agricultura ⓕ a·gree·kool·*too*·ra
ahead em frente eng *freng*·te
AIDS SIDA ⓕ *see*·da
air ar ⓜ aar
air conditioning ar condicionado ⓜ aar kong·dee·syoo·*naa*·doo
airline companhia aérea ⓕ kong·pa·*nyee*·a a·*e*·ree·a
airmail via aérea ⓕ *vee*·a a·e·ree·a
airplane avião ⓜ a·vee·*owng*
airport aeroporto ⓜ a·e·ro·*por*·too
airport tax taxa de aeroporto ⓕ *taa*·sha de a·e·ro·*por*·too

aisle coxia ⓜ koo·*shee*·a
alarm clock despertador ⓜ
desh·per·ta·*dor*
all todo/toda ⓜ/ⓕ *to*·doo/*to*·da
allergy alergia ⓕ a·ler·*zhee*·a
almost quase *kwaa*·ze
alone sozinho/sozinha ⓜ/ⓕ
so·*zee*·nyoo/so·*zee*·nya
already já zhaa
also também tang·*beng*
altitude altitude ⓕ aal·tee·*too*·de
always sempre *seng*·pre
ambassador embaixador/
embaixatriz ⓜ/ⓕ eng·bai·sha·*dor*/
eng·bai·sha·*treesh*
ambulance ambulância ⓕ
ang·boo·*lang*·sya
anaemia anemia ⓕ a·ne·*mee*·a
anarchist anarquista ⓜ&ⓕ
a·nar·*keesh*·ta
ancient antigo/antiga ⓜ/ⓕ
ang·*tee*·goo/ang·*tee*·ga
and e e
angry zangado/zangada ⓜ/ⓕ
zang·*gaa*·doo/zang·*gaa*·da
animal animal ⓜ&ⓕ a·nee·*maal*
ankle tornozelo ⓜ toor·noo·ze·loo
another um outro/uma outra ⓜ/ⓕ
oong oh·troo/oo·ma oh·tra
answer resposta ⓕ rresh·*posh*·ta
antibiotics antibióticos ⓜ pl
ang·tee·bee·o·tee·koosh
antique antiguidade ⓕ
ang·tee·gwee·*daa*·de
antiseptic antiséptico ⓜ
ang·tee·se·tee·koo
apartment apartamento ⓜ
a·par·ta·*meng*·too
appendix (body) apêndice ⓜ
a·*peng*·dee·se
appointment consulta ⓕ kong·*sool*·ta
architect arquitecto/arquitecta ⓜ/ⓕ
ar·kee·te·too/ar·kee·te·ta
architecture arquitectura ⓕ
ar·kee·te·*too*·ra
argue discutir deesh·koo·*teer*
arm (body) braço ⓜ *braa*·soo

aromatherapy aromaterapia ⓕ
a·ro·ma·te·ra·*pee*·a
arrest prender preng·*der*
arrival chegada ⓕ she·*gaa*·da
arrive chegar she·*gaar*
art arte ⓕ *aar*·te
art gallery galeria de arte ⓕ
ga·le·*ree*·a de *aar*·te
artist artista ⓜ&ⓕ ar·*teesh*·ta
ashtray cinzeiro ⓜ seeng·*zay*·roo
ask (a question) perguntar
per·goong·*taar*
ask (for something) pedir pe·*deer*
aspirin aspirina ⓕ ash·pee·*ree*·na
asthma asma ⓕ *ash*·ma
at à a
athletics atletismo ⓜ at·le·*teesh*·moo
atmosphere atmosfera ⓕ
at·moosh·*fe*·ra
aunt tia ⓕ *tee*·a
Australia Austrália ⓕ owsh·*traa*·lya
ATM caixa automático ⓜ *kai*·sha
ow·too·*maa*·tee·koo
avenue avenida ⓕ a·ve·*nee*·da
awful horrível o·*rree*·vel

B

B&W (film) preto e branco *pre*·too e
brang·koo
baby bebé ⓜ&ⓕ be·*be*
baby food comida de bebé ⓕ
koo·*mee*·da de be·*be*
baby powder pó de talco ⓜ po de
taal·koo
babysitter ama ⓕ *a*·ma
back (body) costas ⓕ pl *kosh*·tash
back (position) atrás a·*traash*
backpack mochila ⓕ moo·*shee*·la
bad mau/má ⓜ/ⓕ *ma*·oo/maa
bag saco ⓜ *saa*·koo
baggage bagagem ⓕ ba·*gaa*·zheng
baggage allowance limite de peso ⓜ
lee·*mee*·te de *pe*·zoo
baggage claim balcão de bagagens ⓜ
bal·*kowng* de ba·*gaa*·zhengsh
bakery padaria ⓕ paa·da·*ree*·a
balance (account) saldo ⓜ *saal*·doo

B

balcony varanda ① va·*rang*·da
ball (sport) bola ① *bo*·la
band (music) grupo ⓜ *groo*·poo
bandage ligadura ① lee·ga·*doo*·ra
Band-Aid penso ⓜ *peng*·soo
bank banco ⓜ *bang*·koo
bank account conta bancária ①
kong·ta bang·*kaa*·rya
banknote nota bancária ① *no*·ta
bang·*kaa*·rya
baptism baptismo ⓜ ba·*teezh*·moo
bar bar ⓜ baar
barber barbeiro ⓜ bar·*bay*·roo
bar work trabalho num bar ⓜ
tra·*baa*·lyoo noong baar
basket cesto ① *sesh*·too
basketball basquetebol ⓜ
bash·ke·te·*bol*
bath banho ⓜ *ba*·nyoo
bathroom casa de banho ① *kaa*·za
de *ba*·nyoo
battery pilha ① *pee*·lya
be (ongoing) ser ser
be (temporary) estar shtaar
beach praia ① *prai*·a
beach volleyball vólebol de praia ⓜ
vo·lay·bol de *prai*·a
beautiful bonito/bonita ⓜ/①
boo·*nee*·too/boo·*nee*·ta
beauty salon salão de beleza ⓜ
sa·*lowng* de be·*le*·za
bed cama ① *ka*·ma
bedding lençóis e mantas ① pl
leng·*soysh* ee *mang*·tash
bedroom quarto ⓜ *kwaar*·too
bee abelha ① a·*be*·lya
beer cerveja ① ser·*ve*·zha
beer house cervejaria ①
ser·ve·zha·*ree*·a
before antes *ang*·tesh
beggar pedinte ⓜ&① pe·*deeng*·te
behind atrás a·*traash*
below abaixo a·*bai*·shoo
beside ao lado de ow *laa*·doo de
best o/a melhor ⓜ/① oo/a me·*lyor*
bet aposta ① a·*posh*·ta
better melhor me·*lyor*

between entre *eng*·tre
bicycle bicicleta ① bee·see·*kle*·ta
big grande *grang*·de
bike bicicleta ① bee·see·*kle*·ta
bike chain corrente de bicicleta ①
koo·*rreng*·te de bee·see·*kle*·ta
bike lock cadeado de bicicleta ⓜ
ka·dee·*aa*·doo de bee·see·*kle*·ta
bike path caminho de bicicleta ①
ka·*mee*·nyoo de bee·see·*kle*·ta
bike shop loja de ciclismo ① *lo*·zha
de see·*kleesh*·moo
bill (restaurant) conta ① *kong*·ta
binoculars binóculos ⓜ pl
bee·no·koo·loosh
bird pássaro ① *paa*·sa·roo
birth certificate certidão de
nascimento ① ser·tee·*downg* de
nash·see·*meng*·too
birthday aniversário ⓜ
a·nee·ver·*saa*·ryoo
bite (dog) mordedura ①
moor·de·*doo*·ra
bite (insect) mordida (por um
insecto) ① mor·*dee*·da (poor oong
eeng·se·too)
bitter amargo/amarga ⓜ/①
a·*maar*·goo/a·*maar*·ga
black preto/preta ⓜ/① *pre*·too/*pre*·ta
bladder bexiga ① be·*shee*·ga
blanket cobertor ⓜ koo·ber·*tor*
blind cego/cega ⓜ/① *se*·goo/*se*·ga
blister bolha ① *bo*·lya
blocked bloqueado/bloqueada ⓜ/①
blo·kee·*aa*·doo/blo·kee·*aa*·da
blood sangue ⓜ *sang*·ge
blood pressure tensão arterial ①
teng·*sowng* ar·te·ree·*aal*
blood test análise de sangue ①
a·*naa*·lee·ze de *sang*·ge
blood type grupo sanguíneo ⓜ
groo·poo sang·*gwee*·nee·oo
blue azul a·*zool*
board subir a bordo soo·*beer* a
bor·doo
boarding house pensão ①
peng·*sowng*

boarding pass cartão de embarque ⓜ kar·*towng* de eng·*baar*·ke

boat barco ⓜ *baar*·koo

body corpo ⓜ *kor*·poo

bone osso ⓜ *o*·soo

book livro ⓜ *lee*·vroo

book (reserve) reservar rre·zer·*vaar*

booked out esgotado/esgotada ⓜ/ⓕ shgoo·*taa*·doo/shgoo·*taa*·da

bookshop livraria ⓕ lee·vra·*ree*·a

boots botas ⓕ *bo*·tash

border fronteira ⓕ frong·*tay*·ra

bored aborrecido/aborrecida ⓜ/ⓕ a·boo·rre·*see*·doo/a·boo·rre·see·da

boring chato/chata ⓜ/ⓕ *shaa*·too/*shaa*·ta

borrow pedir emprestado pe·*deer* eng·presh·*taa*·doo

botanic garden jardim botânico ⓜ zhar·*deeng* boo·*ta*·nee·koo

both ambos/ambas ⓜ/ⓕ *ang*·boosh/*ang*·bash

bottle garrafa ⓕ ga·*rraa*·fa

bottle opener saca-rolhas ⓜ saa·ka·*rro*·lyash

bottle shop loja de bebidas ⓕ *lo*·zha de be·*bee*·dash

bottom (body) nádegas ⓕ pl *naa*·de·gash

bottom (position) fundo ⓕ *foong*·doo

bowl tigela ⓕ tee·*zhe*·la

box caixa ⓕ *kai*·sha

boxing boxe ⓜ *bok*·se

boy menino ⓜ me·*nee*·noo

boyfriend namorado ⓜ na·moo·*raa*·doo

bra soutien ⓜ soo·tee·*eng*

brake (car) travão ⓜ tra·*vowng*

brave corajoso/corajosa ⓜ/ⓕ koo·ra·*zho*·zoo/koo·ra·*zho*·za

bread pão ⓜ *powng*

break quebrar ke·*braar*

break down (car) avariar a·va·ree·*aar*

breakfast pequeno almoço ⓜ pe·*ke*·noo aal·*mo*·soo

breast peito ⓜ sg *pay*·too

breasts seios ⓜ *say*·oosh

breathe respirar rresh·pee·*raar*

bribe suborno ⓜ soo·*bor*·noo

bridge (structure) ponte ⓕ *pong*·te

briefcase pasta ⓕ *pash*·ta

bring trazer tra·*zer*

brochure brochura ⓕ broo·*shoo*·ra

broken quebrado/quebrada ⓜ/ⓕ ke·*braa*·doo/ke·*braa*·da

broken down (car, etc) avariado/avariada ⓜ/ⓕ a·va·ree·*aa*·doo/a·va·ree·*aa*·da

bronchitis bronquite ⓕ brong·*kee*·te

brother irmão ⓜ eer·*mowng*

brown castanho/castanha ⓜ/ⓕ kash·*ta*·nyoo/kash·*ta*·nya

bruise nódoa negra ⓕ *no*·doo·a *ne*·gra

brush escova ⓕ *shko*·va

bucket balde ⓜ *baal*·de

Buddhist n&a budista ⓜ&ⓕ boo·*deesh*·ta

budget orçamento ⓜ or·sa·*meng*·too

buffet bufete ⓜ boo·*fe*·te

bug bicho ⓜ *bee*·shoo

build construir kong·shtroo·*eer*

builder construtor ⓜ kong·shtroo·*tor*

building prédio ⓜ *pre*·dyoo

bull touro ⓜ *toh*·roo

bullfight tourada ⓕ toh·*raa*·da

bullfighter cavaleiro ⓜ ka·va·*lay*·roo

bullring praça de touros ⓕ *praa*·sa de *toh*·roosh

burn queimadura ⓕ kay·ma·*doo*·ra

bus autocarro ⓜ ow·to·*kaa*·roo

business negócios ⓜ pl ne·*go*·syoosh

business class classe executiva ⓕ *klaa*·se ee·zhe·koo·*te*·e·va

businessperson homem/mulher de negócios ⓜ/ⓕ *o*·meng/moo·*lyer* de ne·*go*·syoosh

business trip viagem de negócios ⓕ vee·*aa*·zheng de ne·*go*·syoosh

busker artista de rua ⓜ&ⓕ ar·*teesh*·ta de *rroo*·a

C

bus station/stop paragem de autocarros ① pa·*raa*·zheng de ow·to·*kaa*·rroosh
busy ocupado/ocupada ⓜ/① o·koo·*paa*·doo/o·koo·*paa*·da
but mas mash
button botão ⓜ boo·*towng*
buy comprar kong·*praar*

C

cabin camarote ⓜ ka·ma·ro·te
cake shop pastelaria ① pash·te·la·*ree*·a
calculator calculadora ① kaal·koo·la·*do*·ra
calendar calendário ⓜ ka·leng·*daa*·ryoo
call (telephone) telefonar te·le·foo·*naar*
camera máquina fotográfica ① *maa*·kee·na foo·too·*graa*·fee·ka
camera shop loja de equipamentos fotográficos ① *lo*·zha de e·kee·pa·*meng*·toosh foo·too·*graa*·fee·koosh
camp acampar a·kang·*paar*
camping ground acampamento ⓜ a·kang·pa·*meng*·too
camping store loja de campismo ① *lo*·zha de kang·*peezh*·moo
campsite parque de campismo ⓜ *paar*·ke de kang·*peezh*·moo
can (tin) lata ① *laa*·ta
can poder poo·*der*
Canada Canadá ⓜ ka·na·*daa*
cancel cancelar kang·se·*laar*
cancer cancro ⓜ *kang*·kroo
candle vela ① *ve*·la
can opener abre latas ⓜ *aa*·bre *laa*·tash
captain capitão ⓜ ka·pee·*towng*
car carro ⓜ *kaa*·rroo
caravan caravana ① ka·ra·*va*·na
cards (playing) cartas ① pl *kaar*·tash
care (for someone) gostar goosh·*taar*
car hire aluguer de automóvel a·loo·*ger* de ow·too·*mo*·vel

car owner's title título de registo do automóvel ⓜ *tee*·too·loo de rre·*zheesh*·too doo ow·too·*mo*·vel
car park parque de estacionamento ⓜ *paar*·ke de shta·syoo·na·*meng*·too
car registration registo automóvel ⓜ rre·*zheesh*·too ow·too·*mo*·vel
carry carregar ka·rre·*gaar*
carton caixa de papelão ① *kai*·sha de pa·pe·*lowng*
cash dinheiro dee·*nyay*·roo
cash (a cheque) levantar (um cheque) le·vang·*taar* (oong *she*·ke)
cash register caixa registadora ① *kai*·sha rre·zheesh·ta·*do*·ra
cassette cassete ① kaa·se·te
castle castelo ⓜ kash·te·loo
casual work trabalho temporário ⓜ tra·*baa*·lyoo teng·poo·*raa*·ryoo
cat gato/gata ⓜ/① *gaa*·too/*gaa*·ta
cathedral catedral ① ka·te·*draal*
Catholic n&a católico/católica ⓜ/① ka·to·lee·koo/ka·to·lee·ka
cave caverna ① ka·*ver*·na
celebration comemoração ① koo·me·moo·ra·*sowng*
cell phone telemóvel ⓜ te·le·*mo*·vel
cemetery cemitério ⓜ se·mee·*te*·ryoo
cent cêntimo ⓜ *seng*·tee·moo
centimetre centímetro ⓜ seng·*tee*·me·troo
centre centro ⓜ *seng*·troo
certificate certificado ⓜ ser·tee·fee·*kaa*·doo
chain (bike) corrente ① koo·*rreng*·te
chair cadeira ① ka·*day*·ra
chairlift teleférico ⓜ te·le·fe·ree·koo
championships campeonatos ⓜ pl kang·pe·oo·*naa*·toosh
chance oportunidade ① o·poor·too·nee·*daa*·de
change mudança ① moo·*dang*·sa
change (coins) troco ⓜ *tro*·koo
change (money) trocar troo·*kaar*
changing room sala de provas ① *saa*·la de *pro*·vash

charming charmoso/charmosa ⓜ/ⓕ
shar·mo·zoo/shar·mo·za
chat up dar conversa daar kong·ver·sa
cheap barato/barata ba·raa·too/
ba·raa·ta
cheat enganar eng·ga·naar
check verificar ve·ree·fee·kaar
check (banking) cheque ⓜ she·ke
check (bill) conta ⓕ kong·ta
check-in check-in ⓜ shek·eeng
checkpoint ponto de controle ⓜ
pong·too de kong·tro·le
chef cozinheiro/cozinheira chefe ⓜ/ⓕ
koo·zee·nyay·roo/koo·zee·nyay·ra
she·fe
cheque (banking) cheque ⓜ she·ke
chess xadrez ⓜ sha·dresh
chess board tabuleiro de xadrez ⓜ
ta·boo·lay·roo de sha·dresh
chest (body) peito ⓜ pay·too
chewing gum pastilha elástica ⓕ
pash·tee·lya e·laash·tee·ka
chicken galinha ⓕ ga·lee·nya
chicken pox bechigas ⓕ pl
be·shee·gash
child criança ⓜ&ⓕ kree·ang·sa
childminding (service) ama ⓕ a·ma
child seat cadeira de criança ⓕ
ka·day·ra de kree·ang·sa
children crianças ⓜ&ⓕ pl
kree·ang·sash
chocolate chocolate ⓜ
shoo·koo·laa·te
choose escolher shkoo·lyer
Christian n&a Cristão/Cristã ⓜ/ⓕ
kreesh·towng/kreesh·tang
Christmas Natal ⓜ na·taal
church igreja ⓕ ee·gre·zha
cigar charuto ⓜ sha·roo·too
cigarette cigarro ⓜ see·gaa·rroo
cigarette lighter isqueiro ⓜ
eesh·kay·roo
cinema cinema ⓜ see·ne·ma
circus circo ⓜ seer·koo
city cidade ⓕ see·daa·de
city centre centro da cidade ⓜ
seng·troo da see·daa·de

civil rights direitos civis ⓜ pl
dee·ray·toosh see·veesh
class (category) classe ⓕ klaa·se
class system sistema de classes ⓜ
seesh·te·ma de klaa·sesh
clean limpo/limpa ⓜ/ⓕ leeng·poo/
leeng·pa
clean limpar leeng·paar
cleaning limpeza ⓕ leeng·pe·za
client cliente ⓜ&ⓕ klee·eng·te
cliff penhasco ⓜ pe·nyaash·koo
climb subir soo·beer
cloakroom bengaleiro ⓜ
beng·ga·lay·roo
clock relógio ⓜ rre·lo·zhyoo
close perto per·too
close fechar fe·shaar
closed fechado/fechada ⓜ/ⓕ
fe·shaa·doo/fe·shaa·da
clothesline estendal da roupa ⓕ
shteng·daal da rroh·pa
clothing roupas ⓕ pl rroh·pash
clothing store loja de roupas ⓕ
lo·zha de rroh·pash
cloud nuvem ⓕ noo·veng
cloudy nublado/nublada ⓜ/ⓕ
noo·blaa·doo/noo·blaa·da
clutch (car) embraiagem ⓕ
eng·brai·aa·zheng
coach (bus) autocarro ⓜ
ow·to·kaa·rroo
coach (trainer) treinador/
treinadora ⓜ/ⓕ tray·na·dor/
tray·na·do·ra
coat casaco ⓜ ka·zaa·koo
cockroach barata ⓕ ba·raa·ta
coffee café ⓜ ka·fe
coins moedas ⓕ pl moo·e·dash
cold frio/fria ⓜ/ⓕ free·oo/free·a
cold (illness) constipação ⓕ
kong·shtee·pa·sowng
colleague colega ⓜ&ⓕ koo·le·ga
collect call ligação a cobrar ⓕ
lee·ga·sowng a koo·braar
college universidade ⓕ
oo·nee·ver·see·daa·de
colour cor ⓕ kor

comb pente ⓜ *peng*·te
come vir *veer*
comedy comédia ⓕ koo·*me*·dya
comfortable confortável
kong·for·*taa*·vel
commission comissão ⓕ
koo·mee·*sowng*
communion comunhão ⓕ
koo·moo·*nyowng*
communist n&a comunista ⓜ&ⓕ
koo·moo·*neesh*·ta
company (firm) empresa ⓕ
eng·*pre*·za
compass bússola ⓕ *boo*·soo·la
complain reclamar rre·kla·*maar*
complaint reclamação ⓕ
rre·kla·ma·*sowng*
complimentary grátis *graa*·teesh
computer computador ⓜ
kong·poo·ta·*dor*
concert concerto ⓜ kong·*ser*·too
concussion abalo cerebral ⓜ
a·*baa*·loo se·re·*braal*
conditioner (hair) amaciador ⓜ
a·ma·see·a·*dor*
condom preservativo ⓜ
pre·zer·va·*tee*·voo
conference (big) conferência ⓕ
kong·fe·*reng*·sya
conference (small) colóquio ⓜ
koo·*lo*·kyoo
confession confissão ⓕ
kong·fee·*sowng*
confirm confirmar kong·feer·*maar*
conjunctivitis conjuntivite ⓕ
kong·zhoong·tee·*vee*·te
connection ligação ⓕ lee·ga·*sowng*
constipation prisão de ventre ⓕ
pree·*zowng* de *ven*·tre
consulate consulado ⓜ
kong·soo·*laa*·doo
contact lenses lentes de
contacto ⓜ pl *leng*·tesh de
kong·*taak*·too
contact lens solution líquido para
lentes de contacto ⓜ *lee*·kee·doo
pa·ra *leng*·tesh de kong·*taak*·too

contraceptives contraceptivo ⓜ
kong·tra·se·*tee*·voo
contract contrato ⓜ kong·*traa*·too
convenience store loja de
conveniência ⓕ *lo*·zha de
kong·ve·*nyeng*·sya
cook cozinheiro/cozinheira ⓜ/ⓕ
koo·zee·*nyay*·roo/koo·zee·*nyay*·ra
cook cozinhar koo·zee·*nyaar*
cooking cozinha ⓕ koo·*zee*·nya
cool (cold) fresco/fresca ⓜ/ⓕ
fresh·koo/*fresh*·ka
cool (exciting) fixe ⓜ&ⓕ *fee*·she
corkscrew saca-rolhas ⓜ
saa·ka·*rro*·lyash
corner esquina ⓕ *shkee*·na
corrupt corrupto/corrupta ⓜ/ⓕ
koo·*rroop*·too/koo·*rroop*·ta
cost custar koosh·*taar*
cotton algodão ⓜ aal·goo·*downg*
cotton balls bolas de algodão ⓕ pl
bo·lash de aal·goo·*downg*
cotton buds cotonete ⓜ ko·to·*ne*·te
cough tossir too·*seer*
cough medicine xarope ⓜ sha·*ro*·pe
count contar kong·*taar*
counter (at bar) balcão ⓜ
baal·*kowng*
country país ⓜ pa·*eesh*
countryside interior do país ⓜ
eeng·te·ree·*or* doo pa·*eesh*
coupon cupão ⓜ koo·*powng*
court (legal) tribunal ⓜ tree·boo·*naal*
court (sport) campo ⓜ *kang*·poo
cover charge consumo obrigatório ⓜ
kon·*soo*·moo o·bree·ga·*to*·ree·oo
cow vaca ⓕ *vaa*·ka
crafts artesanato ⓜ ar·te·za·*naa*·too
crash (car) acidente ⓜ a·see·*deng*·te
crazy louco/louca ⓜ/ⓕ *loh*·koo/
loh·ka
cream creme ⓜ *kre*·me
crèche infantário ⓜ
eeng·fang·*taa*·ree·oo
credit crédito ⓜ *kre*·dee·too
credit card cartão de crédito ⓜ
kar·*towng* de *kre*·dee·too

cross (religious) cruz ① kroosh
crowded cheio/cheia ⓜ/① shay·oo/
shay·a
cup chávena ① shaa·ve·na
cupboard armário ⓜ ar·maa·ryoo
currency exchange câmbio ⓜ
kang·byoo
current (electricity) corrente ①
koo·rreng·te
current affairs assuntos do dia ⓜ pl
a·soong·toosh doo dee·a
custom costume ⓜ koosh·too·me
customs alfândega ① aal·fang·de·ga
cut cortar koor·taar
cutlery talheres ⓜ pl ta·lye·resh
CV CV ⓜ se·ve
cycle andar de bicicleta ang·daar de
bee·see·kle·ta
cycling ciclismo ⓜ see·kleesh·moo
cyclist ciclista ⓜ&① see·kleesh·ta
cystitis cistite ① seesh·tee·te

D

daily diário/diária ⓜ/① dee·aa·ryoo/
dee·aa·rya
dance dançar dang·saar
dancing dança ① dang·sa
dangerous perigoso/perigosa ⓜ/①
pe·ree·go·zoo/pe·ree·go·za
dark (colour/night) escuro/
escura ⓜ/① shkoo·roo/shkoo·ra
date (appointment) encontro ⓜ
eng·kong·troo
date (day) data ① daa·ta
date (a person) namorar na·moo·raar
date of birth data de nascimento ①
daa·ta de nash·see·meng·too
daughter filha ① fee·lya
dawn madrugada ① ma·droo·gaa·da
day dia ⓜ dee·a
dead morto/morta ⓜ/① mor·too/
mor·ta
deaf surdo/surda ⓜ/① soor·doo/
soor·da
decide decidir de·see·deer
(car) deck convés (de automóveis) ⓜ
kong·vesh (de ow·too·mo·vaysh)

deep profundo/profunda ⓜ/①
proo·foong·doo/proo·foong·da
deforestation desflorestação ⓜ
desh·floo·resh·ta·sowng
degrees (temperature) graus ⓜ pl
growsh
delay atraso ⓜ a·traa·zoo
delicatessen charcutaria ①
shar·koo·ta·ree·a
deliver entregar eng·tre·gaar
democracy democracia ①
de·moo·kra·see·a
demonstration manifestação ①
ma·nee·fesh·ta·sowng
dental dam protector de borracha ⓜ
proo·te·tor de boo·rraa·sha
dental floss fio dental ① fee·oo
deng·taal
dentist dentista ⓜ&① deng·teesh·ta
deodorant desodorizante ⓜ
de·zo·doo·ree·zang·te
depart partir par·teer
departure partida ① par·tee·da
departure gate porta de partida ①
por·ta de par·tee·da
deposit (bank) depósito ⓜ
de·po·zee·too
desert deserto ⓜ de·zer·too
design design ⓜ dee·zain
dessert sobremesa ① soo·bre·me·za
destination destino ⓜ desh·tee·noo
details detalhes ⓜ pl de·taa·lyesh
diabetes diabetes ① dee·a·be·tesh
dial tone sinal da linha telefónica ①
see·naal da lee·nya te·le·fo·nee·ka
diaper fralda ① fraal·da
diaphragm diafragma ⓜ
dee·a·fraa·ge·ma
diarrhoea diarreia ① dee·a·rray·a
diary diário ⓜ dee·aa·ryoo
dice dados ⓜ pl daa·doosh
dictionary dicionário ⓜ
dee·syoo·naa·ryoo
die morrer moo·rrer
diet dieta ① dee·e·ta
different diferente dee·fe·reng·te
difficult difícil dee·fee·seel

E

dining car vagão restaurante ⓜ
va·*gowng* rresh·tow·*rang*·te

dinner jantar ⓜ zhang·*taar*

direct directo/directa ⓜ/ⓕ
dee·re·too/dee·re·ta

direct-dial ligação directa ⓕ
lee·ga·*sowng* dee·*re*·ta

direction direcção ⓕ dee·re·*sowng*

director director/directora ⓜ/ⓕ
dee·re·*tor*/dee·re·*to*·ra

dirty sujo/suja ⓜ/ⓕ *soo*·zhoo/
soo·zha

disabled deficiente de·fee·see·*eng*·te

disco disco ⓜ *deesh*·koo

discount desconto ⓜ desh·*kong*·too

discrimination discriminação ⓕ
deesh·kree·mee·na·*sowng*

disease doença ⓕ doo·*eng*·sa

dish prato ⓜ *praa*·too

diving mergulho ⓜ mer·*goo*·lyoo

diving equipment equipamento de
mergulho ⓜ e·kee·pa·*meng*·too de
mer·*goo*·lyoo

divorced divorciado/divorciada ⓜ/ⓕ
dee·vor·see·*aa*·doo/dee·vor·see·*aa*·da

dizzy tonto/tonta ⓜ/ⓕ *tong*·too/
tong·ta

do fazer fa·*zer*

doctor médico/médica ⓜ/ⓕ
me·dee·koo/*me*·dee·ka

documentary documentário ⓜ
doo·koo·meng·*taa*·ryoo

dog cão ⓜ kowng

dole (welfare) assistência social ⓕ
a·seesh·*teng*·sya soo·see·*aal*

doll boneco/boneca ⓜ/ⓕ
boo·*ne*·koo/boo·*ne*·ka

double duplo/dupla ⓜ/ⓕ *doo*·ploo/
doo·pla

double bed cama de casal ⓕ *ka*·ma
de ka·*zaal*

double room quarto de casal ⓜ
kwaar·too de ka·*zaal*

down baixo *bai*·shoo

downhill para baixo *pa*·ra *bai*·shoo

dream sonho ⓜ *so*·nyoo

dress vestido ⓜ vesh·*tee*·doo

dried seco/seca ⓜ/ⓕ *se*·koo/*se*·ka

drink bebida ⓕ be·*bee*·da

drink (alcoholic) bebida alcoólica ⓕ
be·*bee*·da aal·koo·o·lee·ka

drink beber be·*ber*

drive conduzir kong·doo·*zeer*

drivers licence carta de condução ⓕ
kaar·ta de kong·doo·*sowng*

drug droga ⓕ *dro*·ga

drug addiction vício da droga ⓜ
vee·syoo da *dro*·ga

drug dealer traficante de
drogas ⓜ&ⓕ tra·fee·*kang*·te de
dro·gash

drug trafficking tráfico de drogas ⓜ
traa·fee·koo de *dro*·gash

drug user toxicodependente ⓜ&ⓕ
tok·see·ko·de·peng·*deng*·te

drunk bêbado/bêbada ⓜ/ⓕ
be·ba·doo/be·ba·da

dry seco/seca ⓜ/ⓕ *se*·koo/*se*·ka

dry secar se·*kaar*

dummy (pacifier) chupeta ⓕ
shoo·*pe*·ta

E

each cada *ka*·da

ear orelha ⓕ o·*re*·lya

early cedo *se*·doo

earn ganhar ga·*nyaar*

earplugs tampões para os
ouvidos ⓜ pl tang·*poyngsh* pa·ra
oosh oh·*vee*·doosh

earrings brincos ⓜ pl *breeng*·koosh

earthquake terramoto ⓜ
te·rra·*mo*·too

Easter Páscoa ⓕ *paash*·kwa

easy fácil *faa*·seel

eat comer koo·*mer*

economy class classe económica ⓕ
klaa·se ee·koo·*no*·mee·ka

education educação ⓕ
e·doo·ka·*sowng*

election eleição ⓕ e·lay·*sowng*

electrical store loja de aparelhos
eléctricos ⓕ *lo*·zha de a·pa·*re*·lyoosh
ee·*le*·tree·koosh

electricity electricidade ⓕ
ee·le·tree·see·*daa*·de

elevator elevador ⓜ ee·le·va·*dor*

embassy embaixada ⓕ
eng·bai·*shaa*·da

emergency emergência ⓕ
ee·mer·*zheng*·sya

emotional sensível seng·*see*·vel

employee empregado/
empregada ⓜ/ⓕ eng·pre·*gaa*·doo/
eng·pre·*gaa*·da

employer patrão/patroa ⓜ/ⓕ
pa·*trowng*/pa·*tro*·a

empty vazio/vazia ⓜ/ⓕ va·*zee*·oo/
va·*zee*·a

end fim ⓜ feeng

engaged (phone) ocupado ⓜ
o·koo·*paa*·doo

engaged comprometido/compro-
metida ⓜ/ⓕ kong·proo·me·*tee*·doo/
kong·proo·me·*tee*·da

engagement noivado ⓜ noy·*vaa*·doo

engine motor ⓜ moo·*tor*

engineering engenharia ⓕ
eng·zhe·nya·*ree*·a

England Inglaterra ⓕ eeng·gla·te·rra

English inglês ⓜ eeng·*glesh*

enjoy (oneself) divertir-se
dee·ver·*teer*·se

enough suficiente soo·fee·see·*eng*·te

enter entrar eng·*traar*

entertainment guide guia
de espectáculos ⓕ *gee*·a de
shpe·*taa*·koo·loosh

entry entrada ⓕ eng·*traa*·da

envelope envelope ⓜ eng·ve·*lo*·pe

environment ambiente ⓜ
ang·bee·*eng*·te

epilepsy epilepsia ⓕ e·pee·le·pe·*see*·a

equality igualdade ⓕ ee·gwal·*daa*·de

equal opportunities igualdade de
oportunidades ⓕ ee·gwal·*daa*·de de
o·poor·too·nee·*daa*·desh

equipment equipamento ⓜ
e·kee·pa·*meng*·too

escalator escada rolante ⓕ
shkaa·da rroo·*lang*·te

estate agency agência de
imobiliário ⓕ a·*zheng*·sya de
ee·mo·bee·*lyaa*·ryoo

euro euro ⓜ e·oo·roo

evening da noite ⓜ da *noy*·te

every todo/toda ⓜ/ⓕ *to*·doo/*to*·da

everyone todos/todas ⓜ/ⓕ
to·doosh/*to*·dash

everything tudo ⓜ *too*·doo

exactly exactamente e·za·ta·*meng*·te

example exemplo ⓜ e·*zeng*·ploo

excellent excelente ay·she·*leng*·te

exchange câmbio ⓜ *kang*·byoo

exchange trocar troo·*kaar*

exchange rate taxa de câmbio ⓕ
taa·sha de *kang*·byoo

excluded excluído/excluída ⓜ/ⓕ
aysh·kloo·ee·doo/aysh·kloo·ee·da

exhaust (car) exaustor ⓜ
ee·zowsh·*tor*

exhibition exposição ⓕ
shpoo·zee·*sowng*

exit saída ⓕ saa·ee·da

expensive caro/cara ⓜ/ⓕ *kaa*·roo/
kaa·ra

experience experiência ⓕ
shpe·ree·*eng*·sya

exploitation exploração ⓕ
shplo·ra·*sowng*

express expresso/expressa ⓜ/ⓕ
shpre·soo/*shpre*·sa

express mail correio azul ⓜ
koo·*rray*·oo a·*zool*

extension (visa) extensão ⓕ
shteng·*sowng*

eye olho ⓜ o·*lyoo*

eye drops colírio ⓕ koo·*lee*·ree·oo

F

fabric tecido ⓜ te·*see*·doo

face rosto ⓜ *rrosh*·too

face cloth toalha de rosto ⓕ
twaa·lya de *rrosh*·too

factory fábrica ⓕ *faa*·bree·ka

factory worker operário/
operária ⓜ/ⓕ o·pe·*raa*·ryoo/
o·pe·*raa*·rya

F

fall cair ka·*eer*

family família ⓕ fa·*mee*·lya

family name apelido ⓜ a·pe·*lee*·doo

famous famoso/famosa ⓜ/ⓕ
fa·*mo*·zoo/fa·*mo*·za

fan (machine) ventoínha ⓕ
veng·*too*·ee·nya

fan (sport, etc) adepto/adepta ⓜ/ⓕ
a·*de*·pe·too/a·*de*·pe·ta

fanbelt correia da ventoinha ⓕ
koo·*rray*·a da veng·*too*·ee·nya

far longe *long*·zhe

fare preço da passagem ⓜ *pre*·soo
da pa·*saa*·zheng

farm quinta ⓕ *keeng*·ta

farmer agricultor ⓜ&ⓕ
a·gree·*kool*·*tor*

fashion moda ⓕ *mo*·da

fast a rápido/rápida ⓜ/ⓕ
rraa·pee·doo/*rraa*·pee·da

fast adv depressa de·*pre*·sa

fat gordo/gorda ⓜ/ⓕ *gor*·doo/*gor*·da

father pai ⓜ pai

father-in-law sogro ⓜ *so*·groo

faucet torneira ⓕ toor·*nay*·ra

fault (someone's) culpa ⓕ *kool*·pa

faulty defeituoso/defeituosa ⓜ/ⓕ
de·fay·too·*o*·zoo/de·fay·too·*o*·za

fax fax ⓜ faaks

feed alimentar a·lee·meng·*taar*

feel (touch) tocar too·*kaar*

feeling (physical) sensação ⓕ
seng·sa·*sowng*

feelings sentimentos ⓜ pl
seng·tee·*meng*·toosh

female a feminino/feminina ⓜ/ⓕ
fe·mee·*nee*·noo/fe·mee·*nee*·na

fence cerca ⓕ *ser*·ka

ferry ferryboat ⓜ fe·*rree*·boht

festival festival ⓜ fesh·tee·*vaal*

fever febre ⓕ *fe*·bre

few alguns/algumas ⓜ/ⓕ pl
aal·*goongsh*/aal·*goo*·mash

fiancé/fiancée noivo/noiva ⓜ/ⓕ
noy·voo/*noy*·va

fiction ficção ⓕ feek·*sowng*

fight luta ⓕ *loo*·ta

fill encher eng·*sher*

film filme ⓜ *feel*·me

film speed velocidade do filme ⓕ
ve·loo·see·*daa*·de doo *feel*·me

filtered filtrado/filtrada ⓜ/ⓕ
feel·*traa*·doo/feel·*traa*·da

find encontrar eng·kong·*traar*

fine (payment) multa ⓕ *mool*·ta

fine bom/boa ⓜ/ⓕ bong/*bo*·a

finger dedo ⓜ *de*·doo

finish terminar ter·mee·*naar*

fire fogo ⓜ *fo*·goo

firewood lenha ⓕ *le*·nya

first primeiro/primeira ⓜ/ⓕ
pree·*may*·roo/pree·*may*·ra

first-aid kit estojo de primeiros
socorros ⓜ *shto*·zhoo de
pree·*may*·roosh so·*ko*·rroosh

first class primeira classe ⓕ
pree·*may*·ra *klaa*·se

fish peixe ⓜ *pay*·she

fishing pesca ⓕ *pesh*·ka

fishmonger peixeiro/peixeira ⓜ/ⓕ
pay·*shay*·roo/pay·*shay*·ra

fish shop peixaria ⓕ pay·sha·*ree*·a

flag bandeira ⓕ bang·*day*·ra

flannel (face cloth) toalha de
rosto ⓕ *twaa*·lya de *rrosh*·too

flash (camera) flash ⓜ flaash

flashlight (torch) luz do flash ⓕ
loosh doo flaash

flat (apartment) apartamento ⓜ
a·par·ta·*meng*·too

flat a plano/plana ⓜ/ⓕ *pla*·noo/
pla·na

flea pulga ⓕ *pool*·ga

fleamarket feira da ladra ⓕ *fay*·ra
da *laa*·dra

flight voo ⓜ *vo*·oo

flood inundação ⓕ
ee·noong·da·*sowng*

floor chão ⓜ showng

floor (storey) andar ⓜ ang·*daar*

florist (shop) florista ⓕ floo·*reesh*·ta

flower flor ⓕ flor

flu gripe ⓕ *gree*·pe

fly voar voo·*aar*

foggy enevoado/enevoada ⓜ/ⓕ
e·ne·voo·aa·doo/e·ne·voo·aa·da
folk music música popular ⓕ
moo·zee·ka poo·poo·laar
follow seguir se·geer
food comida ⓕ koo·mee·da
foot pé ⓜ pe
footpath caminho ⓜ ka·mee·nyoo
foreign estrangeiro/estrangeira ⓜ/ⓕ
shtrang·zhay·roo/shtrang·zhay·ra
forest floresta ⓕ floo·resh·ta
forever para sempre pa·ra seng·pre
forget esquecer shke·ser
forgive perdoar per·doo·aar
fork garfo ⓜ gaar·foo
fortnight quinzena ⓕ keeng·ze·na
fortune teller vidente ⓜ&ⓕ
vee·deng·te
foyer sala de estar ⓕ saa·la de shtaar
fragile frágil fraa·zheel
free (available) a disponível
deesh·po·nee·vel
free (gratis) a grátis graa·teesh
free (not bound) a livre lee·vre
freeze congelar kong·zhe·laar
fresh fresco/fresca ⓜ/ⓕ fresh·koo/
fresh·ka
fridge frigorífico ⓜ
free·goo·ree·fee·koo
friend amigo/amiga ⓜ/ⓕ
a·mee·goo/a·mee·ga
from de de
frost geada ⓕ zhee·aa·da
frozen gelado/gelada ⓜ/ⓕ
zhe·laa·doo/zhe·laa·da
fruit-picking colheita de frutas ⓕ
koo·lyay·ta de froo·tash
full cheio/cheia ⓜ/ⓕ shay·oo/shay·a
full-time tempo inteiro teng·poo
eeng·tay·roo
fun divertido/divertida ⓜ/ⓕ
dee·ver·tee·doo/dee·ver·tee·da
funeral funeral ⓜ foo·ne·raal
funny engraçado/engraçada ⓜ/ⓕ
eng·gra·saa·doo/eng·gra·saa·da
furniture móveis ⓜ pl mo·vaysh
future futuro ⓜ foo·too·roo

G

game (sport) jogo ⓜ zho·goo
garage garagem ⓕ ga·raa·zheng
garbage lixo ⓜ lee·shoo
garbage can caixote do lixo ⓜ
kai·sho·te doo lee·shoo
garden jardim ⓜ zhar·deeng
gardening jardinagem ⓕ
zhar·dee·naa·zheng
gas (cooking) gás ⓜ gaash
gas (petrol) gasolina ⓕ
ga·zoo·lee·na
gas cartridge botija de gás ⓜ
boo·tee·zha de gaash
gastroenteritis gastrenterite ⓕ
gash·treng·te·ree·te
gate (airport) portão/porta ⓜ/ⓕ
por·towng/por·ta
gauze gaze ⓕ gaa·ze
gearbox caixa de velocidades ⓕ
kai·sha de ve·loo·see·daa·desh
get agarrar a·ga·rraar
get off (bus, train) descer
desh·ser
gift presente ⓜ pre·zeng·te
girl menina ⓕ me·nee·na
girlfriend namorada ⓕ
na·moo·raa·da
give dar daar
glandular fever febre glandular ⓕ
fe·bre glang·doo·laar
glass (drinking) copo ⓜ ko·poo
glasses (spectacles) óculos ⓜ pl
o·koo·loosh
gloves luvas ⓕ pl loo·vash
gloves (latex) luvas de borracha ⓕ pl
loo·vash de boo·rraa·sha
glue cola ⓕ ko·la
go ir eer
goal (sport) golo ⓜ go·loo
goalkeeper guarda-redes
gwaar·da·rre·desh
goat cabra ⓕ kaa·bra
God (general) Deus ⓜ de·oosh
goggles (skiing) óculos de
esqui ⓜ pl o·koo·loosh de shke

goggles (swimming) óculos de natação ⓜ pl o·koo·loosh de na·ta·sowng

gold ouro ⓜ oh·roo

golf ball bola de golfe ⓕ bo·la de gol·fe

golf course campo de golfe ⓜ kang·poo de gol·fe

good bom/boa ⓜ/ⓕ bong/bo·a

go out (with) sair (com) sa·eer (kong)

go shopping fazer compras fa·zer kong·prash

government governo ⓜ goo·ver·noo

gram grama ⓜ graa·ma

grandchild neto/neta ⓜ/ⓕ ne·too/ ne·ta

grandfather avô ⓜ a·voh

grandmother avó ⓕ a·vo

grass (lawn) relva ⓕ rrel·va

grateful grato/grata ⓜ/ⓕ graa·too/ graa·ta

grave túmulo ⓜ too·moo·loo

great óptimo/óptima ⓜ/ⓕ o·tee·moo/o·tee·ma

green verde ver·de

greengrocer vendedor de hortaliças ⓜ veng·de·dor de or·ta·lee·sash

grey a cinzento/cinzenta ⓜ/ⓕ seeng·zeng·too/seeng·zeng·ta

grocery mercearia ⓕ mer·see·a·ree·a

grow crescer kresh·ser

guaranteed garantido/ garantida ⓜ/ⓕ ga·rang·tee·doo/ ga·rang·tee·da

guess adivinhar a·dee·vee·nyaar

guesthouse casa de hóspedes ⓕ kaa·za de osh·pe·desh

guide (audio) guia auditivo ⓜ gee·a ow·dee·tee·voo

guide (person) guia ⓜ gee·a

guidebook guia de viagem ⓜ gee·a de vee·aa·zheng

guide dog cão-guia ⓜ kowng·gee·a

guided tour excursão guiada ⓕ shkoor·sowng gee·aa·da

guilty culpado/culpada ⓜ/ⓕ kool·paa·doo/kool·paa·da

guitar guitarra ⓕ gee·taa·rra

gun pistola ⓕ peesh·to·la

gym (place) ginásio ⓜ zhee·naa·zyoo

gynaecologist ginecologista ⓜ&ⓕ zhe·ne·koo·loo·zheesh·ta

H

hair cabelo ⓜ ka·be·loo

hairbrush escova ⓕ shko·va

haircut corte de cabelo ⓜ kor·te de ka·be·loo

hairdresser cabeleireiro/ cabeleireira ⓜ/ⓕ ka·be·lay·ray·roo/ ka·be·lay·ray·ra

half a metade ⓕ a me·taa·de

hallucination alucinação ⓕ a·loo·see·na·sowng

hammer martelo ⓜ mar·te·loo

hammock cama de rede ⓕ ka·ma de rre·de

hand mão ⓕ mowng

handbag mala de mão ⓕ maa·la de mowng

handicrafts artesanato ⓜ ar·te·za·naa·too

handkerchief lenço de mão ⓜ leng·soo de mowng

handlebars guiador ⓜ gee·a·dor

handmade feito/feita à mão ⓜ/ⓕ fay·too/fay·ta aa mowng

handsome bonito/bonita ⓜ/ⓕ bo·nee·too/bo·nee·ta

happy feliz fe·leesh

harassment assédio ⓜ a·se·dyoo

harbour porto ⓜ por·too

hard (not soft) duro/dura ⓜ/ⓕ doo·roo/doo·ra

hardware store loja de ferramentas ⓕ lo·zha de fe·rra·meng·tash

hat chapéu ⓜ sha·pe·oo

have ter ter

have fun divertir-se dee·ver·teer·se

hay fever febre dos fenos ⓕ fe·bre doosh fe·noosh

H

he ele *e*·le
head cabeça ① ka·*be*·sa
headache dor de cabeça ① dor de
ka·*be*·sa
headlights faróis ① pl fa·*roysh*
health saúde ① sa·oo·de
hear escutar shkoo·*taar*
hearing aid aparelho auditivo ⓜ
a·pa·*re*·lyoo ow·dee·*tee*·voo
heart coração ⓜ koo·ra·*sowng*
heart attack ataque de coração ⓜ
a·*taa*·ke de koo·ra·*sowng*
heart condition problema de
coração ⓜ proo·*ble*·ma de
koo·ra·*sowng*
heat calor ⓜ ka·*lor*
heated aquecido/aquecida ⓜ/①
a·ke·see·doo/a·ke·see·da
heater aquecedor ⓜ a·ke·se·*dor*
heating aquecimento ⓜ
a·ke·see·*meng*·too
heavy pesado/pesada ⓜ/①
pe·*zaa*·doo/pe·*zaa*·da
helmet capacete ⓜ ka·pa·se·te
help ajuda ① a·*zhoo*·da
help ajudar a·zhoo·*daar*
hepatitis hepatite ① e·pa·*tee*·te
her (possessive) dela *de*·la
herb erva ① *er*·va
here aqui a·*kee*
high alto/alta ⓜ/① *aal*·too/*aal*·ta
highchair cadeira de refeição para
bebé ① ka·*day*·ra de rre·fay·*sowng*
pa·ra be·*be*
high school escola secundária ①
shko·la se·koong·*daa*·ree·a
highway autoestrada ①
ow·to·*shtraa*·da
hike caminhar ka·mee·*nyaar*
hiking caminhada ① ka·mee·*nyaa*·da
hiking boots botas para
caminhadas ① pl *bo*·tash pa·ra
ka·mee·*nyaa*·dash
hiking route rota de caminhada ①
rro·ta de ka·mee·*nyaa*·da
hill colina ① koo·*lee*·na
Hindu n&a hindu ⓜ&① eeng·*doo*

hire alugar a·loo·*gaar*
his (possessive) dele *de*·le
historical histórico/histórica ⓜ/①
shto·ree·koo/*shto*·ree·ka
history história ① *shto*·rya
hitchhike apanhar boleia a·pa·*nyaar*
boo·*lay*·a
HIV VIH ⓜ a·*gaa*
hockey hóquei ⓜ o·*kay*
holiday feriado ⓜ fe·ree·*aa*·doo
holidays férias ① pl *fe*·ryash
home casa ① *kaa*·za
homeless sem abrigo seng a·*bree*·goo
homemaker dona de casa ① *do*·na
de *kaa*·za
homesick com saudades kong
sow·da·desh
homosexual n&a homosexual ⓜ&①
o·mo·sek·soo·*aal*
honeymoon lua de mel ① *loo*·a
de mel
horoscope horóscopo ⓜ
o·*rosh*·koo·poo
horse cavalo ⓜ ka·*vaa*·loo
horseriding hipismo ⓜ
ee·*peezh*·moo
hospital hospital ⓜ osh·pee·*taal*
hospitality hospitalidade ①
osh·pee·ta·lee·*daa*·de
hot quente *keng*·te
hotel hotel ⓜ o·*tel*
hour hora ① *o*·ra
house casa ① *kaa*·za
housework trabalho doméstico ⓜ
tra·*baa*·lyoo doo·*mesh*·tee·koo
how como *ko*·moo
hug abraçar a·bra·*saar*
huge enorme ⓜ&① ee·*nor*·me
human resources recursos
humanos ⓜ pl rre·*koor*·soosh
oo·*ma*·noosh
human rights direitos humanos ⓜ pl
dee·*ray*·toosh oo·*ma*·noosh
hungry faminto/faminta ⓜ/①
fa·*meeng*·too/fa·*meeng*·ta
hurt aleijar a·lay·*zhaar*
husband marido ⓜ ma·*ree*·doo

I

I eu e·oo

ice gelo ⓜ zhe·loo

ice axe machado de gelo ⓜ ma·shaa·doo de zhe·loo

ice hockey hóquei sobre o gelo ⓜ o·kay so·bre oo zhe·loo

identification identificação ⓕ ee·deng·tee·fee·ka·sowng

identification card (ID) bilhete de identidade ⓜ bee·lye·te de ee·deng·tee·daa·de

idiot idiota ⓜ&ⓕ ee·dee·o·ta

if se se

ill doente doo·eng·te

immigration imigração ⓕ ee·mee·gra·sowng

important importante eeng·por·tang·te

impossible impossível eeng·po·see·vel

in em eng

in a hurry com pressa kong pre·sa

included incluído/incluída ⓜ/ⓕ eeng·kloo·ee·doo/eeng·kloo·ee·da

income tax imposto de rendimentos ⓜ eeng·posh·too de rreng·dee·meng·toosh

indigestion indigestão ⓕ eeng·dee·zhesh·towng

indoors no interior noo eeng·te·ree·or

industry indústria ⓕ eeng·doosh·trya

infection infecção ⓕ eeng·fe·sowng

inflammation inflamação ⓕ eeng·fla·ma·sowng

influenza gripe ⓕ gree·pe

information informação ⓕ eeng·for·ma·sowng

in front of na frente de na freng·te de

ingredient ingrediente ⓜ eeng·gre·dee·eng·te

inhaler inalador ⓜ ee·na·la·dor

inject injectar eeng·zhe·taar

injection injecção ⓕ eeng·zhe·sowng

injured ferido/ferida ⓜ/ⓕ fe·ree·doo/fe·ree·da

injury ferimento ⓕ fe·ree·meng·too

inner tube câmara de ar ⓕ ka·ma·ra de aar

innocent inocente ee·noo·seng·te

insect repellant repelente ⓜ rre·pe·leng·te

inside dentro deng·troo

instructor instrutor/instrutora ⓜ/ⓕ eeng·shtroo·tor/eeng·shtroo·to·ra

insurance seguro ⓜ se·goo·roo

interesting interessante eeng·te·re·sang·te

intermission intervalo ⓜ eeng·ter·vaa·loo

international internacional eeng·ter·naa·syoo·naal

internet cafe café da internet ⓜ ka·fe da eeng·ter·net

interpreter intérprete ⓜ&ⓕ eeng·ter·pre·te

interview entrevista ⓕ eng·tre·veesh·ta

invite convidar kong·vee·daar

Ireland Irlanda ⓕ eer·lang·da

iron (clothes) ferro de engomar ⓜ fe·rroo de eng·goo·maar

island ilha ⓕ ee·lya

it ele/ela ⓜ/ⓕ e·le/e·la

IT informática ⓕ eeng·for·maa·tee·ka

itch comichão ⓕ koo·mee·showng

itinerary itinerário ⓜ ee·tee·ne·raa·ryoo

IUD DIU ⓜ de·ee·oo

J

jacket casaco ⓜ ka·zaa·koo

jail prisão ⓕ pree·zowng

jam compota ⓕ kong·po·ta

jar frasco ⓜ fraash·koo

jaw (human) maxilar ⓜ maak·see·laar

jealous ciumento/ciumenta ⓜ/ⓕ see·oo·meng·too/see·oo·meng·ta

jeep jipe ⓜ zhee·pe

jewellery ourivesaria ⓕ oh·ree·ve·za·ree·a

Jewish Judeu/Judia ⓜ/ⓕ zhoo·de·oo/zhoo·dee·a

job emprego ⓜ eng·pre·goo
jogging corrida ⓕ koo·rree·da
joke piada ⓕ pee·aa·da
journalist jornalista ⓜ&ⓕ zhor·na·leesh·ta
journey viagem ⓕ vee·aa·zheng
judge juiz/juiza ⓜ/ⓕ zhoo·eesh/ zhoo·ee·za
jump saltar saal·taar
jumper (sweater) camisola ⓕ ka·mee·zo·la
jumper leads recarregador de bateria ⓜ rre·ka·rre·ga·dor de ba·te·ree·a

K

key chave ⓕ shaa·ve
keyboard teclado ⓜ te·klaa·doo
kick chutar shoo·taar
kidney rim ⓜ rreeng
kill matar ma·taar
kilogram quilograma ⓜ kee·loo·graa·ma
kilometre quilómetro ⓜ kee·lo·me·troo
kind (nice) amável ⓜ&ⓕ a·maa·vel
kindergarten jardim de infância ⓜ zhar·deeng de eeng·fang·sya
king rei ⓜ rray
kiosk quiosque ⓜ kee·osh·ke
kiss beijo ⓜ bay·zhoo
kiss beijar bay·zhaar
kitchen cozinha ⓕ koo·zee·nya
knee joelho ⓜ zhoo·e·lyoo
knife faca ⓕ faa·ka
know saber sa·ber

L

labourer trabalhador/ trabalhadora ⓜ/ⓕ tra·ba·lya·dor/ tra·ba·lya·do·ra
lace renda ⓕ reng·da
lake lago ⓜ laa·goo
lamb (animal) cordeiro ⓜ koor·day·roo
land terra ⓕ te·rra

landlady senhoria se·nyoo·ree·a
landlord senhorio se·nyoo·ree·oo
language língua ⓕ leeng·gwa
laptop computador portátil ⓜ kong·poo·ta·dor por·taa·teel
large grande grang·de
last (final) último/última ⓜ/ⓕ ool·tee·moo/ool·tee·ma
last (previous) passado/ passada ⓜ/ⓕ pa·saa·doo/pa·saa·da
late atrasado/atrasada ⓜ/ⓕ a·tra·zaa·doo/a·tra·zaa·da
later mais tarde maish tar·de
laugh rir rreer
laundry lavandaria ⓕ la·vang·da·ree·a
law lei ⓕ lay
law (study/profession) Direito ⓜ dee·ray·too
lawyer advogado/advogada ⓜ/ⓕ a·de·voo·gaa·doo/a·de·voo·gaa·da
laxative laxante ⓜ la·shang·te
lazy preguiçoso/preguiçosa ⓜ/ⓕ pre·gee·so·zoo/pre·gee·so·za
leader líder ⓜ&ⓕ lee·der
leaf folha ⓕ fo·lya
learn aprender a·preng·der
leather couro ⓜ koh·roo
lecturer professor/professora ⓜ/ⓕ proo·fe·sor/proo·fe·so·ra
ledge parapeito ⓜ pa·ra·pay·too
left (direction) esquerda ⓕ shker·da
left luggage perdidos e achados ⓜ pl per·dee·doosh ee aa·shaa·doosh
leg (body) perna ⓕ per·na
legal legal le·gaal
lens (camera) lente ⓕ leng·te
lesbian n&a lésbica ⓕ lezh·bee·ka
less menos me·noosh
letter (mail) carta ⓕ kaar·ta
liar mentiroso/mentirosa ⓜ/ⓕ meng·tee·ro·zoo/meng·tee·ro·za
library biblioteca ⓕ bee·blee·oo·te·ka
lice piolhos ⓜ pl pee·o·lyoosh
licence licença ⓕ lee·seng·sa
license plate number número da matrícula ⓜ noo·me·roo da ma·tree·koo·la

M

lie (not stand) deitar-se day·*taar*·se

lie (not tell the truth) mentir
meng·*teer*

life ⓕ vida *vee*·da

lifeboat barco salva-vidas ⓜ
baar·koo *saal*·va·va·vee·dash

life jacket colete salva-vidas ⓜ
koo·*le*·te *saal*·va·vee·dash

lift (elevator) elevador ⓜ
ee·le·va·*dor*

light luz ⓕ loosh

light (colour) claro/clara ⓜ/ⓕ
klaa·roo/*klaa*·ra

light (weight) leve *le*·ve

light bulb lâmpada ⓕ *lang*·pa·da

lighter (cigarette) isqueiro ⓜ
eesh·*kay*·roo

light meter fotómetro ⓜ
foo·*to*·me·troo

like gostar goosh·*taar*

linen (material) linho ⓜ *lee*·nyoo

lip balm bálsamo para os lábios ⓜ
baal·sa·moo *pa*·ra oosh *laa*·byoosh

lips lábios ⓜ pl *laa*·byoosh

lipstick batom ⓜ ba·*tong*

liquor store loja de bebidas ⓕ
lo·zha de be·*bee*·dash

listen escutar shkoo·*taar*

little (quantity) pouco/pouca ⓜ/ⓕ
poh·koo/*poh*·ka

little (size) pequeno/pequena ⓜ/ⓕ
pe·*ke*·noo/pe·*ke*·na

live (somewhere) morar moo·*raar*

liver fígado ⓜ *fee*·ga·doo

lizard lagarto ⓜ la·*gaar*·too

local a local loo·*kaal*

lock tranca ⓕ *trang*·ka

lock trancar trang·*kaar*

locked trancado/trancada ⓜ/ⓕ
trang·*kaa*·doo/trang·*kaa*·da

long longo/longa ⓜ/ⓕ *long*·goo/
long·ga

look olhar oo·*lyaar*

look after cuidar kwee·*daar*

look for procurar pro·koo·*raar*

lookout miradouro ⓜ mee·ra·*doh*·roo

loose solto/solta ⓜ/ⓕ *sol*·too/*sol*·ta

loose change trocos ⓜ pl *tro*·koosh

lose perder per·*der*

lost perdido/perdida ⓜ/ⓕ
per·*dee*·doo/per·*dee*·da

lost-property office gabinete de
perdidos e achados ⓜ gaa·bee·*ne*·te
de per·*dee*·doosh ee a·*shaa*·doosh

(a) lot muito/muita ⓜ/ⓕ
mweeng·too/*mweeng*·ta

loud alto/alta ⓜ/ⓕ *aal*·too/*aal*·ta

love amor ⓜ a·*mor*

love amar a·*maar*

lover amante ⓜ&ⓕ a·*maang*·te

low baixo/baixa ⓜ/ⓕ *bai*·shoo/
bai·sha

lubricant lubrificante ⓜ
loo·bree·fee·*kang*·te

luck sorte ⓕ *sor*·te

lucky afortunado/afortunada ⓜ/ⓕ
a·foor·too·*naa*·doo/a·foor·too·*naa*·da

luggage bagagem ⓕ ba·*gaa*·zheng

luggage locker depósito de
bagagens ⓜ de·*po*·zee·too de
ba·*gaa*·zhengsh

luggage tag etiqueta de bagagem ⓕ
e·te·*ke*·ta de ba·*gaa*·zheng

lump nódulo ⓜ *no*·doo·loo

lunch almoço ⓜ aal·*mo*·soo

lung pulmão ⓜ pool·*mowng*

luxury luxo ⓜ *loo*·shoo

M

machine máquina ⓕ *maa*·kee·na

magazine revista ⓕ rre·*veesh*·ta

mail enviar eng·vee·*aar*

mail correio ⓜ koo·*rray*·oo

mailbox caixa do correio ⓕ *kai*·sha
doo koo·*rray*·oo

main principal preeng·see·*paal*

main road rua principal ⓕ *rroo*·a
preeng·see·*paal*

make fazer fa·*zer*

make-up maquilhagem ⓕ
ma·kee·*lyaa*·zheng

mammogram mamograma ⓜ
ma·moo·*graa*·ma

man homem ⓜ *o*·meng

manager (business) gerente
zhe·reng·te

manager (sport) treinador/
treinadora ⓜ/ⓕ tray·na·dor/
tray·na·do·ra

manual worker trabalhador/
trabalhadora ⓜ/ⓕ tra·ba·lya·dor/
tra·ba·lya·do·ra

many vários/várias ⓜ/ⓕ
vaa·ryoosh/vaa·ryash

map mapa ⓜ maa·pa

marital status estado civil ⓜ
shtaa·doo see·veel

market mercado ⓜ mer·kaa·doo

marriage casamento ⓜ
ka·za·meng·too

married casado/casada ⓜ/ⓕ
ka·zaa·doo/ka·zaa·da

marry casar ka·zaar

martial arts artes marciais ⓕ pl
ar·tesh mar·see·aish

mass (Catholic) missa ⓕ mee·sa

massage massagem ⓕ ma·saa·zheng

masseur/masseuse
massagista ⓜ&ⓕ ma·sa·zheesh·ta

mat capacho ⓜ ka·paa·shoo

match (sport) partida ⓕ par·tee·da

matches (for lighting) fósforos ⓜ pl
fosh·foo·roosh

mattress colchão ⓜ kol·showng

maybe talvez tal·vesh

mayor presidente da câmara ⓜ&ⓕ
pre·zee·deng·te da ka·ma·ra

me mim ⓜ&ⓕ meeng

meal refeição ⓕ rre·fay·sowng

measles sarampo ⓜ sa·rang·poo

mechanic mecânico/mecânica ⓜ/ⓕ
me·ka·nee·koo/me·ka·nee·ka

media os meios de
comunicação ⓜ pl oosh may·oosh
de koo·moo·nee·ka·sowng

medicine medicamentos ⓜ pl
me·dee·ka·meng·toosh

medicine (study/profession)
medicina ⓕ me·dee·see·na

meditation meditação ⓕ
me·dee·ta·sowng

meet encontrar eng·kong·traar

meet (first time) conhecer
koo·nye·ser

member membro ⓜ&ⓕ meng·broo

memory card memória ⓕ
me·mo·ree·a

menstruation menstruação ⓕ
meng·shtroo·a·sowng

menu ementa ⓕ ee·meng·ta

message mensagem ⓕ
meng·saa·zheng

metal metal ⓜ me·taal

metre metro ⓜ me·troo

metro (train) metropolitano ⓜ
me·troo·poo·lee·ta·noo

metro station estação de
metropolitano ⓕ shta·sowng de
me·troo·poo·lee·ta·noo

microwave oven microondas ⓜ pl
mee·kro·ong·dash

midday meio-dia ⓜ may·oo·dee·a

midnight meia-noite ⓕ may·a·noy·te

migraine enxaqueca ⓕ eng·sha·ke·ka

military forças armadas ⓕ pl
for·sash ar·maa·dash

milk leite ⓜ lay·te

millimetre milímetro ⓜ
mee·lee·me·troo

minute minuto ⓜ mee·noo·too

mirror espelho ⓜ shpe·lyoo

miscarriage aborto espontâneo ⓜ
a·bor·too shpong·ta·nee·oo

miss (feel absence of) ter saudades
ter sow·daa·desh

mistake erro ⓜ e·rroo

mix misturar meesh·too·raar

mobile phone telemóvel ⓜ
te·le·mo·vel

modem modem ⓜ mo·deng

modern moderno/moderna ⓜ/ⓕ
moo·der·noo/moo·der·na

moisturiser hidratante ⓜ
ee·dra·tang·te

monastery mosteiro ⓜ
moosh·tay·roo

money dinheiro ⓜ dee·nyay·roo

month mês ⓜ mesh

N

monument monumento ⓜ
moo·noo·*meng*·too
moon lua ① *loo*·a
more mais maish
morning manhã ① ma·*nyang*
morning sickness enjoo matinal ⓜ
eng·*zho*·oo ma·tee·*naal*
mosque mesquita ① mesh·*kee*·ta
mosquito coil repelente em espiral ⓜ
rre·pe·*leng*·te eng shpee·*raal*
mosquito net mosquiteiro ⓜ
moosh·kee·*tay*·roo
motel motel ⓜ mo·*tel*
mother mãe ① maing
mother-in-law sogra ① *so*·gra
motorbike mota ① *mo*·ta
motorboat barco a motor ⓜ
baar·koo a moo·*tor*
motorway (tollway) autoestrada ①
ow·to·*shtraa*·da
mountain montanha ①
mong·*ta*·nya
mountain bike bicicleta de
montanha ① bee·see·*kle*·ta de
mong·*ta*·nya
mountaineering montanhismo ⓜ
mong·ta·*nyeezh*·moo
mountain path trilho de montanha ⓜ
tree·lyoo de mong·*ta*·nya
mountain range cordilheira ①
koor·dee·*lyay*·ra
mouse rato ⓜ *rraa*·too
mouth boca ① *bo*·ka
movie filme ⓜ *feel*·me
mud lama ① *la*·ma
mumps papeira ① pa·*pay*·ra
murder assassinato ⓜ
a·sa·see·*naa*·too
murder assassinar a·sa·see·*naar*
muscle músculo ⓜ *moosh*·koo·loo
museum museu ⓜ moo·*ze*·oo
music música ① *moo*·zee·ka
music group tuna ① *too*·na
musician músico/música ⓜ/①
moo·zee·koo/*moo*·zee·ka
music shop loja de música ① *lo*·zha
de *moo*·zee·ka

Muslim n&a muçulmano/
muçulmana ⓜ/① moo·sool·*ma*·noo/
moo·sool·*ma*·na
mute mudo/muda ⓜ/① *moo*·doo/
moo·da
my meu/minha ⓜ/① *me*·oo/*mee*·nya

N

nail clippers corta-unhas ⓜ
kor·ta·*oong*·nyash
name nome ⓜ *no*·me
napkin guardanapo ⓜ
gwar·da·*naa*·poo
nappy (diaper) fralda ① *fraal*·da
nappy rash irritação por causa da
fralda ① ee·rree·ta·*sowng* poor
kow·sa da *fraal*·da
nationality nacionalidade ①
na·syoo·na·lee·*daa*·de
national park parque nacional ⓜ
paar·ke na·syoo·*naal*
nature natureza ① na·too·*re*·za
nausea náusea ① *now*·zee·a
near perto *per*·too
nearby próximo/próxima ⓜ/①
pro·see·moo/*pro*·see·ma
nearby por perto poor *per*·too
nearest o/a mais perto ⓜ/① oo/a
maish *per*·too
necessary necessário/
necessária ⓜ/① ne·se·*saa*·ryoo/
ne·se·*saa*·rya
neck pescoço ⓜ pesh·*ko*·soo
necklace colar ⓜ koo·*laar*
need precisar pre·see·*zaar*
needle (sewing) agulha ① a·*goo*·lya
needle (syringe) seringa ①
se·*reeng*·ga
negatives (film) negativos ⓜ pl
ne·ga·*tee*·voosh
neither nenhum/nenhuma ⓜ/①
neng·*yoong*/neng·*yoo*·ma
net/network rede ① *rre*·de
never nunca *noong*·ka
new novo/nova ⓜ/① *no*·voo/*no*·va
news notícias ① pl noo·*tee*·syash
newspaper jornal ⓜ zhor·*naal*

newsstand quiosque ⓜ kee·*osh*·ke
New Year Ano Novo ⓜ *a*·noo *no*·voo
New Zealand Nova Zelândia ⓕ
no·va ze·*lang*·dya
next próximo/próxima ⓜ/ⓕ
pro·see·moo/*pro*·see·ma
next to ao lado de ow *laa*·doo de
nice simpático/simpática ⓜ/ⓕ
seeng·*paa*·tee·koo/seeng·*paa*·tee·ka
nickname alcunha ⓕ aal·*koo*·nya
night noite ⓕ *noy*·te
nightclub discoteca ⓕ
deesh·koo·*te*·ka
night out saída à noite ⓕ saa·*ee*·da
aa *noy*·te
no não nowng
noisy barulhento/barulhenta ⓜ/ⓕ
ba·roo·*lyeng*·too/ba·roo·*lyeng*·ta
none nenhum/nenhuma ⓜ/ⓕ
neng·*yoong*/neng·*yoo*·ma
nonsmoking não-fumador
nowng·foo·ma·*dor*
noon meio-dia ⓜ *may*·oo·*dee*·a
nose nariz ⓜ na·*reesh*
notebook bloco-notas ⓜ
blo·koo·*no*·tash
nothing nada ⓜ *naa*·da
now agora a·*go*·ra
nuclear energy energia nuclear ⓕ
ee·*ner*·*zhe*·a noo·klee·*aar*
nuclear testing teste nuclear ⓜ
tesh·te noo·klee·*aar*
nuclear waste resíduos
nucleares ⓜ pl rre·*zee*·doo·oosh
noo·klee·*aar*·esh
number número ⓜ *noo*·me·roo
numberplate número de matrícula ⓕ
noo·me·roo de ma·*tree*·koo·la
nurse enfermeiro/enfermeira ⓜ/ⓕ
eng·fer·*may*·roo/eng·fer·*may*·ra

O

oats aveia ⓕ sg a·*vay*·a
ocean oceano ⓜ o·see·*a*·noo
off (spoiled) estragado/
estragada ⓜ/ⓕ shtra·*gaa*·doo/
shtra·*gaa*·da

off (power) desligado/
desligada ⓜ/ⓕ desh·lee·*gaa*·doo/
desh·lee·*gaa*·da
office escritório ⓜ shkree·*to*·ryoo
office worker empregado/
empregada de escritório ⓜ/ⓕ
eng·pre·*gaa*·doo/eng·pre·*gaa*·da de
shkree·*to*·ryoo
often frequentemente
fre·kweng·te·*meng*·te
oil (food) óleo ⓜ *o*·lyoo
oil (petrol) petróleo ⓜ pe·*tro*·lyoo
old (age) velho/velha ⓜ/ⓕ *ve*·lyoo/
ve·lya
old (former) antigo/antiga ⓜ/ⓕ
ang·*tee*·goo/ang·*tee*·ga
on sobre *so*·bre
on (power) ligado/ligada ⓜ/ⓕ
lee·*gaa*·doo/lee·*gaa*·da
once uma vez *oo*·ma vezh
one-way (ticket) só de ida so de *ee*·da
only somente so·*meng*·te
on time a horas a o·*rash*
open a aberto/aberta ⓜ/ⓕ
a·*ber*·too/a·*ber*·ta
open abrir a·*breer*
opening hours horário de
expediente ⓜ o·*raa*·ryoo de
shpe·dee·*eng*·te
operation (medical) cirurgia ⓕ
see·roor·*zhe*·a
operator (phone) telefonista ⓜ&ⓕ
te·le·foo·*neesh*·ta
opinion opinião ⓕ o·pee·nee·*owng*
opposite oposto/oposta ⓜ/ⓕ
o·*posh*·too/o·*posh*·ta
optometrist optometrista ⓜ&ⓕ
o·to·me·*treesh*·ta
or ou oh
orange (colour) cor de laranja kor de
la·*rang*·zha
orchestra orquestra ⓕ or·*kesh*·tra
order pedido ⓜ pe·*dee*·doo
order pedir pe·*deer*
ordinary comum koo·*moong*
orgasm orgasmo ⓜ or·*gaazh*·moo
original a original o·ree·zhee·*naal*

P

other n&a outro/outra ⓜ/ⓕ
oh·troo/oh·tra

our (one thing) nosso/nossa ⓜ/ⓕ
no·soo/no·sa

our (more than one thing) nossos/
nossas ⓜ/ⓕ no·soosh/no·sash

out of order avariado/avariada ⓜ/ⓕ
a·va·ree·aa·doo/a·va·ree·aa·da

outside fora fo·ra

ovarian cyst cisto no ovário ⓜ
seesh·too noo o·vaa·ryoo

ovary ovário ⓜ o·vaa·ryoo

oven forno ⓜ for·noo

overdose dose excessiva ⓕ do·ze
she·see·va

overnight de noite de noy·te

overseas no estrangeiro noo
shtrang·zhay·roo

owe dever de·ver

owner dono/dona ⓜ/ⓕ do·noo/do·na

oxygen oxigénio ⓜ ok·see·zhe·nyoo

ozone layer camada de ozono ⓕ
ka·maa·da de o·zo·noo

P

package embrulho ⓜ eng·broo·lyoo

packet pacote ⓜ pa·ko·te

padlock cadeado ⓜ ka·dee·aa·doo

page página ⓕ paa·zhee·na

pain dor ⓕ dor

painkiller analgésico ⓜ
a·nal·zhe·zee·koo

painter pintor/pintora ⓜ/ⓕ
peeng·tor/peeng·to·ra

painting pintura ⓕ peeng·too·ra

pair (couple) casal ⓜ ka·zaal

palace palácio ⓜ pa·laa·syoo

pan panela ⓕ pa·ne·la

pants (trousers) calças ⓕ pl
kaal·sash

pantyhose collants ⓜ pl ko·langsh

panty liner penso higiénico ⓜ
peng·soo ee·zhee·e·nee·koo

paper papel ⓜ pa·pel

paperwork papelada ⓕ pa·pe·laa·da

pap smear exame papa nicolau ⓜ
e·za·me paa·pa ne·koo·low

parcel encomenda ⓕ
eng·koo·meng·da

parents pais ⓜ pl paish

park parque ⓜ paar·ke

park (a car) estacionar shta·syoo·naar

parliament parlamento ⓜ
par·la·meng·too

part (component) parte ⓕ paar·te

part-time meio tempo may·oo
teng·poo

party (night out) festa ⓕ fesh·ta

party (politics) partido ⓜ par·tee·doo

passenger passageiro/passageira
pa·sa·zhay·roo/pa·sa·zhay·ra

passport passaporte ⓜ paa·sa·por·te

past passado ⓜ pa·saa·doo

pastry shop pastelaria ⓕ
pash·te·la·ree·a

path caminho ⓜ ka·mee·nyoo

pay pagar pa·gaar

payment pagamento ⓜ
pa·ga·meng·too

peace paz ⓕ pash

peak (mountain) pico ⓜ pee·koo

pedal pedal ⓜ pe·daal

pedestrian peão ⓜ pee·owng

pen caneta ⓕ ka·ne·ta

pencil lápis ⓜ laa·peesh

penis pénis ⓜ pe·neesh

penknife canivete ⓜ ka·nee·ve·te

pensioner pensionista ⓜ&ⓕ
peng·syoo·neesh·ta

people pessoas ⓕ pl pe·so·ash

per (day) por poor

per cent por cento poor seng·too

perfect perfeito/perfeita ⓜ/ⓕ
per·fay·too/per·fay·ta

performance actuação ⓕ
a·too·a·sowng

perfume perfume ⓜ per·foo·me

period pain dor menstrual ⓕ dor
meng·shtroo·aal

permission licença ⓕ lee·seng·sa

permit licença ⓕ lee·seng·sa

person pessoa ⓕ pe·so·a

petition petição ① pe·tee·*sowng*
petrol gasolina ① ga·zoo·*lee*·na
petrol station posto de gasolina ⓜ
posh·too de ga·zoo·*lee*·na
pharmacist farmacêutico/farma-
cêutica ⓜ/① far·ma·se·oo·tee·koo/
far·ma·se·oo·*tee*·ka
pharmacy farmácia ① far·*maa*·sya
phone book lista telefónica ①
leesh·ta te·le·*fo*·nee·ka
phone box telefone público ⓜ
te·le·*fo*·ne poo·*blee*·koo
phonecard cartão telefónico ⓜ
kar·*towng* te·le·*fo*·nee·koo
photo fotografar foo·too·gra·*faar*
photographer fotógrafo/
fotógrafa ⓜ/① foo·*to*·gra·foo/
foo·*to*·gra·fa
photography fotografia ①
foo·too·gra·*fee*·a
phrasebook livro de frases ⓜ
lee·vroo de *fraa*·zesh
pickaxe picareta ① pee·ka·*re*·ta
picnic piquenique ⓜ pee·ke·*nee*·ke
piece pedaço ⓜ pe·*daa*·soo
pig porco/porca ⓜ/① *por*·koo/*por*·ka
pill comprimido ⓜ
kong·pree·*mee*·doo
(the) pill pílula ① *pee*·loo·la
pillory (column) pilar ⓜ pee·*laar*
pillow almofada ① al·moo·*faa*·da
pillowcase fronha ① *fro*·nya
pink cor-de-rosa kor·de·*rro*·za
place lugar ⓜ loo·*gaar*
place of birth local de nascimento ⓜ
loo·*kaal* de nash·see·*meng*·too
plane avião ⓜ a·vee·*owng*
plant planta ① *plang*·ta
plate prato ⓜ *praa*·too
plateau planalto ⓜ pla·*naal*·too
platform plataforma ① pla·ta·*for*·ma
play (theatre) peça ① *pe*·sa
play (cards, etc) jogar zhoo·*gaar*
play (guitar, etc) tocar too·*kaar*
plug (bath) tampão ⓜ tang·*powng*
plug (electricity) tomada ①
too·*maa*·da

pocket bolso ⓜ *bol*·soo
pocketknife canivete ⓜ ka·nee·*ve*·te
poetry poesia ① po·ee·*zee*·a
point ponto ⓜ *pong*·too
point apontar a·pong·*taar*
poisonous venenoso/venenosa ⓜ/①
ve·ne·*no*·zoo/ve·ne·*no*·za
police polícia ① poo·*lee*·sya
police officer polícia poo·*lee*·sya
police station esquadra da polícia ①
shkwaa·dra da poo·*lee*·sya
policy política ① poo·*lee*·tee·ka
politician político/política ⓜ/①
poo·*lee*·tee·koo/poo·*lee*·tee·ka
politics política ① poo·*lee*·tee·ka
pollen pólen ⓜ *po*·leng
pollution poluição ①
poo·loo·ee·*sowng*
pool (game) bilhar ⓜ bee·*lyaar*
pool (swimming) piscina ①
pesh·*see*·na
poor pobre *po*·bre
popular popular poo·poo·*laar*
port (river/sea) porto ⓜ *por*·too
Portugal Portugal ⓜ poor·too·*gaal*
Portuguese português ⓜ
poor·too·*gesh*
positive positivo/positiva ⓜ/①
poo·zee·*tee*·voo/poo·zee·*tee*·vaa
possible possível poo·*see*·vel
post enviar eng·vee·*aar*
postage tarifa postal ① ta·*ree*·fa
poosh·*taal*
postcode código postal ⓜ
ko·dee·goo poosh·*taal*
poster cartaz ⓜ kar·*taash*
post office correio ⓜ koo·*rray*·oo
pot (cooking) panela ① pa·*ne*·la
pottery cerâmica ① se·raa·*mee*·ka
pound (weight) libra ① *lee*·bra
poverty pobreza ① poo·*bre*·za
powder pó ⓜ po
power poder ⓜ poo·*der*
prayer oração ① o·ra·*sowng*
prefer preferir pre·fe·*reer*
pregnancy test kit teste de
gravidez ⓜ *tesh*·te de gra·vee·*desh*

pregnant grávida *graa·vee·da*
premenstrual tension tensão
pré-menstrual ① *teng·sowng
pre·meng·shtroo·aal*
prepare preparar *pre·pa·raar*
prescription receita médica ①
rre·say·ta me·dee·ka
present (gift/time) presente ⑩
pre·zeng·te
president presidente ⑩&①
pre·zee·deng·te
pressure (tyre) pressão ① *pre·sowng*
pretty bonito/bonita ⑩/①
boo·nee·too/boo·nee·ta
price preço ⑩ *pre·soo*
priest padre ⑩ *paa·dre*
prime minister primeiro ministro/
primeira ministra ⑩/① *pree·may·roo
mee·nee·shtroo/pree·may·ra
mee·nee·shtra*
printer (computer) impressora ①
eeng·pre·so·ra
prison prisão ① *pree·zowng*
private privado/privada
pree·vaa·doo/pree·vaa·da
produce produzir *proo·doo·zeer*
profit lucro ⑩ *loo·kroo*
program programa ⑩ *proo·gra·ma*
projector projector ⑩ *proo·zhe·tor*
promise prometer *proo·me·ter*
prostitute prostituto/prostituta ⑩/①
proosh·tee·too·too/proosh·tee·too·ta
protect proteger *proo·te·zher*
protected (species) protegido/
protegida ⑩/① *proo·te·zhee·doo/
proo·te·zhee·da*
protest manifestação ①
ma·nee·fesh·ta·sowng
protest protestar *proo·tesh·taar*
provisions provisões ① pl
proo·vee·zoyngsh
pub (bar) bar ⑩ *baar*
public gardens jardins públicos ⑩ pl
zhar·deengzh poo·blee·koosh
public relations relações
públicas ① pl *rre·la·soyngsh
poo·blee·kash*

public telephone telefone público ⑩
te·le·fo·ne poo·blee·koo
public toilet casa de banho pública ①
kaa·za de ba·nyoo poo·blee·ka
pull puxar *poo·shaar*
pump bomba ① *bong·ba*
puncture furo ⑩ *foo·roo*
pure puro/pura ⑩/① *poo·roo/poo·ra*
purple roxo/roxa ⑩/① *rro·shoo/
rro·sha*
purse bolsa ① *bol·sa*
push empurrar *eng·poo·rraar*
put colocar *koo·loo·kaar*

qualifications qualificações ① pl
kwa·lee·fee·ka·soyngsh
quality qualidade ① *kwa·lee·daa·de*
quarantine quarentena ①
kwa·reng·te·na
queen rainha ① *rra·ee·nya*
question pergunta ① *per·goong·ta*
queue fila ① *fee·la*
quick rápido/rápida ⑩/①
rraa·pee·doo/rraa·pee·da
quiet calado/calada ⑩/①
ka·laa·doo/ka·laa·da
quit desistir *de·zeesh·teer*

rabbit coelho ⑩ *koo·e·lyoo*
race (sport) corrida ① *koo·rree·da*
racetrack pista de corridas ①
peesh·ta de koo·rree·dash
racing bike bicicleta de corrida ①
bee·see·kle·ta de koo·rree·da
racism racismo ⑩ *rra·seezh·moo*
racquet raquete ① *rra·ke·te*
radiator radiador ⑩ *rra·dee·a·dor*
radio rádio *rraa·dyoo*
railway station estação de caminhos
de ferro ① *shta·sowng de
ka·mee·nyoosh de fe·rroo*
rain chuva ① *shoo·va*
raincoat gabardina ①
gaa·baar·dee·na

rape violação ⓕ vee·oo·la·*sowng*
rare (uncommon) raro/rara ⓜ/ⓕ
rraa·roo/*rraa*·ra
rash irritação da pele ⓕ
ee·rree·ta·*sowng* da *pe*·le
rat ratazana ⓜ&ⓕ rra·ta·*za*·na
raw cru/crua ⓜ/ⓕ kroo/*kroo*·a
razor gilete ⓕ zhee·*le*·te
razor blade lâmina de barbear ⓕ
la·mee·na de bar·bee·*aar*
read ler ler
reading leitura ⓕ lay·*too*·ra
ready pronto/pronta ⓜ/ⓕ
prong·too/*prong*·ta
real estate agent agente
imobiliário ⓜ&ⓕ a·*zheng*·te
ee·moo·bee·*lyaa*·ryoo
realistic realista rree·a·*leesh*·ta
reason razão ⓕ rra·*zowng*
receipt recibo ⓜ rre·*see*·boo
recently recentemente
rre·seng·te·*meng*·te
recommend recomendar
rre·koo·meng·*daar*
record gravar gra·*vaar*
recording gravação ⓕ gra·va·*sowng*
recyclable reciclável rre·see·*klaa*·vel
recycle reciclar rre·see·*klaar*
red vermelho/vermelha ⓜ/ⓕ
ver·me·*lyoo*/ver·me·*lya*
referee juiz/juiza ⓜ/ⓕ zhoo·*eesh*/
zhoo·ee·za
reference referência ⓕ rre·fe·*reng*·sya
refrigerator frigorífico ⓜ
free·goo·*ree*·fee·koo
refugee refugiado/refugiada ⓜ/ⓕ
rre·foo·zhee·*aa*·doo/rre·foo·zhee·*aa*·da
refund reembolso ⓜ rre·eng·*bol*·soo
refuse recusar rre·koo·*zaar*
regional regional rre·zhyoo·*naal*
registered mail correio registado ⓜ
koo·*rray*·oo re·zhee·*shtaa*·doo
rehydration salts sais de
hidratação ⓜ pl saish de
ee·dra·ta·*sowng*
relationship relacionamento ⓜ
rre·la·syoo·na·*meng*·too

relax relaxar rre·laa·*shaar*
relic relíquia ⓕ rre·*lee*·kya
religion religião ⓕ rre·lee·zhee·*owng*
religious religioso/religiosa ⓜ/ⓕ
rre·lee·zhee·o·*zoo*/rre·lee·zhee·o·*za*
remote remoto/remota ⓜ/ⓕ
rre·*mo*·too/rre·*mo*·ta
remote control telecomando ⓜ
te·le·koo·*mang*·doo
rent alugar a·loo·*gaar*
repair consertar kong·ser·*taar*
reservation reserva ⓕ rre·*zer*·va
rest descansar desh·kang·*saar*
restaurant restaurante ⓜ
rresh·tow·*rang*·te
résumé currículo ⓜ koo·*rree*·koo·loo
retired aposentado/aposentada ⓜ/ⓕ
a·poo·zeng·*taa*·doo/a·poo·zeng·*taa*·da
return (ticket) a ida e volta ee·da
ee *vol*·ta
return voltar vol·*taar*
review revisão ⓕ rre·vee·*zowng*
rhythm ritmo ⓜ *rret*·moo
rib costela ⓕ koosh·*te*·la
rich (wealthy) rico/rica ⓜ/ⓕ
rree·koo/*rree*·ka
ride (car) boleia ⓕ boo·*lay*·a
ride andar
ride a bike andar de bicicleta
ang·*daar* de bee·see·*kle*·ta
ride a horse andar a cavalo ang·*daar*
a ka·*vaa*·loo
right (correct) a correcto/
correcta ⓜ/ⓕ koo·*rre*·too/koo·*rre*·ta
right (direction) (à) direita (aa)
dee·*ray*·ta
ring (jewellery) anel ⓜ a·*nel*
rip-off roubo ⓜ *rroh*·boo
risk risco ⓜ *rreesh*·koo
river rio ⓜ *rree*·oo
road estrada ⓕ *shtraa*·da
road map mapa de estradas ⓜ
maa·pa de *shtraa*·dash
rob roubar rroh·*baar*
rock pedra ⓕ *pe*·dra
rock climbing alpinismo ⓜ
aal·pee·*neezh*·moo

S

rock group banda de rock ⓕ *baang*·da de *rro*·ke
rollerblading patins em linha ⓜ pl pa·*teengzh* eng *lee*·nya
romantic romântico/romântica ⓜ/ⓕ rroo·*maang*·tee·koo/rroo·*maang*·tee·ka
room quarto ⓜ *kwaar*·too
room number número do quarto ⓜ *noo*·me·roo doo *kwaar*·too
rope corda ⓕ *kor*·da
round redondo/redonda ⓜ/ⓕ rre·*dong*·doo/rre·*dong*·da
roundabout rotunda ⓕ rroo·*toong*·da
route rota ⓕ *rro*·ta
rubbish lixo ⓜ *lee*·shoo
rubella rubéola ⓕ rroo·*be*·o·la
rug tapete ⓜ ta·*pe*·te
ruins ruínas ⓕ pl rroo·ee·nash
rule regra ⓕ *rre*·gra
run correr koo·*rrer*
running corrida ⓕ koo·*rree*·da
runny nose nariz a pingar ⓜ na·*reesh* a peeng·*gaar*

S

sad triste *treesh*·te
safe cofre ⓜ *ko*·fre
safe seguro/segura ⓜ/ⓕ se·*goo*·roo/se·*goo*·ra
safe sex sexo protegido ⓜ *sek*·soo proo·te·*zhee*·doo
sailboarding windsurf ⓕ *weend*·sarf
saint n santo/santa ⓜ/ⓕ *sang*·too/ *sang*·ta
salary salário ⓜ sa·*laa*·ryoo
sale liquidação ⓕ lee·kee·da·*sowng*
sales tax IVA ⓜ *ee*·va
same mesmo/mesma ⓜ/ⓕ *mezh*·moo/*mezh*·ma
sand areia ⓕ a·*ray*·a
sandal sandália ⓕ sang·*daa*·lya
sanitary napkin penso higiénico ⓜ *peng*·soo ee·zhee·e·nee·koo
sauna sauna ⓕ *sow*·na
say dizer dee·*zer*
scalp couro cabeludo ⓜ *koh*·roo ka·be·*loo*·doo

scarf lenço ⓜ *leng*·soo
school escola ⓕ *shko*·la
science ciências ⓕ pl see·*eng*·syash
scientist cientista ⓜ&ⓕ see·eng·*teesh*·ta
scissors tesoura ⓕ sg te·*zoh*·ra
score (a goal) marcar mar·*kaar*
scoreboard placar ⓜ pla·*kaar*
Scotland Escócia ⓕ *shko*·sya
sculpture escultura ⓕ shkool·*too*·ra
sea mar ⓜ maar
seasick enjoado/enjoada ⓜ/ⓕ eng·*zhoo*·aa·doo/eng·*zhoo*·aa·da
seaside beira mar ⓕ *bay*·ra maar
season estação ⓕ shta·*sowng*
seat assento ⓜ a·*seng*·too
seatbelt cinto de segurança ⓜ *seeng*·too de se·goo·*raang*·sa
second (time) segundo ⓜ se·*goong*·doo
second segundo/segunda ⓜ/ⓕ se·*goong*·doo/se·*goong*·da
second class segunda classe ⓕ se·*goong*·da *klaa*·se
second-hand em segunda mão eng se·*goong*·da mowng
second-hand shop loja de segunda mão ⓕ *lo*·zha de se·*goon*·da mowng
secretary secretário/secretária ⓜ/ⓕ se·kre·*taa*·ryoo/se·kre·*taa*·rya
see ver ver
self-employed person empregado/ empregada por conta própria ⓜ/ⓕ eng·pre·*gaa*·doo/eng·pre·*gaa*·da poor *kong*·ta *pro*·pree·a
selfish egoísta e·goo·*eesh*·ta
sell vender veng·*der*
send enviar eng·vee·*aar*
sensible razoável rra·zoo·*aa*·vel
sensual sensual seng·soo·*aal*
separate separado/separada ⓜ/ⓕ se·pa·*raa*·doo/se·pa·*raa*·da
serious sério/séria ⓜ/ⓕ *se*·ryoo/ *se*·rya
service serviço ⓜ ser·*vee*·soo
service charge taxa de serviço ⓕ *taa*·sha de ser·*vee*·soo

serviette guardanapo ⓜ
gwar·da·naa·poo

several vários/várias ⓜ/ⓕ pl
vaa·ryoosh/vaa·ryash

sew coser koo·zer

sex sexo ⓜ sek·soo

sexism machismo ⓜ ma·sheezh·moo

sexy sexy sek·see

shadow sombra ⓕ song·bra

shampoo champô ⓜ shang·poo

shape forma ⓕ for·ma

share (a room) partilhar par·tee·lyaar

shave fazer a barba fa·zer a baar·ba

shaving cream creme de barbear ⓜ
kre·me de bar·bee·aar

she ela e·la

sheep ovelha ⓕ oo·ve·lya

sheet (bed) lençol ⓜ leng·sol

shingles (illness) zona ⓕ zo·na

ship navio ⓜ na·vee·oo

shirt camisa ⓕ ka·mee·za

shoe sapato ⓜ sa·paa·too

shoe shop sapataria ⓕ sa·pa·ta·ree·a

shoot atirar a·tee·raar

shop loja ⓕ lo·zha

shop fazer compras fa·zer kong·prash

shopping compras ⓕ pl kong·prash

shopping centre centro comercial ⓜ
seng·troo koo·mer·see·aal

short (length) curto/curta ⓜ/ⓕ
koor·too/koor·ta

shorts calções ⓜ pl kaal·soyngsh

shoulder ombro ⓜ ong·broo

shout gritar gree·taar

show espectáculo ⓜ shpe·taa·koo·loo

show mostrar moosh·traar

shower chuveiro ⓜ shoo·vay·roo

shrine santuário ⓜ sang·too·aa·ryoo

shut fechado/fechada ⓜ/ⓕ
fe·shaa·doo/fe·shaa·da

shy tímido/tímida ⓜ/ⓕ
tee·mee·doo/tee·mee·da

sick doente doo·eng·te

side lado ⓜ laa·doo

sign sinal ⓜ see·naal

signature assinatura ⓕ
a·see·na·too·ra

silk seda ⓕ se·da

silver prata ⓕ praa·ta

SIM card cartão SIM ⓜ kar·towng
seeng

similar parecido/parecida ⓜ/ⓕ
pa·re·see·doo/pa·re·see·da

simple simples seeng·plesh

since (time) desde dezh·de

singer cantor/cantora ⓜ/ⓕ
kang·tor/kang·to·ra

single (person) a solteiro/
solteira ⓕ/ⓕ sol·tay·roo/sol·tay·ra

single room quarto de solteiro ⓜ
kwaar·too de sol·tay·roo

sister irmã ⓕ eer·mang

sit sentar seng·taar

size tamanho ⓜ ta·ma·nyoo

skate patinar pa·tee·naar

skateboarding skate ⓜ skay·te

ski esquiar shkee·aar

skiing esqui ⓜ shkee

skim milk leite magro ⓕ lay·te
maa·groo

skin pele ⓕ pe·le

skirt saia ⓕ sai·a

skull crânio ⓜ kra·nyoo

sky céu ⓜ se·oo

sleep dormir door·meer

sleeping bag saco de dormir ⓜ
saa·koo de dor·meer

sleeping car vagão cama ⓜ
va·gowng ka·ma

sleeping pills pílula para dormir ⓕ
pee·loo·laa pa·ra door·meer

sleepy sonolento/sonolenta ⓜ/ⓕ
soo·noo·leng·too/soo·noo·leng·ta

slice fatia ⓕ fa·tee·a

slide (transparency) diapositivo ⓜ
dee·a·po·zee·tee·voo

slide film filme de diapositivos ⓜ
feel·me de dee·a·po·zee·tee·voosh

slow (down) devagar de·va·gaar

slowly vagarosamente
va·ga·ro·za·meng·te

small pequeno/pequena ⓜ/ⓕ
pe·ke·noo/pe·ke·na

smell cheiro ⓜ shay·roo

S

smile sorrir so·*rreer*

smoke fumar foo·*maar*

snack refeição ligeira ⓕ rre·fay·*sowng* lee·*zhay*·ra

snake cobra ⓕ *ko*·bra

snorkelling snorkel ⓜ *snor*·kel

snow neve ⓕ *ne*·ve

soap sabonete ⓜ sa·boo·*ne*·te

soap opera telenovela ⓕ te·le·noo·*ve*·la

soccer futebol ⓜ foo·te·*bol*

socialist n&a socialista ⓜ&ⓕ soo·see·a·*leesh*·ta

sock meia ⓕ *may*·a

soft drink refrigerante ⓜ rre·free·zhe·*rang*·te

soldier soldado ⓜ&ⓕ sol·*daa*·doo

some uns/umas ⓜ/ⓕ pl oongsh/ oo·mash

someone alguém ⓜ&ⓕ aal·*geng*

something alguma coisa ⓕ aal·goo·ma *koy*·za

sometimes às vezes aash *ve*·zesh

son filho ⓜ *fee*·lyoo

song canção ⓕ kang·*sowng*

soon em breve eng *bre*·ve

sore a dorido/dorida ⓜ/ⓕ doo·*ree*·doo/doo·*ree*·da

souvenir lembrança ⓕ leng·*brang*·sa

souvenir shop loja de lembranças ⓕ *lo*·zha de leng·*brang*·sash

soy milk leite de soja ⓜ *lay*·te de *so*·zha

space (room) espaço ⓜ *shpaa*·soo

Spain Espanha ⓕ *shpa*·nya

speak falar fa·*laar*

special especial shpe·see·*aal*

specialist especialista ⓜ&ⓕ shpe·see·a·*leesh*·ta

speed (velocity) velocidade ⓕ ve·loo·see·*daa*·de

speed limit limite de velocidade ⓜ lee·*mee*·te de ve·loo·see·*daa*·de

speedometer mostrador de velocidade ⓜ moosh·tra·*dor* de ve·loo·see·*daa*·de

spider aranha ⓕ a·*ra*·nya

spoilt (person) mimado/mimada ⓜ/ⓕ mee·*maa*·doo/mee·*maa*·da

spoke raio de roda ⓜ *rraa*·yoo de *rro*·da

spoon colher ⓕ koo·*lyer*

sport desporto ⓜ desh·*por*·too

sportsperson desportista ⓜ&ⓕ desh·poor·*teesh*·ta

sports store loja de desporto ⓕ *lo*·zha de desh·*por*·too

sprain entorse ⓕ eng·*tor*·se

spring (coil) molas ⓕ pl *mo*·lash

square (town) praça ⓕ *praa*·sa

stadium estádio ⓜ *shtaa*·dyoo

stairway escadaria ⓕ shka·da·*ree*·a

stale seco/seca ⓜ/ⓕ *se*·koo/*se*·ka

stamp (postage) selo ⓜ *se*·loo

stand-by ticket bilhete sem garantia ⓜ bee·*lye*·te seng ga·rang·*tee*·a

star estrela ⓕ *shtre*·la

(four-)star (quatro) estrelas ⓕ pl (*kwaa*·troo) *shtre*·lash

start começo ⓜ koo·*me*·soo

start começar koo·me·*saar*

station estação ⓕ shta·*sowng*

stationery shop papelaria ⓕ pa·pe·la·*ree*·a

statue estátua ⓕ *shtaa*·too·a

stay ficar fee·*kaar*

steal roubar rroh·*baar*

steep íngreme *eeng*·gre·me

step passo ⓜ *paa*·soo

stereo estéreo ⓜ *shte*·ree·oo

stockings meias de vidro ⓕ pl *may*·ash de *vee*·droo

stolen roubado/roubada ⓜ/ⓕ rroh·*baa*·doo/rroh·*baa*·da

stomach estômago ⓜ *shto*·ma·goo

stomachache dor de estômago ⓕ dor de *shto*·ma·goo

stone pedra ⓕ *pe*·dra

stoned (drugged) drogado/drogada ⓜ/ⓕ droo·*gaa*·doo/droo·*gaa*·da

stop parar pa·*raar*

storm tempestade ⓕ
teng·pesh·*taa*·de

story história ⓕ *shto*·rya

stove fogão ⓜ foo·*gowng*

straight directo/directa ⓜ/ⓕ
dee·*re*·too/dee·*re*·ta

strange estranho/estranha ⓜ/ⓕ
shtra·nyoo/*shtra*·nya

stranger estranho/estranha ⓜ/ⓕ
shtra·nyoo/*shtra*·nya

stream ribeiro ⓜ rree·*bay*·roo

street rua ⓕ *rroo*·a

street market feira ⓕ *fay*·ra

street party festa na rua ⓕ *fesh*·ta
na *rroo*·a

strike greve ⓕ *gre*·ve

string cordel ⓜ koor·*del*

stroke (health) trombose ⓕ
trong·*bo*·ze

strong forte *for*·te

stubborn teimoso/teimosa ⓜ/ⓕ
tay·*mo*·zoo/tay·*mo*·za

student estudante ⓜ&ⓕ
shtoo·*dang*·te

studio estúdio ⓜ *shtoo*·dyoo

stupid burro/burra ⓜ/ⓕ *boo*·rroo/
boo·rra

style estilo ⓜ *shtee*·loo

subtitles legendas ⓕ pl
le·*zheng*·dash

suburb bairro ⓜ *bai*·rroo

subway (train) metropolitano ⓜ
me·troo·poo·lee·*ta*·no

suit bag saco de fatos ⓜ *saa*·koo de
faa·toosh

suitcase mala de viagem ⓕ *maa*·la
de vee·*aa*·zheng

sun sol ⓜ sol

sunblock protecção anti-solar ⓕ
proo·te·*sowng* ang·tee·soo·*laar*

sunburnt queimado/queimada do
sol ⓜ/ⓕ kay·*maa*·doo/kay·*maa*·da
doo sol

sunglasses óculos de sol ⓜ pl
o·koo·loosh de sol

sunny ensolarado/ensolarada ⓜ/ⓕ
eng·soo·la·*raa*·doo/eng·soo·la·*raa*·da

sunrise nascer do sol ⓜ *nash*·ser
doo sol

sunset pôr do sol ⓜ por doo sol

sunstroke insolação ⓕ
eeng·soo·la·*sowng*

supermarket supermercado ⓜ
soo·per·mer·*kaa*·doo

superstition superstição ⓕ
soo·persh·tee·*sowng*

supporter (politics) partidário/
partidária ⓜ/ⓕ par·tee·*daa*·ryoo/
par·tee·*daa*·rya

supporter (sport) adepto/
adepta ⓜ/ⓕ a·*de*·pe·too/a·*de*·pe·ta

surf fazer surf fa·*zer* sarf

surfboard prancha de surf ⓕ
prang·sha de sarf

surfing surf ⓜ sarf

surname apelido ⓜ a·pe·*lee*·doo

surprise surpresa ⓕ soor·*pre*·za

sweater camisola ⓕ ka·mee·*zo*·la

sweet a doce *do*·se

swelling inchaço ⓜ eeng·*shaa*·soo

swim nadar na·*daar*

swimming natação ⓕ na·ta·*sowng*

swimming pool piscina ⓕ
pesh·*see*·na

swimsuit fato de banho ⓜ *faa*·too
de *ba*·nyoo

synagogue sinagoga ⓕ see·na·*go*·ga

synthetic sintético/sintética ⓜ/ⓕ
seeng·*te*·tee·koo/seeng·*te*·tee·ka

syringe seringa ⓕ se·*reeng*·ga

T

table mesa ⓕ *me*·za

tablecloth toalha de mesa ⓕ
twaa·lya de *me*·za

table tennis ténis de mesa ⓜ
te·neesh de *me*·za

tail cauda ⓕ *kow*·da

tailor alfaiate ⓜ aal·fai·*aa*·te

take levar le·*vaar*

take a photo tirar uma foto tee·*raar*
oo·ma *fo*·too

talk falar fa·*laar*

tall alto/alta ⓜ/ⓕ *aal*·too/*aal*·ta

tampon tampão ⓜ tang·*powng*

tap torneira ⓕ toor·*nay*·ra

tasty gostoso/gostosa ⓜ/ⓕ goosh·to·*zoo*/goosh·to·za

tax imposto ⓜ eeng·*posh*·too

taxi rank praça de táxis ⓕ *praa*·sa de *taak*·seesh

tea chá ⓜ shaa

teacher professor/professora ⓜ/ⓕ proo·fe·*sor*/proo·fe·*so*·ra

tea house casa de chá ⓕ *kaa*·za de shaa

team equipa ⓕ e·*kee*·pa

teaspoon colher de chá ⓕ koo·*lyer* de shaa

technique técnica ⓕ *tek*·nee·ka

teeth dentes ⓜ pl *deng*·tesh

telephone telefone ⓜ te·le·*fo*·ne

telephone telefonar te·le·foo·*naar*

telescope telescópio ⓜ te·lesh·*ko*·pyoo

television televisão ⓕ te·le·vee·*zowng*

tell dizer dee·*zer*

temperature (fever) febre ⓕ *fe*·bre

temperature (weather) temperatura ⓕ teng·pe·ra·*too*·ra

tennis ténis ⓜ *te*·neesh

tennis court campo de ténis ⓜ *kang*·poo de *te*·neesh

tent tenda ⓕ *teng*·da

tent peg estaca ⓕ *shtaa*·ka

terrible terrível te·*rree*·vel

terrorism terrorismo ⓜ te·rroo·*reezh*·moo

test teste ⓜ *tesh*·te

thank agradecer a·gra·de·*ser*

that aquele/aquela ⓜ/ⓕ a·*ke*·le/a·*ke*·la

theatre teatro ⓜ te·*aa*·troo

their deles *de*·lesh

there (where neither of us is) lá *laa*

there (where you are) aí a·*ee*

thermometer termómetro ⓜ ter·*mo*·me·troo

they eles/elas ⓜ/ⓕ *e*·lesh/*e*·lash

thick grosso/grossa ⓜ/ⓕ *gro*·soo/*gro*·sa

thief ladrão/ladra ⓜ/ⓕ la·*drowng*/*laa*·dra

thin fino/fina ⓜ/ⓕ *fee*·noo/*fee*·na

think pensar peng·*saar*

thirsty sedento/sedenta ⓜ/ⓕ se·*deng*·too/se·*deng*·ta

this este/esta ⓜ/ⓕ *esh*·te/*esh*·ta

thread linha de coser ⓕ *lee*·nya de koo·*zer*

throat garganta ⓕ gar·*gang*·ta

thrush (health) corrimento ⓜ koo·rree·*meng*·too

thunderstorm trovoada ⓕ troo·voo·*aa*·da

ticket bilhete ⓜ bee·*lye*·te

ticket collector cobrador ⓜ koo·bra·*dor*

ticket machine máquina de vender bilhetes ⓕ *maa*·kee·na de veng·*der* bee·*lye*·tesh

ticket office bilheteira ⓕ bee·lye·*tay*·ra

tide maré ⓕ ma·*re*

tight apertado/apertada ⓜ/ⓕ a·per·*taa*·doo/a·per·*taa*·da

time tempo ⓜ *teng*·poo

time difference diferença horária ⓕ dee·fe·*reng*·sa o·*raa*·rya

timetable horário ⓜ o·*raa*·ryoo

tin (can) lata ⓕ *laa*·ta

tin opener abre latas ⓜ *aa*·bre *laa*·tash

tiny minúsculo/minúscula ⓜ/ⓕ mee·*noosh*·koo·loo/mee·*noosh*·koo·la

tip (gratuity) gorjeta ⓕ gor·*zhe*·ta

tire pneu ⓜ pe·*ne*·oo

tired cansado/cansada ⓜ/ⓕ kang·*saa*·doo/kang·*saa*·da

tissue lenço de papel ⓜ *leng*·soo de pa·*pel*

to a a·tash

toaster torradeira ⓕ too·rra·*day*·ra

tobacco tabaco ⓜ ta·*baa*·koo

tobacconist tabacaria ⓕ ta·ba·ka·*ree*·a

tobogganing tobogã ⓜ to·bo·*gang*

today hoje o·*zhe*

toe dedo do pé ⓜ *de·doo doo pe*
together junto/junta ⓜ/ⓕ
zhoong·too/zhoong·ta
toilet casa de banho ⓕ *kaa·za de
ba·nyoo*
toilet paper papel higiénico ⓜ
pa·pel ee·zhee·e·nee·koo
toiletry bag necessaire ⓜ *ne·se·ser*
tomorrow amanhã *aa·ma·nyang*
tonight hoje à noite *o·zhe aa noy·te*
too (also) também *tang·beng*
too (much) demais *de·maish*
tooth dente ⓜ *deng·te*
toothache dor de dentes ⓕ *dor de
deng·tesh*
toothbrush escova de dentes ⓕ
shko·va de deng·tesh
toothpaste pasta de dentes ⓕ
paash·ta de deng·tesh
toothpick palito ⓜ *pa·lee·too*
torch (flashlight) lanterna
eléctrica ⓕ *lang·ter·na ee·le·tree·ka*
touch tocar *too·kaar*
tour excursão ⓕ *shkoor·sowng*
tourist turista ⓜ&ⓕ *too·reesh·ta*
tourist office escritório de turismo ⓜ
shkree·to·ryoo de too·reezh·moo
towel toalha ⓕ *twaa·lya*
tower torre ⓕ *to·rre*
toy shop loja de brinquedos ⓕ
lo·zha de breeng·ke·doosh
track (path) caminho ⓜ *ka·mee·nyoo*
track (sport) pista ⓕ *peesh·ta*
tradesperson comerciante ⓜ&ⓕ
koo·mer·see·aang·te
traffic tráfico ⓜ *traa·fee·koo*
traffic light semáforo ⓜ
se·maa·foo·roo
trail atalho ⓜ *a·taa·lyoo*
train comboio ⓜ *kong·boy·oo*
train station estação de caminhos
de ferro ⓕ *shta·sowng de
ka·mee·nyoosh de fe·rroo*
tram eléctrico ⓜ *ee·le·tree·koo*
transit lounge sala de trânsito ⓕ
saa·la de trang·zee·too
translate traduzir *tra·doo·zeer*

transport transporte ⓜ
transh·por·te
travel viajar *vee·a·zhaar*
travel agency agência de viagens ⓕ
a·zheng·sya de vee·aa·zhengsh
travellers cheques travellers
cheques ⓜ pl *tra·ve·ler she·kesh*
travel sickness enjoo de viagem ⓜ
eng·zho·oo de vee·aa·zheng
tree árvore ⓕ *aar·vo·re*
trip viagem ⓕ *vee·aa·zheng*
trolley carrinho ⓜ *ka·rree·nyoo*
trousers calças ⓕ pl *kaal·sash*
truck camião ⓜ *ka·mee·yowng*
trust confiar *kong·fee·aar*
try (attempt) tentar *teng·taar*
tube (tyre) câmara ⓕ *ka·ma·ra*
tumour tumor ⓜ *too·mor*
tune melodia ⓕ *me·loo·dee·a*
turn virar *vee·raar*
TV televisão ⓕ *te·le·vee·zowng*
tweezers pinça ⓕ *peeng·sa*
twice duas vezes *doo·ash ve·zesh*
twin beds camas gémeas ⓕ pl
ka·mash zhe·me·ash
twins gémeos/gémeas ⓜ/ⓕ
zhe·mee·oosh/zhe·mee·ash
type tipo ⓜ *tee·poo*
typical típico/típica ⓜ/ⓕ
tee·pee·koo/tee·pee·ka
tyre pneu ⓜ *pe·ne·oo*

U

ultrasound ultrasom ⓜ *ool·tra·song*
umbrella guarda-chuva ⓜ
gwaar·da·shoo·va
uncomfortable desconfortável
desh·kong·foor·taa·vel
understand compreender
kong·pree·eng·der
underwear roupa interior ⓕ *rroh·pa
eeng·te·ree·or*
unemployed desempregado/desem-
pregada ⓜ/ⓕ *de·zeng·pre·gaa·doo/
de·zeng·pre·gaa·da*
unfair injusto/injusta ⓜ/ⓕ
eeng·zhoosh·too/eeng·zhoosh·ta

V

uniform farda ⓕ *faar·da*
universe universo ⓜ *oo·nee·ver·soo*
university universidade ⓕ
oo·nee·ver·see·daa·de
unsafe inseguro/insegura ⓜ/ⓕ
eeng·se·goo·roo/eeng·se·goo·ra
until até *a·te*
unusual invulgar *eeng·vool·gaar*
up para cima *pa·ra see·ma*
urgent urgente *oor·zheng·te*
urinary infection infecção urinária ⓕ
eeng·fek·sowng oo·ree·naa·rya
USA EUA ⓜ pl *e·oo·aa*
useful útil *oo·teel*

V

vacancy vaga ⓕ *vaa·ga*
vacant vago/vaga ⓜ/ⓕ *vaa·goo/ vaa·ga*
vacation férias ⓕ pl *fe·ree·ash*
vaccination vacina ⓕ *va·see·na*
validate validar *va·lee·daar*
valley vale ⓜ *vaa·le*
valuable valioso/valiosa ⓜ/ⓕ
va·lee·o·zoo/va·lee·o·za
value valor ⓜ *va·lor*
van carrinha ⓕ *ka·rree·nya*
vegetarian n&a vegetariano/ vegetariana ⓜ/ⓕ *ve·zhe·ta·ree·a·noo/ ve·zhe·ta·ree·a·na*
vein veia ⓕ *vey·a*
venereal disease doença venérea ⓕ
do·eng·sa ve·ne·ree·a
venue local ⓜ *loo·kaal*
very muito *mweeng·too*
video camera câmara de vídeo ⓕ
ka·ma·ra de vee·dee·oo
video recorder gravador de
vídeo ⓜ *gra·va·dor de vee·dee·oo*
video tape cassete de vídeo ⓕ
ka·se·te de vee·dee·oo
view vista ⓕ *veesh·ta*
village aldeia ⓕ *aal·day·a*
vineyard vinha ⓕ *vee·nya*
virus vírus ⓜ *vee·roosh*
visa visto ⓜ *veesh·too*
visit visitar *vee·zee·taar*

vitamin vitamina ⓕ *vee·ta·mee·na*
voice voz ⓕ *vosh*
volleyball (sport) vóleibol ⓜ
vo·lay·bol
volume volume ⓜ *voo·loo·me*
vote votar *voo·taar*

W

wage salário ⓜ *sa·laa·ryoo*
wait (for) esperar *shpe·raar*
waiter criado/criada de mesa ⓜ/ⓕ
kree·aa·doo/kree·aa·da de me·za
waiting room sala de espera ⓕ
saa·la de shpe·ra
wake (someone) up acordar
a·koor·daar
Wales País de Gales ⓜ *pa·eesh de gaa·lesh*
walk caminhar *ka·mee·nyaar*
wall (outer) parede ⓕ *pa·re·de*
want querer *ke·rer*
war guerra ⓕ *ge·rra*
wardrobe guarda-roupa ⓜ
gwaar·da·rroh·pa
warm morno/morna ⓜ/ⓕ *mor·noo/ mor·na*
warn avisar *a·vee·zaar*
wash lavar *la·vaar*
wash (oneself) lavar-se *la·vaar·se*
washing machine máquina de lavar
roupa ⓕ *maa·kee·na de la·vaar rroh·pa*
watch relógio ⓜ *rre·lo·zhyoo*
watch (look after) vigiar *vee·zhee·aar*
watch (television, etc) ver *ver*
water água ⓕ *aa·gwa*
water bottle garrafa de água ⓕ
ga·rraa·fa de aa·gwa
waterfall cascata ⓕ *kash·kaa·ta*
waterproof à prova d'água aa *pro·va daa·gwa*
water-skiing esqui aquático ⓜ
shkee a·kwaa·tee·koo
wave (ocean) onda ⓕ *ong·da*
way caminho ⓜ *ka·mee·nyoo*
we nós *nosh*
weak fraco/fraca ⓜ/ⓕ *fraa·koo/ fraa·ka*

wealthy rico/rica ⓜ/ⓕ rree·koo/rree·ka

wear usar oo·zaar

weather tempo ⓜ teng·poo

wedding casamento ⓜ ka·za·meng·too

week semana ⓕ se·ma·na

weekend fim-de-semana ⓜ feeng·de·se·ma·na

weigh pesar pe·zaar

weight peso ⓜ pe·zoo

welcome receber rre·se·ber

welfare seguro social ⓜ se·goo·roo soo·see·aal

well bem beng

wet molhado/molhada ⓜ/ⓕ moo·lyaa·doo/moo·lyaa·da

what que ke

wheel roda ⓕ rro·da

wheelchair cadeira de rodas ⓕ ka·day·ra de rro·dash

when quando kwang·doo

where onde ong·de

which qual kwaal

white branco/branca ⓜ/ⓕ brang·koo/brang·ka

who quem keng

why porquê poor·ke

wide largo/larga ⓜ/ⓕ laar·goo/laar·ga

wife esposa ⓕ shpo·za

win ganhar ga·nyaar

wind vento ⓜ veng·too

window janela ⓕ zha·ne·la

windscreen (windshield) pára-brisas ⓜ pl pa·ra·bree·zash

wine vinho ⓜ vee·nyoo

winner vencedor/vencedora ⓜ/ⓕ veng·se·dor/veng·se·do·ra

wish desejar de·ze·zhaar

with com kong

within (time) dentro de deng·troo de

without sem seng

woman mulher ⓕ moo·lyer

wonderful maravilhoso/maravilhosa ⓜ/ⓕ ma·ra·vee·lyo·zoo/ma·ra·vee·lyo·za

wood madeira ⓕ ma·day·ra

wool lã ⓕ lang

word palavra ⓕ pa·laa·vra

work trabalho ⓜ tra·baa·lyoo

work trabalhar tra·ba·lyaar

work experience experiência de trabalho ⓕ shpe·ree·eng·sya de tra·baa·lyoo

workout treinamento ⓜ tre·na·meng·too

work permit licença de trabalho ⓕ lee·seng·sa de tra·baa·lyoo

workshop oficina ⓕ o·fe·see·na

world mundo ⓜ moong·doo

worms (intestinal) lombrigas ⓕ pl long·bree·gash

worried preocupado/preocupada ⓜ/ⓕ pree·o·koo·paa·doo/pree·o·koo·paa·da

worship reverenciar rre·ve·reng·see·aar

wrist pulso ⓜ pool·soo

write escrever shkre·ver

writer escritor/escritora ⓜ/ⓕ shkree·tor/shkree·to·ra

wrong errado/errada ⓜ/ⓕ e·rraa·doo/e·rraa·da

yacht iate ⓜ ee·aat

year ano ⓜ a·noo

yellow amarelo/amarela ⓜ/ⓕ a·ma·re·loo/a·ma·re·la

yes sim seeng

yesterday ontem ong·teng

you inf sg/pl tu/vocês too/vo·sesh

you pol sg/pl você/vós vo·se/vosh

young jovem zho·veng

youth hostel pousada de juventude ⓕ poh·zaa·da de zhoo·veng·too·de

zipper fecho écler ⓜ fe·shoo e·kler

zoo jardim zoológico ⓜ zhar·deeng zoo·oo·lo·zhee·koo

A

Dictionary
PORTUGUESE *to* ENGLISH
português – inglês

Portuguese nouns have their gender indicated with ⓜ (masculine)
and ⓕ (feminine). Where adjectives or nouns have separate
masculine and feminine forms, these are divided by a slash and
marked ⓜ/ⓕ. You'll also see words marked as v (verb), n (noun), a
(adjective), pl (plural), sg (singular), inf (informal) and pol (polite)
where necessary. Verbs are given in the infinitive – for details on
how to change verbs for use in a sentence, see **grammar** (p25). For
food and drink terms, see the **menu decoder** (p194).

A

a a to
à a at
abaixo a-*bai*-shoo below
abalo cerebral ⓜ a-*baa*-loo
se-re-*braal* concussion
abelha ⓕ a-*be*-lya bee
aberto/aberta ⓜ/ⓕ a-*ber*-too/
a-*ber*-ta open a
a bordo a *bor*-doo aboard
aborrecido/aborrecida ⓜ/ⓕ
a-boo-rre-*see*-doo/a-boo-rre-*see*-da
bored
aborto ⓜ a-*bor*-too abortion
— espontâneo shpong-*ta*-nee-oo
miscarriage
abraçar a-bra-*saar* hug
abrir a-*breer* open
acampamento ⓜ
a-kang-pa-*meng*-too campsite
acampar a-kang-*paar* camp
acidente ⓜ a-see-*deng*-te accident

acordar a-koor-*daar* wake up
actor/actriz ⓜ/ⓕ aa-*tor*/aa-*treesh*
actor
actuação ⓕ a-too-a-*sowng*
performance
adepto/adepta ⓜ/ⓕ a-de-pe-too/
a-*de*-pe-ta supporter (sport)
adivinhar a-dee-vee-*nyaar* guess
admitir a-de-mee-*teer* acknowledge •
let in
adulto/adulta ⓜ/ⓕ a-*dool*-too/
a-*dool*-ta adult n&a
advogado/advogada
a-de-voo-*gaa*-doo/a-de-voo-*gaa*-da
lawyer
aeroporto ⓜ a-e-ro-*por*-too airport
afortunado/afortunada ⓜ/ⓕ
a-foor-too-*naa*-doo/a-foor-too-*naa*-da
lucky
agarrar a-ga-*rraar* get
agência ⓕ a-*zheng*-sya agency
— de imobiliário de
ee-mo-bee-*lyaa*-ryoo real estate agency

— de viagens de vee·*aa*·zhengsh travel agency

— noticiosa noo·tee·see·*o*·za newsagency

agora a·*go*·ra now

agradecer a·gra·de·*ser* thank

agricultor ⓜ&ⓕ a·gree·kool·*tor* farmer

agricultura ⓕ a·gree·kool·*too*·ra agriculture

água ⓕ *aa*·gwa water

agulha ⓕ a·*goo*·lya needle (sewing)

a horas a o·rash on time

aí a·*ee* there (where you are)

ajuda ⓕ a·*zhoo*·da help

ajudar a·zhoo·*daar* help

alcunha ⓕ aal·*koo*·nya nickname

aldeia ⓕ aal·*day*·a village

aleijar a·lay·*zhaar* hurt

alfândega ⓕ aal·*fang*·de·ga customs

algodão ⓜ aal·goo·*downg* cotton

alguém ⓜ&ⓕ aal·*geng* someone

alguma coisa ⓕ aal·*goo*·ma *koy*·za something

alguns/algumas ⓜ/ⓕ pl aal·*goongsh*/aal·*goo*·mash few · some

alimentar a·lee·meng·*taar* feed

almoço ⓜ aal·*mo*·soo lunch

almofada ⓕ al·moo·*faa*·da pillow

alto/alta ⓜ/ⓕ *aal*·too/*aal*·ta high · loud · tall

alugar a·loo·*gaar* hire (rent)

aluguer de automóvel ⓜ a·loo·*ger* de ow·too·mo·vel car hire

ama ⓕ *a*·ma babysitter · childminding

amaciador ⓜ a·ma·see·a·*dor* hair conditioner

amanhã aa·ma·*nyang* tomorrow

amante ⓜ&ⓕ a·*maang*·te lover

amar a·*maar* love

amarelo/amarela ⓜ/ⓕ a·ma·re·*loo*/ a·ma·re·la yellow

amável ⓜ&ⓕ a·*maa*·vel kind (nice)

ambiente ⓜ ang·bee·*eng*·te environment

ambos/ambas ⓜ/ⓕ ang·boosh/ ang·bash both

ambulância ⓕ ang·boo·*lang*·sya ambulance

amigo/amiga ⓜ/ⓕ a·*mee*·goo/ a·*mee*·ga friend

amor ⓜ a·*mor* love

analgésico ⓜ a·nal·*zhe*·zee·koo painkiller

análise de sangue ⓕ a·*naa*·lee·ze de *sang*·ge blood test

andar ⓜ ang·*daar* floor (storey)

andar ang·*daar* ride

— a cavalo a ka·*vaa*·loo ride a horse

— de bicicleta de bee·see·*kle*·ta ride a bicycle

anel ⓜ a·*nel* ring (jewellery)

anemia ⓕ a·ne·*mee*·a anaemia

aniversário ⓜ a·nee·ver·*saa*·ryoo birthday

ano ⓜ a·noo year

anteontem ang·tee·*ong*·teng day before yesterday

antes ang·tesh before

antibióticos ⓜ pl ang·tee·bee·o·tee·koosh antibiotics

antigo/antiga ⓜ/ⓕ ang·tee·goo/ ang·tee·ga ancient · antique · old

antiguidade ⓕ ang·tee·gwee·*daa*·de antique

antiséptico ⓜ ang·tee·se·tee·koo antiseptic

anúncio ⓜ a·*noong*·syoo advertisement

ao ow at

ao lado de ow *laa*·doo de next to

apanhar boleia a·pa·*nyaar* boo·*lay*·a hitchhike

aparelho auditivo ⓜ a·pa·re·*lyoo* ow·dee·*tee*·voo hearing aid

apelido ⓜ a·pe·*lee*·doo family name

apertado/apertada ⓜ/ⓕ a·per·*taa*·doo/a·per·*taa*·da tight

apontar a·pong·*taar* point

aposentado/aposentada ⓜ/ⓕ a·poo·zeng·*taa*·doo/ a·poo·zeng·*taa*·da retired

B

aposta ① a·*posh*·ta bet
aprender a·preng·*der* learn
à prova d'água aa pro·va daa·gwa waterproof
aquecedor ⑩ a·ke·se·*dor* heater
aquecido/aquecida ⑩/① a·ke·*see*·doo/a·ke·*see*·da heated
aquecimento ⑩ a·ke·see·*meng*·too heating
aquele/aquela ⑩/① a·ke·le/a·ke·la that
aqui a·*kee* here
ar ⑩ aar air
— condicionado kong·dee·syoo·*naa*·doo air-con
aranha ① a·ra·nya spider
areia ① a·*ray*·a sand
arquitectura ① ar·kee·te·*too*·ra architecture
arte ① aar·te art
artesanato ⑩ ar·te·za·*naa*·too crafts
artes marciais ① pl ar·tesh mar·see·*aish* martial arts
árvore ① *aar*·vo·re tree
asma ① *ash*·ma asthma
aspirina ① ash·pee·*ree*·na aspirin
assassinato ⑩ a·sa·see·*naa*·too murder
assédio ⑩ a·se·*dyoo* harassment
assento ⑩ a·*seng*·too seat
assinar a·see·*naar* sign
assinatura ① a·see·na·*too*·ra signature
assistência social ① a·seesh·*teng*·sya soo·see·*aal* welfare
às vezes aash ve·zesh sometimes
atalho ⑩ a·*taa*·lyoo trail
ataque de coração ⑩ a·*taa*·ke de koo·ra·*sowng* heart attack
até a·te until
atirar a·tee·*raar* shoot
atmosfera ① at·moosh·*fe*·ra atmosphere
atrás a·*traash* back (position) • behind
atrasado/atrasada ⑩/① a·tra·*zaa*·doo/a·tra·*zaa*·da late
atraso ⑩ a·*traa*·zoo delay

através a·tra·*vesh* across
autocarro ⑩ ow·to·*kaa*·roo bus
autoestrada ① ow·to·*shtraa*·da highway • motorway (tollway)
avariado/avariada ⑩/① a·va·ree·*aa*·doo/a·va·ree·*aa*·da broken down (car) • out of order
avariar a·va·ree·*aar* break down (car)
avenida ① a·ve·*nee*·da avenue
avião ⑩ a·vee·*owng* airplane
avisar a·vee·*zaar* warn
avó ① a·*vo* grandmother
avô ⑩ a·*voh* grandfather
azul a·*zool* blue
azulejo ⑩ a·zoo·*le*·zhoo painted tile

B

bagagem ① ba·*gaa*·zheng baggage
baixo *bai*·shoo down
baixo/baixa ⑩/① *bai*·shoo/*bai*·sha low
balcão ⑩ bal·*kowng* counter (at bar)
— de bagagens de ba·*gaa*·zhengsh baggage claim
balde ⑩ *baal*·de bucket
banco ⑩ *bang*·koo bank
bandeira ① bang·*day*·ra flag
banho ⑩ ba·*nyoo* bath
baptismo ⑩ ba·*teezh*·moo baptism
barata ① ba·*raa*·ta cockroach
barato/barata ⑩/① ba·*raa*·too/ba·*raa*·ta cheap
barbeiro ⑩ bar·*bay*·roo barber
barco ⑩ *baar*·koo boat
— a motor a moo·*tor* motorboat
barulhento/barulhenta ⑩/① ba·roo·*lyeng*·too/ba·roo·*lyeng*·ta noisy
basquetebol ⑩ bash·ke·te·*bol* basketball
batom ⑩ ba·*tong* lipstick
bêbado/bêbada ⑩/① be·ba·doo/be·ba·da drunk
bebé ⑩&① be·*be* baby
beber be·*ber* drink
bechigas ① pl be·*shee*·gash chicken pox
beijo ⑩ *bay*·zhoo kiss

beira mar ⓕ *bay*·ra maar seaside
bem beng well
bengaleiro ⓜ beng·ga·*lay*·roo cloakroom
bexiga ⓕ be·*shee*·ga bladder
biblioteca ⓕ bee·blee·oo·*te*·ka library
bicho ⓜ *bee*·shoo bug
bicicleta ⓕ bee·see·*kle*·ta bicycle
— de corrida de koo·*rree*·da racing bike
— de montanha de mong·*ta*·nya mountain bike
bilhar ⓜ bee·*lyaar* pool (game)
bilhete ⓜ bee·*lye*·te ticket
— de identidade de ee·deng·tee·*daa*·de ID card
— sem garantia seng ga·rang·*tee*·a stand-by ticket
bilheteira ⓕ bee·lye·*tay*·ra ticket office
binóculos ⓜ pl bee·*no*·koo·loosh binoculars
bloco-notas ⓜ *blo*·koo·no·tash notebook
bloqueado/bloqueada ⓜ/ⓕ blo·kee·*aa*·doo/blo·kee·*aa*·da blocked
boca ⓕ *bo*·ka mouth
bola ⓕ *bo*·la ball (sport)
bolas de algodão ⓕ pl *bo*·lash de aal·goo·*downg* cotton balls
boleia ⓕ boo·*lay*·a ride (car, etc)
bolha ⓕ *bo*·lya blister
bolo ⓜ *bo*·loo cake
bolsa ⓕ *bol*·sa purse
bolso ⓜ *bol*·soo pocket
bom/boa ⓜ/ⓕ bong/*bo*·a fine • good
bomba ⓕ *bong*·ba pump
boneco/boneca ⓜ/ⓕ boo·*ne*·koo/boo·*ne*·ka doll
bonito/bonita ⓜ/ⓕ boo·*nee*·too/boo·*nee*·ta beautiful • handsome
botão ⓜ boo·*towng* button
botas ⓕ *bo*·tash boots
— para caminhadas *pa*·ra ka·mee·*nyaa*·dash hiking boots
botija de gás ⓕ boo·*tee*·zha de gaash gas cartridge

boxe ⓜ *bok*·se boxing
braço ⓜ *braa*·soo arm (body)
branco/branca ⓜ/ⓕ *brang*·koo/*brang*·ka white
brincos ⓜ pl *breeng*·koosh earrings
brochura ⓕ broo·*shoo*·ra brochure
bronquite ⓕ brong·*kee*·te bronchitis
budista ⓜ&ⓕ boo·*deesh*·ta Buddhist
bufete ⓜ boo·*fe*·te buffet
burro/burra ⓜ/ⓕ *boo*·rroo/*boo*·rra stupid
bússola ⓕ *boo*·soo·la compass

C

cabeça ⓕ ka·*be*·sa head
cabeleireiro/cabeleireira ⓜ/ⓕ ka·be·lay·*ray*·roo/ka·be·lay·*ray*·ra hairdresser
cabelo ⓜ ka·*be*·loo hair
cabra ⓕ *kaa*·bra goat
caça ⓕ *kaa*·sa hunting
cada *ka*·da each
cadeado ⓜ ka·dee·*aa*·doo padlock
cadeira ⓕ ka·*day*·ra chair
— de criança de kree·*ang*·sa child seat
— de rodas de *rro*·dash wheelchair
cair ka·*eer* fall
caixa ⓕ *kai*·sha box
— automático ow·too·*maa*·tee·koo automated teller machine (ATM)
— de papelão de pa·pe·*lowng* carton
— de velocidades de ve·loo·see·*daa*·desh gearbox
— do correio doo koo·*rray*·oo mailbox
— registadora rre·zheesh·ta·*do*·ra cash register
caixote do lixo ⓜ kai·*sho*·te doo *lee*·shoo garbage can • rubbish bin
calado/calada ⓜ/ⓕ ka·*laa*·doo/ka·*laa*·da quiet
calças ⓕ pl *kaal*·sash trousers
calções ⓜ pl kaal·*soyngsh* shorts
calculadora ⓕ kaal·koo·la·*do*·ra calculator
calendário ⓜ ka·leng·*daa*·ryoo calendar

C

calor ⓜ ka·*lor* heat
cama ① *ka*·ma bed
— de casal de ka·*zaal* double bed
— de rede de *rre*·de hammock
câmara ① *ka*·ma·ra tube (tyre)
câmara de vídeo ① *ka*·ma·ra de *vee*·dee·oo video camera
camas gémeas ① pl *ka*·mash *zhe*·me·ash twin beds
câmbio ⓜ *kang*·byoo currency exchange
camião ⓜ ka·mee·*yowng* truck
caminhada ① ka·mee·*nyaa*·da hiking
caminhar ka·mee·*nyaar* hike • walk
caminho ⓜ ka·*mee*·nyoo path • way
camisa ① ka·*mee*·za shirt
camisola ① ka·mee·zo·la sweater
campeonatos ⓜ pl kang·pe·oo·*naa*·toosh championships
campo de golfe ⓜ *kang*·poo de *gol*·fe golf course
campo de ténis ⓜ *kang*·poo de *te*·neesh tennis court
canção ① kang·*sowng* song
cancelar kang·se·*laar* cancel
cancro ⓜ *kang*·kroo cancer
caneta ① ka·*ne*·ta pen
canivete ⓜ ka·nee·*ve*·te pocketknife
cansado/cansada ⓜ/① kang·*saa*·doo/kang·*saa*·da tired
cantor/cantora ⓜ/① kang·*tor*/kang·*to*·ra singer
cão ⓜ kowng dog
cão-guia ⓜ kowng·*gee*·a guide dog
capacete ⓜ ka·pa·*se*·te helmet
capacho ⓜ ka·*paa*·shoo mat
caro/cara ⓜ/① *kaa*·roo/*kaa*·ra expensive
carregar ka·rre·*gaar* carry
carrinha ① ka·*rree*·nya van
carrinho ⓜ ka·*rree*·nyoo trolley
— de bebé de be·*be* stroller
carro ⓜ *kaa*·rroo car
carta ① *kaar*·ta letter (mail)
carta de condução ① *kaar*·ta de kong·doo·*sowng* drivers licence

cartão ⓜ kar·*towng* card
— de crédito de *kre*·dee·too credit card
— de embarque de eng·*baar*·ke boarding pass
— telefónico te·le·fo·nee·koo phonecard
cartas ① pl *kaar*·tash playing cards
cartaz ⓜ kar·*taash* poster
casa ① *kaa*·za home • house
— de banho de ba·*nyoo* bathroom • toilet
— de chá de shaa tea house
— de fados de *faa*·doosh fado house
— de hóspedes de *osh*·pe·desh guesthouse
casaco ⓜ ka·*zaa*·koo coat • jacket
casado/casada ⓜ/① ka·*zaa*·doo/ka·*zaa*·da married
casal ⓜ ka·*zaal* pair (couple)
casamento ⓜ ka·za·*meng*·too marriage • wedding
casar ka·*zaar* marry
cascata ① kash·*kaa*·ta waterfall
cassete ① kaa·*se*·te cassette
— de vídeo de *vee*·dee·oo video tape
castanho/castanha ⓜ/① kash·*ta*·nyoo/kash·*ta*·nya brown
castelo ⓜ kash·*te*·loo castle
catedral ① ka·te·*draal* cathedral
católico/católica ⓜ/① ka·to·lee·koo/ka·to·lee·ka Catholic
cauda ① *kow*·da tail
cavaleiro ⓜ ka·va·*lay*·roo bullfighter
cavalo ⓜ ka·*vaa*·loo horse
caverna ① ka·*ver*·na cave
cedo *se*·doo early
cego/cega ⓜ/① *se*·goo/*se*·ga blind
cemitério ⓜ se·mee·*te*·ryoo cemetery
centímetro ⓜ seng·*tee*·me·troo centimetre
cêntimo ⓜ *seng*·tee·moo cent
centro ⓜ *seng*·troo centre
— comercial koo·mer·see·*aal* shopping centre
— da cidade da see·*daa*·de city centre
cerâmica ① se·*raa*·mee·ka pottery

cerca ① *ser*·ka fence

cerca de *ser*·ka de about

certidão de nascimento ①
ser·tee·*downg* de nash·see·*meng*·too
birth certificate

cesto ⑩ *sesh*·too basket

céu ⑩ *se*·oo sky

champô ⑩ shang·*poo* shampoo

chão ⑩ showng floor

chapéu ⑩ sha·*pe*·oo hat

charcutaria ① shar·koo·ta·ree·a
delicatessen

charmoso/charmosa ⑩/①
shar·mo·*zoo*/shar·mo·*za* charming

charuto ⑩ sha·*roo*·too cigar

chato/chata ⑩/① *shaa*·too/*shaa*·ta
boring

chave ① *shaa*·ve key

chávena ① *shaa*·ve·na cup

chegada ① she·*gaa*·da arrival

chegar she·*gaar* arrive

cheio/cheia ⑩/① *shay*·oo/*shay*·a
crowded • full

cheiro ⑩ *shay*·roo smell

chupeta ① shoo·*pe*·ta dummy
(pacifier)

chutar shoo·*taar* kick

chuva ① *shoo*·va rain

chuveiro ⑩ shoo·*vay*·roo shower

ciclismo ⑩ see·*kleesh*·moo cycling

cidadania ① see·da·da·*nee*·a
citizenship

cidade ① see·*daa*·de city

ciências ① pl see·*eng*·syash science

cigarro ⑩ see·*gaa*·rroo cigarette

cinema ⑩ see·*ne*·ma cinema

cinto de segurança ⑩ *seeng*·too de
se·goo·*raang*·sa seatbelt

cinzeiro ⑩ seeng·*zay*·roo ashtray

cinzento/cinzenta ⑩/①
seeng·*zeng*·too/seeng·*zeng*·ta grey

circo ⑩ *seer*·koo circus

cirurgia ① see·roor·*zhee*·a
operation (medical)

ciumento/ciumenta ⑩/①
see·oo·*meng*·too/see·oo·*meng*·ta
jealous

claro/clara ⑩/① *klaa*·roo/*klaa*·ra
light (colour)

classe ① *klaa*·se class (category)

— económica ee·koo·*no*·mee·ka
economy class

— executiva ee·zhe·koo·*tee*·va
business class

— primeira pree·*may*·ra first class

— segunda se·*goong*·da second
class

cliente ⑩&① klee·*eng*·te client

cobertor ⑩ koo·ber·*tor* blanket

cobra ① *ko*·bra snake

cobrador ⑩ koo·bra·*dor* ticket
collector

código postal ⑩ *ko*·dee·goo
poosh·*taal* postcode

coelho ⑩ koo·*e*·lyoo rabbit

cofre ⑩ *ko*·fre safe

cola ① *ko*·la glue

colar ⑩ koo·*laar* necklace

colchão ⑩ kol·*showng* mattress

colega ⑩&① koo·*le*·ga colleague

colete salva-vidas ⑩ koo·*le*·te
saal·va·*vee*·dash life jacket

colher ① koo·*lyer* spoon

— de chá de shaa teaspoon

colina ① koo·*lee*·na hill

colírio ⑩ koo·*lee*·ree·oo eye drops

collants ⑩ pl ko·*langsh* pantyhose

colocar koo·loo·*kaar* put

colóquio ⑩ koo·*lo*·kyoo small
conference

com kong with

— pressa *pre*·sa in a hurry

— saudades sow·*da*·desh homesick

comboio ⑩ kong·*boy*·oo train

começar koo·me·*saar* start

começo ⑩ koo·*me*·soo start

comédia ① koo·*me*·dya comedy

comemoração ①
koo·me·moo·ra·*sowng* celebration

comer koo·*mer* eat

comerciante ⑩&①
koo·mer·see·*aang*·te tradesperson

comércio ⑩ koo·*mer*·syoo trade

comichão ① koo·mee·*showng* itch

C

comida ① koo·*mee*·da food
— de bebé de be·*be* baby food
comissão ① koo·mee·*sowng* commission
como *ko*·moo how
companheiro/companheira ⑩/① kong·pa·*nyay*·roo/kong·pa·*nyay*·ra companion
companhia aérea ① kong·pa·*nyee*·a a·e·ree·a airline
compota ① kong·*po*·ta jam
comprar kong·*praar* buy
compras ① pl kong·*prash* shopping
compreender kong·pree·eng·*der* understand
comprimido ⑩ kong·pree·*mee*·doo pill
computador ⑩ kong·poo·ta·*dor* computer
— portátil por·*taa*·teel laptop
comum koo·*moong* ordinary
comunhão ① koo·moo·*nyowng* communion
concerto ⑩ kong·*ser*·too concert
concordar kong·koor·*daar* agree
conduzir kong·doo·*zeer* drive
conferência ① kong·fe·*reng*·sya big conference
confiar kong·fee·*aar* trust
confirmar kong·feer·*maar* confirm
confissão ① kong·fee·*sowng* confession
confortável kong·for·*taa*·vel comfortable
congelar kong·zhe·*laar* freeze
conhecer koo·nye·*ser* meet (first time)
conjuntivite ①
kong·zhoong·tee·*vee*·te conjunctivitis
conselho ⑩ kong·se·*lyoo* advice
consertar kong·ser·*taar* repair
conservador/conservadora ⑩/①
kong·ser·va·*dor*/kong·ser·va·*do*·ra conservative n&a
constipação ①
kong·shtee·pa·*sowng* cold (illness)
construir kong·shtroo·*eer* build
construtor ⑩ kong·shtroo·*tor* builder

consulado ⑩ kong·soo·*laa*·doo consulate
consulta ① kong·*sool*·ta appointment
consumo obrigatório ⑩
kon·*soo*·moo o·bree·ga·to·ree·oo cover charge
conta ① *kong*·ta bill • account
— bancária bang·*kaa*·rya bank account
contar kong·*taar* count
contraceptivo ⑩
kong·tra·se·*tee*·voo contraceptives
contrato ⑩ kong·*traa*·too contract
convidar kong·vee·*daar* invite
copo ⑩ *ko*·poo glass (drinking)
cor ① kor colour
— de laranja de la·*rang*·zha orange (colour)
coração ① koo·ra·*sowng* heart
corajoso/corajosa ⑩/①
koo·ra·*zho*·zoo/koo·ra·*zho*·za brave
corda ① *kor*·da rope
cordeiro ⑩ koor·*day*·roo lamb
cordel ⑩ koor·*del* string
cor-de-rosa kor·de·*rro*·za pink
cordilhelra ① koor·dee·*lyay*·ra mountain range
corpo ⑩ *kor*·poo body
correcto/correcta ⑩/①
koo·*rre*·too/koo·*rre*·ta right (correct)
correia da ventoinha ① koo·*rray*·a da veng·*too*·ee·nya fanbelt
correio ⑩ koo·*rray*·oo mail • post office
— azul a·*zool* express mail
— registado re·zhee·*shtaa*·doo registered mail
corrente ① koo·*rreng*·te current (electricity)
corrente de bicicleta ①
koo·*rreng*·te de bee·see·*kle*·ta bike chain
correr koo·*rrer* run
correspondência ①
koo·rresh·pong·*deng*·sya mail (letters)
— por via marítima poor *vee*·a ma·*ree*·tee·ma surface mail (sea)

— por via terrestre poor *vee*·a te·*rresh*·tre surface mail (land)
corrida ① koo·*rree*·da jogging • race (sport)
corrimento ⓜ koo·rree·*meng*·too thrush (health)
corrupto/corrupta ⓜ/①
koo·*rroop*·too/koo·*rroop*·ta corrupt
cortar koor·*taar* cut
corta-unhas ⓜ *kor*·ta·*oong*·nyash nail clippers
corte de cabelo ⓜ *kor*·te de ka·*be*·loo haircut
coser koo·*zer* sew
costas ① pl *kosh*·tash back (body)
costela ① koosh·*te*·la rib (body)
costume ⓜ koosh·*too*·me custom
cotonete ⓜ ko·to·*ne*·te cotton buds
couro cabeludo ⓜ *koh*·roo ka·be·*loo*·doo scalp
couro ⓜ *koh*·roo leather
coxia ① koo·*shee*·a aisle
cozinha ① koo·*zee*·nya cooking • kitchen
cozinhar koo·zee·*nyaar* cook
cozinheiro/cozinheira ⓜ/①
koo·zee·*nyay*·roo/koo·zee·*nyay*·ra cook
crânio ⓜ *kra*·nyoo skull
crédito ⓜ *kre*·dee·too credit
creme ⓜ *kre*·me cream
— de barbear de bar·bee·*aar* shaving cream
crescer kresh·*ser* grow
criado/criada de mesa ⓜ/①
kree·*aa*·doo/kree·*aa*·da de *me*·za waiter/waitress
criança ⓜ&① kree·*ang*·sa child
Cristão/Cristã ⓜ/① kreesh·*towng*/ kreesh·*tang* Christian
cru/crua ⓜ/① kroo/*kroo*·a raw
cruz ① kroosh cross (religious)
cuidar kwee·*daar* look after
culpa ① *kool*·pa fault (someone's)
culpado/culpada ⓜ/①
kool·*paa*·doo/kool·*paa*·da guilty
cupão ⓜ koo·*powng* coupon

currículo ⓜ koo·*rree*·koo·loo résumé
curto/curta ⓜ/① *koor*·too/*koor*·ta short (length)
custar koosh·*taar* cost

D

dança ① *dang*·sa dance • dancing
dançar dang·*saar* dance
da noite da *noy*·te evening
dar daar give • deal (cards)
dar conversa daar kong·*ver*·sa chat up (flirt)
data ① *daa*·ta date (day)
— de nascimento de nash·see·*meng*·too date of birth
de de from
decidir de·see·*deer* decide
dedo ⓜ *de*·doo finger
— do pé doo pe toe
defeituoso/defeituosa ⓜ/①
de·fay·*too*·o·zoo/de·fay·*too*·o·za faulty
deficiente de·fee·see·*eng*·te disabled
deitar-se day·*taar*·se lie (not stand)
demais de·*maish* too (much)
democracia ① de·moo·kra·*see*·a democracy
de noite de *noy*·te overnight
dente ⓜ *deng*·te tooth
dentes ⓜ pl *deng*·tesh teeth
dentista ⓜ&① deng·*teesh*·ta dentist
dentro *deng*·troo inside
dentro de *deng*·troo de within (time)
depois de·*poysh* after
— de amanhã de aa·ma·*nyang* day after tomorrow
depósito ⓜ de·po·zee·too deposit (bank)
— de bagagens de·po·zee·too de ba·*gaa*·zhengsh luggage locker
depressa de·*pre*·sa fast adv
descansar desh·kang·*saar* rest
descer desh·*ser* get off (bus, train)
desconfortável desh·kong·foor·*taa*·vel uncomfortable
desconto ⓜ desh·*kong*·too discount
desde *dezh*·de since (time)
desejar de·ze·*zhaar* wish

desempregado/desempregada
ⓜ/ⓕ de·zeng·pre·*gaa*·doo/
de·zeng·pre·*gaa*·da unemployed
deserto ⓜ de·*zer*·too desert
desistir de·zeesh·*teer* quit
desligado/desligada ⓜ/ⓕ
desh·lee·*gaa*·doo/desh·lee·*gaa*·da
off (power)
desodorizante ⓜ
de·zo·doo·ree·*zang*·te deodorant
despertador ⓜ desh·per·ta·*dor*
alarm clock
desportista ⓜ&ⓕ
desh·poor·*teesh*·ta sportsperson
desporto ⓜ desh·*por*·too sport
destino ⓜ desh·*tee*·noo destination
detalhes ⓜ pl de·*taa*·lyesh details
Deus ⓜ de·oosh God (general)
devagar de·va·*gaar* slow (down) v
dever de·*ver* owe
dia ⓜ *dee*·a day
diafragma ⓜ dee·a·*fraa*·ge·ma
diaphragm
diapositivo ⓜ dee·a·po·zee·*tee*·voo
slide (transparency)
diário ⓜ dee·*aa*·ryoo diary
diário/diária ⓜ/ⓕ dee·*aa*·ryoo/
dee·*aa*·rya daily
dicionário ⓜ dee·syoo·*naa*·ryoo
dictionary
dieta ⓕ dee·e·ta diet
diferença horária ⓕ dee·fe·*reng*·sa
o·*raa*·rya time difference
diferente dee·fe·*reng*·te different
difícil dee·*fee*·seel difficult
dinheiro ⓜ dee·*nyay*·roo money
direcção ⓕ dee·re·*sowng* direction
directo/directa ⓜ/ⓕ dee·re·*too*/
dee·re·ta direct • straight
director/directora ⓜ/ⓕ dee·re·*tor*/
dee·re·*to*·ra director
direita dee·*ray*·ta right (direction)
Direito ⓜ dee·*ray*·too law (profession)
direitos ⓜ pl dee·*ray*·toosh rights
— civis see·*veesh* civil rights
— humanos oo·*ma*·noosh human
rights

discoteca ⓕ deesh·koo·*te*·ka
nightclub
discutir deesh·koo·*teer* argue
disponível deesh·po·*nee*·vel available
DIU ⓜ de·ee·oo IUD
divertido/divertida ⓜ/ⓕ
dee·ver·*tee*·doo/dee·ver·*tee*·da fun
divertir-se dee·ver·*teer*·se enjoy
(oneself)
divorciado/divorciada ⓜ/ⓕ
dee·vor·see·*aa*·doo/
dee·vor·see·*aa*·da divorced
dizer dee·*zer* say • tell
doce *do*·se sweet
documentário ⓜ
doo·koo·meng·*taa*·ryoo documentary
doença ⓕ doo·*eng*·sa disease
— venérea ve·*ne*·ree·a venereal
disease
doente doo·*eng*·te sick
doloroso/dolorosa ⓜ/ⓕ
doo·loo·ro·zoo/doo·loo·ro·za painful
dona de casa ⓕ *do*·na de *kaa*·za
homemaker
dono/dona ⓜ/ⓕ *do*·noo/*do*·na
owner
dor ⓕ dor pain
— de cabeça de ka·*be*·sa headache
— de dentes de *deng*·tesh toothache
— de estômago de shto·ma·goo
stomachache
— menstrual meng·shtroo·*aal*
period pain
dorido/dorida ⓜ/ⓕ doo·ree·doo/
doo·ree·da sore
dormir door·*meer* sleep
dose excessiva ⓕ *do*·ze she·see·va
overdose
droga ⓕ *dro*·ga drug
drogado/drogada ⓜ/ⓕ
droo·*gaa*·doo/droo·*gaa*·da stoned
(drugged)
duas vezes doo·ash *ve*·zesh twice
duplo/dupla ⓜ/ⓕ *doo*·ploo/*doo*·pla
double
duro/dura ⓜ/ⓕ *doo*·roo/*doo*·ra
hard (not soft)

E

e e and
educação ⓕ e·doo·ka·*sowng* education
egoísta e·goo·*eesh*·ta selfish
ela *e*·la she
ele *e*·le he
electricidade ⓕ ee·le·tree·see·*daa*·de electricity
eléctrico ⓜ ee·*le*·tree·koo tram
eleição ⓕ e·lay·*sowng* election
eles/elas *e*·lesh/*e*·lash they
elevador ⓜ ee·le·va·*dor* lift (elevator)
em eng at • in
— breve *bre*·ve soon
— frente *freng*·te ahead
— segunda mão se·*goong*·da mowng second-hand
embaixada ⓕ eng·bai·*shaa*·da embassy
embaixador/embaixatriz ⓜ/ⓕ eng·bai·sha·*dor*/eng·bai·sha·*treesh* ambassador
embraiagem ⓕ eng·brai·*aa*·zheng clutch (car)
embrulho ⓜ eng·*broo*·lyoo package
ementa ⓕ ee·*meng*·ta menu
emergência ⓕ ee·mer·*zheng*·sya emergency
empregado/empregada ⓜ/ⓕ eng·pre·*gaa*·doo/eng·pre·*gaa*·da employee
—de escritório de shkree·*to*·ryoo office worker
— por conta própria poor *kong*·ta *pro*·pree·a self-employed person
emprego ⓜ eng·*pre*·goo job
empresa ⓕ eng·*pre*·za company (firm)
empurrar eng·poo·*rraar* push
encher eng·*sher* fill
encomenda ⓕ eng·koo·*meng*·da parcel
encontrar eng·kong·*traar* find • meet
encontro ⓜ eng·*kong*·troo date (appointment)

endereço ⓜ eng·de·*re*·soo address
enevoado/enevoada ⓜ/ⓕ e·ne·voo·*aa*·doo/e·ne·voo·*aa*·da foggy
enfermeiro/enfermeira ⓜ/ⓕ eng·fer·*may*·roo/eng·fer·*may*·ra nurse
engenharia ⓕ eng·zhe·nya·*ree*·a engineering
engraçado/engraçada ⓜ/ⓕ eng·gra·*saa*·doo/eng·gra·*saa*·da funny
enjoado/enjoada ⓜ/ⓕ eng·zhoo·*aa*·doo/eng·zhoo·*aa*·da seasick
enjoo ⓜ eng·*zho*·oo nausea
— de viagem de vee·*aa*·zheng travel sickness
— matinal ma·tee·*naal* morning sickness
enorme ee·*nor*·me huge
ensolarado/ensolarada ⓜ/ⓕ eng·soo·la·*raa*·doo/eng·soo·la·*raa*·da sunny
entorse ⓜ eng·*tor*·se sprain
entrada ⓕ eng·*traa*·da entry
entrar eng·*traar* enter
entre *eng*·tre between
entregar eng·tre·*gaar* deliver
entrevista ⓕ eng·tre·*veesh*·ta interview
envergonhado/envergonhada ⓜ/ⓕ en·ver·goo·*nya*·doo/en·ver·goo·*nya*·da embarrassed
enviar eng·vee·*aar* post • send
enxaqueca ⓕ eng·sha·*ke*·ka migraine
equipa ⓕ e·*kee*·pa team
equipamento ⓜ e·kee·pa·*meng*·too equipment
— de mergulho de mer·*goo*·lyoo diving equipment
errado/errada ⓜ/ⓕ e·*rraa*·doo/e·*rraa*·da wrong
erro ⓜ e·*rroo* mistake
escadaria ⓕ shka·da·*ree*·a stairway
escada rolante ⓕ *shkaa*·da rroo·*lang*·te escalator
escola ⓕ *shko*·la school
— secundária se·koong·*daa*·ree·a high school

E

escolher shkoo·*lyer* choose
escova ① *shko*·va hairbrush
— de dentes de *deng*·tesh toothbrush
escrever shkre·*ver* write
escritor/escritora ⓜ/① shkree·*tor*/
shkree·*to*·ra writer
escritório ⓜ shkree·*to*·ryoo office
— de turismo de too·*reezh*·moo
tourist office
escultura ① shkool·*too*·ra sculpture
escuro/escura ⓜ/① *shkoo*·roo/
shkoo·ra dark (colour/night)
escutar shkoo·*taar* hear · listen
esgotado/esgotada ⓜ/①
shgoo·*taa*·doo/shgoo·*taa*·da booked
out
espaço ⓜ *shpaa*·soo space (room)
Espanha ① *shpa*·nya Spain
espanhol ⓜ shpa·*nyol* Spanish
especial shpe·see·*aal* special
especialista ⓜ&①
shpe·see·a·*leesh*·ta specialist
espectáculo ⓜ shpe·*taa*·koo·loo
show
espelho ⓜ *shpe*·lyoo mirror
esperar shpe·*raar* wait (for)
esposa ① *shpo*·za wife
esquadra da polícia ① *shkwaa*·dra
da poo·*lee*·sya police station
esquecer shke·*ser* forget
esquerda ① *shker*·da left (direction)
esqui ⓜ shkee ski · skiing
— aquático a·*kwaa*·tee·koo
waterskiing
esquiar shkee·*aar* ski
esquina ① *shkee*·na corner
estaca ① *shtaa*·ka tent peg
estação ① shta·*sowng* season ·
station
— de caminhos de ferro de
ka·*mee*·nyoosh de *fe*·rroo train station
— de metropolitano de
me·troo·poo·lee·*ta*·noo metro station
estacionar shta·syoo·*naar* park (a car)
estádio ⓜ *shtaa*·dyoo stadium
estado civil ⓜ *shtaa*·doo see·*veel*
marital status

estar shtaar be (temporary)
— constipado/constipada ⓜ/①
kong·shtee·*paa*·doo/
kong·shtee·*paa*·da have a cold
estátua ① *shtaa*·too·a statue
este/esta ⓜ/① *esh*·te/*esh*·ta this
estendal da roupa ① shteng·*daal*
da *rroh*·pa clothesline
estéreo ① *shte*·ree·oo stereo
estilo ⓜ *shtee*·loo style
estojo de primeiros socorros ⓜ
shto·zhoo de pree·*may*·roosh
so·*ko*·rroosh first-aid kit
estômago ⓜ *shto*·ma·goo stomach
estrada ① *shtraa*·da road
estrangeiro/estrangeira ⓜ/①
shtrang·*zhay*·roo/shtrang·*zhay*·ra
foreign
estranho/estranha ⓜ/① *shtra*·nyoo/
shtra·nya strange · stranger
estrela ① *shtre*·la star
estudante ⓜ&① shtoo·*dang*·te
student
estúdio ⓜ *shtoo*·dyoo studio
etiqueta de bagagem ① e·tee·*ke*·ta
do ba·*gaa*·zhong luggage tag
eu *e*·oo I
EUA ⓜ pl e·oo·*aa* USA
euro ⓜ *e*·oo·roo euro
exactamente e·za·ta·*meng*·te exactly
exame papa nicolau ⓜ e·*za*·me
paa·pa nee·koo·*low* pap smear
exaustor ⓜ ee·*zowsh*·tor exhaust
(car)
excelente ay·she·*leng*·te excellent
excluído/excluída ⓜ/①
aysh·kloo·*ee*·doo/aysh·kloo·*ee*·da
excluded
excursão ① shkoor·*sowng* tour
— guiada gee·*aa*·da guided tour
exemplo ⓜ e·*zeng*·ploo example
experiência ① shpe·ree·*eng*·sya
experience
— de trabalho ① de tra·*baa*·lyoo
work experience
exploração ① shplo·ra·*sowng*
exploitation

exposição ① shpoo·zee·*sowng* exhibition

expresso/expressa ⓜ/① *shpre*·soo/esh·*pre*·sa express

extensão ① shteng·*sowng* extension (visa)

F

fábrica ① *faa*·bree·ka factory

faca ① *faa*·ka knife

fácil *faa*·seel easy

fado ⓜ *faa*·doo fado (music)

falar fa·*laar* speak · talk

falta ① *faal*·ta foul (soccer)

família ① fa·*mee*·lya family

faminto/faminta ⓜ/①
fa·*meeng*·too/fa·*meeng*·ta hungry

famoso/famosa ⓜ/① fa·*mo*·zoo/
fa·*mo*·za famous

farda ① *faar*·da uniform

farinha ① fa·*ree*·nya flour

farmacêutico/farmacêutica ⓜ/①
far·ma·se·*oo*·tee·koo/
far·ma·se·*oo*·tee·ka pharmacist

farmácia ① far·*maa*·sya pharmacy

faróis ⓜ pl fa·*roysh* headlights

fatia ① fa·*tee*·a slice

fato de banho ⓜ *faa*·too de *ba*·nyoo swimsuit

fazer fa·*zer* do · make

— a barba a *baar*·ba shave

— a contagem a kong·*taa*·zheng score (keep)

— compras *kong*·prash go shopping

— surf sarf surf

febre ① *fe*·bre fever

— dos fenos doosh fe·*noosh* hay fever

— glandular glang·doo·*laar* glandular fever

fechado/fechada ⓜ/①
fe·*shaa*·doo/fe·*shaa*·da closed

fechar fe·*shaar* close

fecho écler ⓜ *fe*·shoo e·*kler* zipper

feira ① *fay*·ra fair · street market

— da ladra da *laa*·dra fleamarket

feito/feita à mão ⓜ/① *fay*·too/
fay·ta aa mowng handmade

feliz fe·*leesh* happy

feminino/feminina ⓜ/①
fe·mee·*nee*·noo/fe·mee·*nee*·na female

feriado ⓜ fe·ree·*aa*·doo holiday

férias ① pl fe·*ryash* vacation

ferido/ferida ⓜ/① fe·*ree*·doo/
fe·*ree*·da injured

ferimento ⓜ fe·ree·*meng*·too injury

ferro de engomar ⓜ *fe*·rroo de
eng·goo·*maar* iron (clothes)

festa ① *fesh*·ta party (night out)

— na rua na *rroo*·a street party

festival ⓜ fesh·tee·*vaal* festival

ficar fee·*kaar* stay

ficção ① feek·*sowng* fiction

fígado ⓜ *fee*·ga·doo liver

fila ① *fee*·la queue

filha ① *fee*·lya daughter

filho ① *fee*·lyoo son

filme ⓜ *feel*·me film

— de diapositivos de
dee·a·po·zee·*tee*·voosh slide film

filtrado/filtrada ⓜ/① feel·*traa*·doo/
feel·*traa*·da filtered

fim ⓜ feeng end

fim-de-semana ⓜ
feeng·de·se·*ma*·na weekend

fino/fina ⓜ/① *fee*·noo/*fee*·na thin

fio dental ⓜ *fee*·oo deng·*taal* dental floss

fixe *fee*·she cool (exciting)

flor ① flor flower

floresta ① floo·*resh*·ta forest

florista ① floo·*reesh*·ta florist (shop)

fogão ⓜ foo·*gowng* stove

fogo ⓜ *fo*·goo fire

folha ① *fo*·lya leaf

fora *fo*·ra outside

forças armadas ① pl *for*·sash
ar·*maa*·dash military

forma ① *for*·ma shape

forno ⓜ *for*·noo oven

forte *for*·te strong

fósforos ⓜ pl *fosh*·foo·roosh
matches (for lighting)

fotografar foo·too·gra·*faar*
photograph

fotografia ① foo·too·gra·*fee*·a photography

fotógrafo/fotógrafa ⓜ/① foo·to·gra·foo/foo·to·gra·fa photographer

fotómetro ⓜ foo·to·me·troo light meter

fraco/fraca ⓜ/① *fraa*·koo/*fraa*·ka weak

frágil *fraa*·zheel fragile

fralda ① *fraal*·da nappy (diaper)

frequentemente fre·kweng·te·*meng*·te often

fresco/fresca ⓜ/① *fresh*·koo/ *fresh*·ka cool (cold) • fresh

frigorífico ① free·goo·*ree*·fee·koo refrigerator

frio/fria ⓜ/① *free*·oo/*free*·a cold

fronha ① *fro*·nya pillowcase

fronteira ① frong·*tay*·ra border

fumar foo·*maar* smoke

fundo ⓜ *foong*·doo bottom (position)

funeral ⓜ foo·ne·*raal* funeral

furo ⓜ *foo*·roo puncture

futuro ⓜ foo·*too*·roo future

G

gabardina ① gaa·baar·*dee*·na raincoat

gabinete de perdidos e achados ⓜ gaa·bee·*ne*·te de per·*dee*·doosh ee a·*shaa*·doosh lost property office

galeria de arte ① ga·le·*ree*·a de *aar*·te art gallery

galinha ① ga·*lee*·nya chicken

ganhar ga·*nyaar* earn • win

garagem ① ga·*raa*·zheng garage

garantido/garantida ⓜ/① ga·rang·*tee*·doo/ga·rang·*tee*·da guaranteed

garfo ⓜ *gaar*·foo fork

garganta ① gar·*gang*·ta throat

garrafa ① ga·*rraa*·fa bottle

gás ⓜ gaash gas (cooking)

gasolina ① ga·zoo·*lee*·na gas (petrol)

gastrenterite ① gash·treng·te·*ree*·te gastroenteritis

gato/gata ⓜ/① *gaa*·too/*gaa*·ta cat

gaze ① *gaa*·ze gauze

geada ① zhee·*aa*·da frost

gelado/gelada ⓜ/① zhe·*laa*·doo/ zhe·*laa*·da frozen

gelo ⓜ *zhe*·loo ice

gémeos/gémeas ⓜ/① *zhe*·mee·oosh/*zhe*·mee·ash twins

gerente ⓜ zhe·*reng*·te manager

gilete ① zhee·*le*·te razor

ginásio ⓜ zhee·*naa*·zyoo gym (place)

golo ⓜ *go*·loo goal (sport)

gordo/gorda ⓜ/① *gor*·doo/*gor*·da fat

gorjeta ① gor·*zhe*·ta tip (gratuity)

gostar goosh·*taar* care for • like

gostoso/gostosa ⓜ/① goosh·to·*zoo*/goosh·to·za tasty

governo ⓜ goo·ver·*noo* government

grama ⓜ *graa*·ma gram

grande *grang*·de big

grátis *graa*·teesh complimentary

grato/grata ⓜ/① *graa*·too/*graa*·ta grateful

graus ⓜ pl growsh degrees (temperature)

gravação ① gra·va·*sowng* recording

gravador de vídeo ⓜ gra·va·*dor* de *vee*·dee·oo video recorder

gravar gra·*vaar* record

grávida *graa*·vee·da pregnant

greve ① *gre*·ve strike

gripe ① *gree*·pe influenza

gritar gree·*taar* shout

grosso/grossa ⓜ/① *gro*·soo/ *gro*·sa thick

grupo ⓜ *groo*·poo band • group

— sanguíneo sang·*gwee*·nee·oo blood type

guarda-chuva ⓜ *gwaar*·da·*shoo*·va umbrella

guardanapo ⓜ gwar·da·*naa*·poo napkin

guarda-redes *gwaar*·da·*rre*·desh goalkeeper

guarda-roupa ⓜ *gwaar*·da·*rroh*·pa wardrobe

guerra ① *ge*·rra war
guia ⓜ *gee*·a guide (person)
— auditivo ow·dee·*tee*·voo audio guide
— de espectáculos de shpe·*taa*·koo·loosh entertainment guide
— de viagem de vee·*aa*·zheng guidebook

H

hepatite ① e·pa·*tee*·te hepatitis
hidratante ① ee·dra·*tang*·te moisturiser
hindu ⓜ&① eeng·*doo* Hindu
hipismo ⓜ ee·*peezh*·moo horseriding
história ① *shto*·rya history • story
hoje *o*·zhe today
— à noite aa *noy*·te tonight
homem ⓜ *o*·meng man
— de negócios de ne·*go*·syoosh businessman
homosexual ⓜ&① o·mo·sek·soo·*aal* homosexual n&a
hóquei ⓜ *o*·kay hockey
— sobre o gelo *so*·bre oo *zhe*·loo ice hockey
hora ① *o*·ra hour
horário ⓜ o·*raa*·ryoo timetable
— de expediente de shpe·dee·*eng*·te opening hours
horóscopo ⓜ o·*rosh*·koo·poo horoscope
horrível o·*rree*·vel awful
hospedagem ① osh·pe·*daa*·zheng accommodation
hospital ⓜ osh·pee·*taal* hospital
hospitalidade ① osh·pee·ta·lee·*daa*·de hospitality
hotel ⓜ o·*tel* hotel

I

idade ① ee·*daa*·de age
ida e volta *ee*·da ee *vol*·ta return (ticket)

identificação ① ee·deng·tee·fee·ka·*sowng* identification
igreja ① ee·*gre*·zha church
igualdade ① ee·gwal·*daa*·de equality
— de oportunidades de o·poor·too·nee·*daa*·desh equal opportunity
ilha ① *ee*·lya island
imigração ① ee·mee·gra·*sowng* immigration
importante eeng·por·*tang*·te important
impossível eeng·po·*see*·vel impossible
imposto ⓜ eeng·*posh*·too tax
— de rendimentos de rreng·dee·*meng*·toosh income tax
impressora ① eeng·pre·*so*·ra printer (computer)
inchaço ⓜ eeng·*shaa*·soo swelling
incluído/incluída ⓜ/①
eeng·kloo·*ee*·doo/eeng·kloo·*ee*·da included
indigestão ① eeng·dee·zhesh·*towng* indigestion
indústria ① eeng·*doosh*·trya industry
infantário ⓜ eeng·fang·*taa*·ree·oo crèche
infecção ① eeng·fe·*sowng* infection
— urinária oo·ree·*naa*·rya urinary infection
inflamação ① eeng·fla·ma·*sowng* inflammation
informação ① eeng·for·ma·*sowng* information
informática ① eeng·for·*maa*·tee·ka IT
Inglaterra ① eeng·gla·*te*·rra England
inglês ⓜ eeng·*glesh* English
ingrediente ⓜ eeng·gre·dee·*eng*·te ingredient
íngreme *eeng*·gre·me steep
injecção ① eeng·zhe·*sowng* injection
injectar eeng·zhe·*taar* inject
injusto/injusta ⓜ/①
eeng·*zhoosh*·too/eeng·*zhoosh*·ta unfair
inocente ee·noo·*seng*·te innocent

J

inseguro/insegura ⓜ/ⓕ
eeng·se·*goo*·roo/eeng·se·*goo*·ra unsafe

insolação ⓕ eeng·soo·la·*sowng*
sunstroke

instrutor/instrutora ⓜ/ⓕ
eeng·shtroo·*tor*/eeng·shtroo·*to*·ra
instructor

interessante eeng·te·re·*sang*·te
interesting

interior do país ⓜ eeng·te·ree·*or*
doo pa·*eesh* countryside

internacional eeng·ter·naa·syoo·*naal*
international

intervalo ⓜ eeng·ter·*vaa*·loo
intermission

inundação ⓕ ee·noong·da·*sowng*
flood

inverno ⓜ eeng·*ver*·noo winter

invulgar eeng·vool·*gaar* unusual

ir eer go

irmã ⓕ eer·*mang* sister

irmão ⓜ eer·*mowng* brother

irritação da pele ⓕ
ee·rre·ta·*sowng* da *pe*·le rash

irritação por causa da fralda ⓕ
ee·rre·ta·*sowng* poor *kow*·sa da
fraal·da nappy rash

isqueiro ⓜ eesh·*kay*·roo cigarette
lighter

itinerário ⓜ ee·tee·ne·*raa*·ryoo
itinerary

IVA ⓕ *ee*·va sales tax

J

já zhaa already

janela ⓕ zha·*ne*·la window

jantar ⓜ zhang·*taar* dinner

jardim ⓜ zhar·*deeng* garden

— botânico boo·*ta*·nee·koo botanic
garden

— de infância de eeng·*fang*·sya
kindergarten

— zoológico zoo·oo·*lo*·zhee·koo zoo

jardinagem ⓕ zhar·dee·*naa*·zheng
gardening

jardins públicos ⓜ pl zhar·*deengzh*
poo·blee·koosh public gardens

jipe ⓜ *zhee*·pe jeep

joelho ⓜ zhoo·e·*lyoo* knee

jogar zhoo·*gaar* play (cards, etc)

jogo ⓜ *zho*·goo game (sport)

— de computador de
kong·poo·ta·*dor* computer game

jornal ⓜ zhor·*naal* newspaper

jornalista ⓜ&ⓕ zhor·na·*leesh*·ta
journalist

jovem *zho*·veng young

Judeu/Judia ⓜ/ⓕ zhoo·*de*·oo/
zhoo·*dee*·a Jewish

juiz/juíza ⓜ/ⓕ zhoo·*eesh*/
zhoo·ee·za judge • referee

junto/junta ⓜ/ⓕ *zhoong*·too/
zhoong·ta together

L

lá laa there (where neither of us is)

lã ⓕ lang wool

lábios ⓜ pl *laa*·byoosh lips

lado ⓜ *laa*·doo side

ladrão/ladra ⓜ/ⓕ la·*drowng*/
laa·dra thief

lagarto ⓜ la·*gaar*·too lizard

lago ⓜ *laa*·goo lake

lama ⓕ *la*·ma mud

lâmina de barbear ⓕ *la*·mee·na de
bar·bee·*aar* razor blade

lâmpada ⓕ *lang*·pa·da light bulb

lanterna eléctrica ⓕ lang·*ter*·na
ee·*le*·tree·ka torch (flashlight)

lápis ⓜ *laa*·peesh pencil

largo/larga ⓜ/ⓕ *laar*·goo/*laar*·ga
wide

lata ⓕ *laa*·ta tin (can)

lavandaria ⓕ la·vang·da·*ree*·a
laundry (clothes/place)

lavar la·*vaar* wash

lavar-se la·*vaar*·se wash (oneself)

laxante ⓜ la·*shang*·te laxative

legal le·*gaal* legal

legendas ⓕ pl le·*zheng*·dash subtitles

legislação ⓕ le·zheezh·la·*sowng*
legislation

lei ⓕ lay law (legislation)

leitura ⓕ lay·*too*·ra reading

lembrança ① leng·*brang*·sa souvenir
lenço ⓜ *leng*·soo scarf
— de mão de mowng handkerchief
— de papel de pa·*pel* tissue
lençóis e mantas ① pl leng·*soysh* ee *mang*·tash bedding
lençol ⓜ leng·*sol* sheet (bed)
lenha ① *le*·nya firewood
lente ① *leng*·te lens (camera)
lentes de contacto ⓜ pl *leng*·tesh de kong·*taak*·too contact lenses
ler ler read
lésbica ① *lezh*·bee·ka lesbian
levantar (um cheque) le·vang·*taar* (oong *she*·ke) cash (a cheque)
levar le·*vaar* take
leve *le*·ve light (weight)
libra ① *lee*·bra pound (weight)
licença ① lee·*seng*·sa licence • permit
— de trabalho de tra·*baa*·lyoo work permit
ligação ① lee·ga·*sowng* connection
— a cobrar a koo·*braar* collect call
— directa dee·re·ta direct-dial
ligado/ligada ⓜ/① lee·*gaa*·doo/lee·*gaa*·da on (power)
ligadura ① lee·ga·*doo*·ra bandage
limite de peso ⓜ lee·*mee*·te de *pe*·zoo baggage allowance
limite de velocidade ⓜ lee·*mee*·te de ve·loo·see·*daa*·de speed limit
limpar leeng·*paar* clean
limpeza ① leeng·*pe*·za cleaning
limpo/limpa ⓜ/① *leeng*·poo/*leeng*·pa clean
língua ① *leeng*·gwa language
liquidação ① lee·kee·da·*sowng* sale
lista telefónica ① *leesh*·ta te·le·*fo*·nee·ka phone book
livraria ① lee·vra·*ree*·a book shop
livre *lee*·vre free (not bound)
livro ⓜ *lee*·vroo book
— de frases de *fraa*·zesh phrasebook
lixo ⓜ *lee*·shoo garbage • rubbish
local ⓜ loo·*kaal* venue
— de nascimento de nash·see·*meng*·too place of birth

local ⓜ&① loo·*kaal* local
loja ① *lo*·zha shop
— de aparelhos eléctricos de a·pa·re·*lyoosh* ee·*le*·tree·koosh electrical store
— de bebidas de be·*bee*·dash liquor store
— de brinquedos de breeng·*ke*·doosh toy shop
— de campismo de kang·*peezh*·moo camping store
— de ciclismo de see·*kleesh*·moo bike shop
— de conveniência de kong·ve·*nyeng*·sya convenience store
— de desporto de desh·*por*·too sports store
— de equipamentos fotográficos de e·kee·pa·*meng*·toosh foo·too·*graa*·fee·koosh camera shop
— de ferramentas de fe·rra·*meng*·tash hardware store
— de lembranças de leng·*brang*·sash souvenir shop
— de música de *moo*·zee·ka music shop
— de roupas de *rroh*·pash clothing store
— de segunda mão de se·*goon*·da mowng second-hand shop
lombrigas ① pl long·*bree*·gash worms (intestinal)
longe *long*·zhe far
longo/longa ⓜ/① *long*·goo/*long*·ga long
louco/louca ⓜ/① *loh*·koo/*loh*·ka crazy
lua ① *loo*·a moon
— de mel de mel honeymoon
lubrificante ⓜ loo·bree·fee·*kang*·te lubricant
lucro ⓜ *loo*·kroo profit
lugar ⓜ loo·*gaar* place
luta ① *loo*·ta fight
luvas ① pl *loo*·vash gloves
— de borracha de boo·*rra*·sha gloves (latex)

luxo ⓜ *loo·shoo* luxury
luz ⓕ *loosh* light
— do flash *doo flaash* flashlight
(torch)

M

machado de gelo ⓜ *ma·shaa·doo
de zhe·loo* ice axe
machismo ⓜ *ma·sheezh·moo* sexism
madeira ⓕ *ma·day·ra* wood
madrugada ⓕ *ma·droo·gaa·da* dawn
mãe ⓕ *maing* mother
maior *may·or* bigger
mais *maish* more
— tarde *tar·de* later
mala de mão ⓕ *maa·la de mowng*
handbag
mala de viagem ⓕ *maa·la de
vee·aa·zheng* suitcase
manhã ⓕ *ma·nyang* morning
manifestação ⓕ
ma·nee·fesh·ta·sowng demonstration
Manuelino/Manuelina ⓜ/ⓕ
man·wel·ee·noo/man·wel·ee·na
Manueline (art)
mão ⓕ *mowng* hand
mapa ⓜ *maa·pa* map
— de estradas *de shtraa·dash* road
map
maquilhagem ⓕ *ma·kee·lyaa·zheng*
make-up
máquina ⓕ *maa·kee·na* machine
— de lavar roupa *de la·vaar rroh·pa*
washing machine
— de vender bilhetes *de veng·der
bee·lye·tesh* ticket machine
— fotográfica *foo·too·graa·fee·ka*
camera
mar ⓜ *maar* sea
maravilhoso/maravilhosa ⓜ/ⓕ
ma·ra·vee·lyo·zoo/ma·ra·vee·lyo·za
wonderful
marcar *mar·kaar* score (a goal)
maré ⓕ *ma·re* tide
marido ⓜ *ma·ree·doo* husband
martelo ⓜ *mar·te·loo* hammer
mas *mash* but

massagem ⓕ *ma·saa·zheng* massage
matar *ma·taar* kill
mau/má ⓜ/ⓕ *ma·oo/maa* bad
maxilar ⓜ *maak·see·laar* jaw (human)
mecânico/mecânica ⓜ/ⓕ
me·ka·nee·koo/me·ka·nee·ka
mechanic
medicamentos ⓜ pl
me·dee·ka·meng·toosh medication
medicina ⓕ *me·dee·see·na*
medicine (profession)
médico/médica ⓜ/ⓕ *me·dee·koo/
me·dee·ka* doctor
meditação ⓕ *me·dee·ta·sowng*
meditation
meia ⓕ *may·a* sock
meia-noite ⓕ *may·a·noy·te* midnight
meias de vidro ⓕ pl *may·ash de
vee·droo* stockings
meio-dia ⓜ *may·oo·dee·a* midday
meio tempo *may·oo teng·poo*
part-time
melhor *me·lyor* better
melodia ⓕ *me·loo·dee·a* tune
membro ⓜ&ⓕ *meng·broo* member
memória ⓕ *me·mo·ree·a* memory
card
menina ⓕ *me·nee·na* girl
Menina *me·nee·na* Miss (title)
menino ⓜ *me·nee·noo* boy
menor *me·nor* smaller
menos *me·noosh* less
mensagem ⓕ *meng·saa·zheng*
message
menstruação ⓕ
meng·shtroo·a·sowng menstruation
mentir *meng·teer* lie (not tell the truth)
mentiroso/mentirosa ⓜ/ⓕ
meng·tee·ro·zoo/meng·tee·ro·za liar
mercado ⓜ *mer·kaa·doo* market
mercearia ⓕ *mer·see·a·ree·a* grocery
mergulho ⓜ *mer·goo·lyoo* diving
mês ⓜ *mesh* month
mesa ⓕ *me·za* table
mesmo/mesma ⓜ/ⓕ *mezh·moo/
mezh·ma* same
mesquita ⓕ *mesh·kee·ta* mosque

metro ⓜ *me*·troo metre
metropolitano ⓜ
me·troo·poo·lee·*ta*·no subway (train)
meu/minha ⓜ/ⓕ *me*·oo/*mee*·nya
my
microondas ⓜ pl mee·kro·*ong*·dash
microwave oven
milímetro ⓜ mee·*lee*·me·troo
millimetre
mim ⓜ&ⓕ meeng me
mimado/mimada ⓜ/ⓕ
mee·*maa*·doo/mee·*maa*·da spoiled
(person)
minúsculo/minúscula ⓜ/ⓕ
mee·*noosh*·koo·loo/mee·*noosh*·koo·la
tiny
minuto ⓜ mee·*noo*·too minute
miradouro ⓜ mee·ra·*doh*·roo lookout
missa ⓕ *mee*·sa mass (Catholic)
misturar meesh·too·*raar* mix
mochila ⓕ moo·*shee*·la backpack
moda ⓕ *mo*·da fashion
moderno/moderna ⓜ/ⓕ
moo·*der*·noo/moo·*der*·na modern
moedas ⓕ pl moo·*e*·dash coins
molas ⓕ pl *mo*·lash spring (coil)
molhado/molhada ⓜ/ⓕ
moo·*lyaa*·doo/moo·*lyaa*·da wet
montanha ⓕ mong·*ta*·nya mountain
montanhismo ⓜ
mong·ta·*nyeezh*·moo mountaineering
monumento ⓜ moo·noo·*meng*·too
monument
morar moo·*raar* live (somewhere)
mordedura ⓕ moor·de·*doo*·ra bite
(dog)
mordida ⓕ mor·*dee*·da bite (insect)
morno/morna ⓜ/ⓕ *mor*·noo/
mor·na warm
morrer moo·*rrer* die
morto/morta ⓜ/ⓕ *mor*·too/*mor*·ta
dead
mosquiteiro ⓜ moosh·kee·*tay*·roo
mosquito net
mosquito ⓜ moosh·*kee*·too mosquito
mosteiro ⓜ moosh·*tay*·roo
monastery

mostrador de velocidade ⓜ
moosh·tra·*dor* de ve·loo·see·*daa*·de
speedometer
mostrar moosh·*traar* show
mota ⓕ *mo*·ta motorbike
motor ⓜ moo·*tor* engine
mourisco/mourisca ⓜ/ⓕ
moh·*reesh*·koo/moh·*reesh*·ka Moorish
móveis ⓜ pl *mo*·vaysh furniture
muçulmano/muçulmana ⓜ/ⓕ
moo·sool·*ma*·noo/moo·sool·*ma*·na
Muslim
mudança ⓕ moo·*dang*·sa change
mudo/muda ⓜ/ⓕ *moo*·doo/
moo·da mute
muito *mweeng*·too very
muito/muita ⓜ/ⓕ *mweeng*·too/
mweeng·ta (a) lot
mulher ⓕ moo·*lyer* woman
— de negócios de ne·*go*·syoosh
businesswoman
multa ⓕ *mool*·ta fine (payment)
mundo ⓕ *moong*·doo world
músculo ⓜ *moosh*·koo·loo muscle
museu ⓜ moo·ze·oo museum
música ⓕ *moo*·zee·ka music
— popular poo·poo·*laar* folk music
músico/música ⓜ/ⓕ *moo*·zee·koo/
moo·zee·ka musician

N

na frente de na *freng*·te de in front of
nacionalidade ⓕ
na·syoo·na·lee·*daa*·de nationality
nada ⓜ *naa*·da nothing
nadar na·*daar* swim
nádegas ⓕ pl *naa*·de·gash bottom
(body)
namorada ⓕ na·moo·*raa*·da
girlfriend
namorado ⓜ na·moo·*raa*·doo
boyfriend
namorar na·moo·*raar* date (a
person)
não nowng no • not
não-fumador nowng·foo·ma·*dor*
nonsmoking

nariz ⓜ na·*reesh* nose
— a pingar a peeng·*gaar* runny nose
nascer do sol ⓜ *nash*·ser doo sol sunrise
natação ⓕ na·ta·*sowng* swimming
Natal ⓜ na·*taal* Christmas
natureza ⓕ na·too·*re*·za nature
navio ⓜ na·vee·oo ship
necessário/necessária ⓜ/ⓕ ne·se·*saa*·ryoo/ne·se·*saa*·rya necessary
negativos ⓜ pl ne·ga·*tee*·voosh negatives (photos)
negócios ⓜ pl ne·*go*·syoosh business
nenhum/nenhuma ⓜ/ⓕ neng·*yoong*/neng·*yoo*·ma neither • none
neto/neta ⓜ/ⓕ *ne*·too/*ne*·ta grandchild
neve ⓕ *ne*·ve snow
nódoa negra ⓕ *no*·doo·a *ne*·gra bruise
nódulo ⓜ *no*·doo·loo lump
no estrangeiro noo shtrang·*zhay*·roo abroad • overseas
no interior noo eeng·te·tee·*or* indoors
noite ⓕ *noy*·te night
noivado ⓜ noy·*vaa*·doo engagement
noivo/noiva ⓜ/ⓕ *noy*·voo/*noy*·va fiancé/fiancée
nome ⓜ *no*·me name
nós nosh we
nosso/nossa ⓜ/ⓕ *no*·soo/*no*·sa our (one thing)
nossos/nossas ⓜ/ⓕ *no*·soosh/*no*·sash our (more than one thing)
nota bancária ⓕ *no*·ta bang·*kaa*·rya banknote
notícias ⓕ pl noo·*tee*·syash news
novamente no·va·*meng*·te again
novo/nova ⓜ/ⓕ *no*·voo/*no*·va new
nublado/nublada ⓜ/ⓕ noo·*blaa*·doo/noo·*blaa*·da cloudy
número ⓜ *noo*·me·roo number
— da matrícula da ma·*tree*·koo·la license plate number (car)

— do passaporte doo paa·sa·*por*·te passport number
— do quarto doo *kwaar*·too room number
nunca *noong*·ka never
nuvem ⓕ noo·*veng* cloud

O

oceano ⓜ o·see·a·noo ocean
óculos ⓜ pl o·*koo*·loosh glasses (eye)
— de esqui de shkee goggles (skiing)
— de natação de na·ta·*sowng* goggles (swimming)
— de sol de sol sunglasses
ocupado ⓜ o·koo·*paa*·doo engaged (phone)
ocupado/ocupada ⓜ/ⓕ o·koo·*paa*·doo/o·koo·*paa*·da busy
oficina ⓕ o·fe·*see*·na workshop
olhar oo·*lyaar* look
olho ⓜ o·lyoo eye
ombro ⓜ *ong*·broo shoulder
onda ⓕ *ong*·da wave (ocean)
onde *ong*·de where
ontem *ong*·teng yesterday
operário/operária ⓜ/ⓕ o·pe·*raa*·ryoo/o·pe·*raa*·rya factory worker
opinião ⓕ o·pee·nee·*owng* opinion
oportunidade ⓕ o·poor·too·nee·*daa*·de chance
oposto/oposta ⓜ/ⓕ o·*posh*·too/o·*posh*·ta opposite
óptimo/óptima ⓜ/ⓕ o·tee·moo/o·tee·ma great (fantastic)
oração ⓕ o·ra·*sowng* prayer
orçamento ⓜ or·sa·*meng*·too budget
orelha ⓕ o·re·lya ear
orgasmo ⓜ or·*gaazh*·moo orgasm
orquestra ⓕ or·*kesh*·tra orchestra
o senhor/a senhora ⓜ/ⓕ oo seng·*yor*/a seng·*yo*·ra you pol sg
os senhores/as senhoras ⓜ/ⓕ oosh seng·*yo*·resh/ash seng·*yo*·rash you pol pl
osso ⓜ o·soo bone
ou oh or

ourivesaria ① oh·ree·ve·za·ree·a
jewellery
ouro ⓜ oh·roo gold
outro/outra ⓜ/① oh·troo/oh·tra
other n&a
ovário ⓜ o·vaa·ryoo ovary
ovelha ① oo·ve·lya sheep
oxigénio ⓜ ok·see·zhe·nyoo oxygen

P

pacote ⓜ pa·ko·te packet
padre ⓜ paa·dre priest
pagamento ⓜ pa·ga·meng·too
payment
pagar pa·gaar pay
página ① paa·zhee·na page
pai ⓜ pai father
país ⓜ pa·eesh country
pais ⓜ pl paish parents
palácio ⓜ pa·laa·syoo palace
palavra ① pa·laa·vra word
palito ⓜ pa·lee·too toothpick
panela ① pa·ne·la pan • pot (cooking)
papeira ① pa·pay·ra mumps
papel ⓜ pa·pel paper
— higiénico ee·zhee·e·nee·koo toilet
paper
papelada ① pa·pe·laa·da paperwork
papelaria ① pa·pe·la·ree·a stationery
shop
para baixo pa·ra bai·shoo downhill
parabéns ⓜ pl pa·ra·bengzh
congratulations
pára-brisas ⓜ pl pa·ra·bree·zash
windscreen (windshield)
para cima pa·ra see·ma up
paragem de autocarros ①
pa·raa·zheng de ow·to·kaa·rroosh
bus station/stop
parapeito ⓜ pa·ra·pay·too ledge
parar pa·raar stop
para sempre pa·ra seng·pre forever
parecido/parecida ⓜ/①
pa·re·see·doo/pa·re·see·da similar
parede ① pa·re·de wall (outer)
parlamento ⓜ par·la·meng·too
parliament

parque ⓜ paar·ke park
— de campismo de kang·peezh·moo
campsite
— de estacionamento de
shta·syoo·na·meng·too car park
— nacional na·syoo·naal national park
parte ① paar·te part (component)
partida ① par·tee·da departure •
match (sport)
partidário/partidária ⓜ/①
par·tee·daa·ryoo/par·tee·daa·rya
supporter (politics)
partido ⓜ par·tee·doo party (politics)
partilhar par·tee·lyaar share (a room)
partir par·teer depart (leave)
Páscoa ① paash·kwa Easter
passado ⓜ pa·saa·doo past
passado/passada ⓜ/①
pa·saa·doo/pa·saa·da last (previous)
passageiro/passageira ⓜ/①
pa·sa·zhay·roo/pa·sa·zhay·ra
passenger
passar pa·saar pass (kick/throw)
— por poor pass (go by)
pássaro ⓜ paa·sa·roo bird
passo ⓜ paa·soo step
pasta ① pash·ta briefcase
pasta de dentes ① paash·ta de
deng·tesh toothpaste
patinar pa·tee·naar skate
patins em linha ⓜ pl pa·teengzh
eng·lee·nya rollerblading
pato/pata ⓜ/① paa·too/paa·ta duck
patrão/patroa ⓜ/① pa·trowng/
pa·tro·a employer
paz ① pash peace
pé ⓜ pe foot (body)
peão ⓜ pee·owng pedestrian
peça ① pe·sa play (theatre)
pedaço ⓜ pe·daa·soo piece
pedido ⓜ pe·dee·doo order
pedinte ⓜ&① pe·deeng·te beggar
pedir pe·deer ask (for something) •
order
— emprestado eng·presh·taa·doo
borrow
pedra ① pe·dra stone

peito ⓜ *pay*·too breast • chest (body)
peixe ⓜ *pay*·she fish
pele ⓕ *pe*·le skin
penhasco ⓜ pe·*nyaash*·koo cliff
Península Ibérica ⓕ pe·*neeng*·soo·la ee·*be*·ree·ka Iberian Peninsula
pénis ⓜ *pe*·neesh penis
pensar peng·*saar* think
penso ⓜ *peng*·soo Band-Aid
— higiénico ee·zhee·e·nee·koo panty liner • sanitary napkin
pente ⓜ *peng*·te comb
pequeno/pequena ⓜ/ⓕ pe·*ke*·noo/pe·*ke*·na small
pequeno almoço ⓜ pe·*ke*·noo aal·*mo*·soo breakfast
perder per·*der* lose • miss (lose/overlook)
perdido/perdida ⓜ/ⓕ per·*dee*·doo/per·*dee*·da lost
perdidos e achados ⓜ pl per·*dee*·doosh ee aa·*shaa*·doosh left luggage
perdoar per·doo·*aar* forgive
perfeito/perfeita ⓜ/ⓕ per·*fay*·too/per·*fay*·ta perfect
perfume ⓜ per·*foo*·me perfume
pergunta ⓕ per·*goong*·ta question
perguntar per·goong·*taar* ask (a question)
perigoso/perigosa ⓜ/ⓕ pe·ree·*go*·zoo/pe·ree·*go*·za dangerous
perna ⓕ *per*·na leg (body)
perto *per*·too close • near
pesado/pesada ⓜ/ⓕ pe·*zaa*·doo/pe·*zaa*·da heavy (weight)
pesca ⓕ *pesh*·ka fishing
pescoço ⓜ pesh·*ko*·soo neck
peso ⓜ *pe*·zoo weight
pessoa ⓕ pe·*so*·a person
pessoas ⓕ pl pe·*so*·ash people
petróleo ⓜ pe·*tro*·lyoo petrol (gas)
piada ⓕ pee·*aa*·da joke
picareta ⓕ pee·ka·*re*·ta pickaxe
pico ⓜ *pee*·koo mountain peak
pilar ⓜ pee·*laar* pillory (column)
pilha ⓕ *pee*·lya battery

pílula ⓕ *pee*·loo·la the pill
— para dormir *pa*·ra door·*meer* sleeping pills
pinça ⓕ *peeng*·sa tweezers
pintor/pintora ⓜ/ⓕ peeng·*tor*/peeng·*to*·ra painter
pintura ⓕ peeng·*too*·ra painting
piolhos ⓜ pl pee·*o*·lyoosh lice
piscina ⓕ pesh·*see*·na swimming pool
pista ⓕ *peesh*·ta track (sport)
pistola ⓕ peesh·*to*·la gun
placar ⓜ pla·*kaar* scoreboard
planalto ⓜ pla·*naal*·too plateau
plano/plana ⓜ/ⓕ *pla*·noo/*pla*·na flat
planta ⓕ *plang*·ta plant
plástico/plástica ⓜ/ⓕ *plash*·tee·koo/*plash*·tee·ka plastic
plataforma ⓕ pla·ta·*for*·ma platform
pneu ⓜ pe·ne·oo tyre (tire)
pó ⓜ po powder
— de talco de *taal*·koo baby powder
pobre *po*·bre poor (wealth)
pobreza ⓕ poo·*bre*·za poverty
poder poo·*der* power
poder poo·*der* can
poesia ⓕ po·ee·*zee*·a poetry
pólen ⓜ *po*·leng pollen
polícia ⓕ poo·*lee*·sya police (officer)
política ⓕ poo·*lee*·tee·ka policy • politics
político/política ⓜ/ⓕ poo·*lee*·tee·koo/poo·*lee*·tee·ka politician
poluição ⓕ poo·loo·ee·*sowng* pollution
ponte ⓕ *pong*·te bridge (structure)
ponto ⓜ *pong*·too point
— de controle de kong·*tro*·le checkpoint
popular poo·poo·*laar* popular
por poor per (day)
— cento *seng*·too per cent
— cima de *see*·ma de above
— perto *per*·too nearby
pôr do sol ⓜ por doo sol sunset
porco/porca ⓜ/ⓕ *por*·koo/*por*·ka pig

porquê poor·*ke* why

porta de partida ① *por*·ta de par·*tee*·da departure gate

portão/porta ⑩/① por·*towng*/ *por*·ta gate (airport)

porto ⑩ *por*·too harbour • port

Portugal ⑩ poor·too·*gaal* Portugal

português ⑩ poor·too·*gesh* Portuguese

positivo/positiva ⑩/① poo·zee·*tee*·voo/poo·zee·*tee*·vaa positive

possível poo·*see*·vel possible

pouco/pouca ⑩/① *poh*·koo/*poh*·ka little (quantity)

pousada de juventude ① poh·*zaa*·da de zhoo·veng·*too*·de youth hostel

praça ① *praa*·sa square (town)

— de táxis de *taak*·seesh taxi stand

— de touros de *toh*·roosh bullring

praia ① *prai*·a beach

prancha de surf ① *prang*·sha de sarf surfboard

prata ① *praa*·ta silver

prateleira ① pra·te·*lay*·ra shelf

prato ⑩ *praa*·too dish • plate

precisar pre·see·*zaar* need

preço ⑩ *pre*·soo price

— da passagem da pa·*saa*·zheng fare

prédio ⑩ *pre*·dyoo building

preferir pre·fe·*reer* prefer

preguiçoso/preguiçosa ⑩/① pre·gee·so·*zoo*/pre·gee·so·*za* lazy

prender preng·*der* arrest

preocupado/preocupada ⑩/① pree·o·koo·*paa*·doo/ pree·o·koo·*paa*·da worried

preparar pre·pa·*raar* prepare

presente ⑩ pre·*zeng*·te gift • present (time)

preservativo ⑩ pre·zer·va·*tee*·voo condom

presidente ⑩&① pre·zee·*deng*·te president

— da câmara da *ka*·ma·ra mayor

pressão ① pre·*sowng* pressure (tyre)

preto/preta ⑩/① *pre*·too/*pre*·ta black

preto e branco *pre*·too e *brang*·koo B&W (film)

primeiro/primeira ⑩/① pree·*may*·roo/pree·*may*·ra first

primeiro ministro/primeira ministra ⑩/① pree·*may*·roo mee·*nee*·shtroo/pree·*may*·ra mee·*nee*·shtra prime minister

primeiro nome ⑩ pree·*may*·roo *no*·me Christian name

principal preeng·see·*paal* main

prisão ① pree·*zowng* jail (prison)

— de ventre pree·*zowng* de *ven*·tre constipation

prisioneiro/prisioneira ⑩/① pree·zyoo·*nay*·roo/pree·zyoo·*nay*·ra prisoner

privado/privada ⑩/① pree·*vaa*·doo/pree·*vaa*·da private

problema de coração ⑩ proo·*ble*·ma de koo·ra·*sowng* heart condition

procurar pro·koo·*raar* look for

produzir proo·doo·*zeer* produce

professor/professora ⑩/① proo·fe·*sor*/proo·fe·so·*ra* teacher

profundo/profunda ⑩/① proo·*foong*·doo/proo·*foong*·da deep

programa ⑩ proo·*gra*·ma program

projector ⑩ proo·zhe·*tor* projector

prometer proo·me·*ter* promise

pronto/pronta ⑩/① *prong*·too/ *prong*·ta ready

prostituto/prostituta ⑩/① proosh·tee·*too*·too/proosh·tee·*too*·ta prostitute

protecção anti-solar ① proo·te·*sowng* ang·tee·soo·*laar* sunblock

protector de borracha ⑩ proo·te·*tor* de boo·*rra*·sha dental dam

proteger proo·te·*zher* protect

protegido/protegida ⑩/① proo·te·*zhee*·doo/proo·te·*zhee*·da protected (species)

protestar proo·tesh·*taar* protest
provisões ① pl proo·vee·*zoyngsh* provisions
próximo/próxima ⓜ/①
pro·see·moo/pro·see·ma nearby • next
pulga ① *pool*·ga flea
pulmão ⓜ pool·*mowng* lung
pulso ⓜ *pool*·soo wrist
puro/pura ⓜ/① *poo·roo/poo*·ra pure
puxar poo·*shaar* pull

Q

qual kwaal which
qualidade ① kwa·lee·*daa*·de quality
qualificações ① pl
kwa·lee·fee·ka·*soyngsh* qualifications
qualquer kwaal·*ker* any
quando *kwang*·doo when
quarentena ① kwa·reng·*te*·na quarantine
quarto ⓜ *kwaar*·too bedroom • room
— de casal de ka·*zaal* double room
— de solteiro de sol·*tay*·roo single room
quase *kwaa·ze* almost
que ke what
quebrado/quebrada ⓜ/①
ke·*braa*·doo/ke·*braa*·da broken
quebrar ke·*braar* break
queimadura ① kay·ma·*doo*·ra burn
quem keng who
quente *keng*·te hot
querer ke·*rer* want
quilograma ⓜ kee·loo·*graa*·ma kilogram
quilómetro ⓜ kee·*lo*·me·troo kilometre
quinta ① *keeng*·ta farm
quinzena ① keeng·*ze*·na fortnight
quiosque ⓜ kee·*osh*·ke kiosk • newsstand

R

racismo ⓜ rra·*seezh*·moo racism
radiador ⓜ rra·dee·a·*dor* radiator
rádio *rraa*·dyoo radio

rainha ① rra·ee·*nya* queen
raio de roda ⓜ *rraa*·yoo de *rro*·da spoke (wheel)
rápido/rápida ⓜ/① *rraa*·pee·doo/ *rraa*·pee·da fast
raquete ① rra·*ke*·te racquet
raro/rara ⓜ/① *rraa*·roo/*rraa*·ra rare (uncommon)
ratazana ⓜ&① rra·ta·*za*·na rat
rato ⓜ *rraa*·too mouse
rave ① rrayv rave (party)
razão ① rra·*zowng* reason
razoável rra·zoo·*aa*·vel sensible
realista ree·a·*leesh*·ta realistic
recarregador de bateria ⓜ
rre·ka·rre·ga·*dor* de ba·te·*ree*·a jumper leads
receber rre·se·*ber* welcome
receita médica ① rre·*say*·ta *me*·dee·ka prescription
recentemente rre·seng·te·*meng*·te recently
recibo ⓜ rre·*see*·boo receipt
reciclar rre·see·*klaar* recycle
reciclável rre·see·*klaa*·vel recyclable
reclamação ① rre·kla·ma·*sowng* complaint
reclamar rre·kla·*maar* complain
recomendar rre·koo·meng·*daar* recommend
recursos humanos ⓜ pl
rre·*koor*·soosh oo·*ma*·noosh human resources
recusar rre·koo·*zaar* refuse
rede ① *rre*·de net • network (phone)
redondo/redonda ⓜ/①
rre·*dong*·doo/rre·*dong*·da round
reembolso ⓜ rre·eng·*bol*·soo refund
refeição ① rre·fay·*sowng* meal
— ligeira lee·*zhay*·ra snack
referência ① rre·fe·*reng*·sya reference
refrigerante ⓜ rre·free·zhe·*rang*·te soft drink
regional rre·zhyoo·*naal* regional
registo automóvel ⓜ rre·*zheesh*·too ow·too·*mo*·vel car registration
regra ① *rre*·gra rule

regressar rre·gre·*saar* return

rei m rray king

relacionamento m
rre·la·*syoo*·na·*meng*·too relationship

relações públicas ① pl rre·la·*soyngsh*
poo·blee·kash public relations

relaxar rre·laa·*shaar* relax

religião ① rre·lee·zhee·*owng* religion

religioso/religiosa m/①
rre·lee·zhee·o·*zoo*/rre·lee·zhee·o·*za*
religious

relíquia ① rre·*lee*·kya relic

relógio m rre·*lo*·zhyoo clock • watch

relva ① *rrel*·va grass (lawn)

remoto/remota m/① rre·*mo*·too/
rre·*mo*·ta remote

renda ① *rreng*·da lace

repelente m rre·pe·*leng*·te insect
repellant

— em espiral eng shpee·*raal*
mosquito coil

reserva ① rre·*zer*·va reservation

reservar rre·zer·*vaar* book (reserve)

respirar rresh·pee·*raar* breathe

resposta ① rresh·*posh*·ta answer

restaurante m rresh·tow·*rang*·te
restaurant

reverenciar rre·ve·reng·see·*aar*
worship

revisão ① rre·vee·*zowng* review

revista ① rre·*veesh*·ta magazine

ribeiro m rree·*bay*·roo stream

rico/rica m/① *rree*·koo/*rree*·ka rich

rim m rreeng kidney

rio m *rree*·oo river

rir rreer laugh

risco m *rreesh*·koo risk

ritmo m *rreet*·moo rhythm

roda ① *rro*·da wheel

romântico/romântica m/①
rroo·*maang*·tee·koo/
rroo·*maang*·tee·ka romantic

rosto m *rrosh*·too face

rota ① *rro*·ta route

— de caminhada de ka·mee·*nyaa*·da
hiking route

rotunda ① rroo·*toong*·da roundabout

roubado/roubada m/①
rroh·*baa*·doo/rroh·*baa*·da stolen

roubar rroh·*baar* steal

roubo m *rroh*·boo rip-off

roupa interior ① *rroh*·pa
eeng·te·ree·*or* underwear

roupas ① pl *rroh*·pash clothing

roxo/roxa m/① *rro*·shoo/*rro*·sha
purple

rua ① *rroo*·a street

— principal preeng·see·*paal* main
road

rubéola ① rroo·be·o·la rubella

ruínas ① pl rroo·ee·nash ruins

S

saber sa·*ber* know

sabonete m sa·boo·*ne*·te soap

saca-rolhas ① *saa*·ka·rro·lyash
bottle opener • corkscrew

saco m *saa*·koo bag

— de dormir de dor·*meer* sleeping
bag

— saco de fatos de *faa*·toosh suit bag

saia ① *sai*·a skirt

saída ① saa·ee·da exit

— à noite aa *noy*·te night out

sair sa·*eer* go out

sais de hidratação m pl saish de
ee·dra·ta·*sowng* rehydration salts

sala ① *saa*·la room

— de espera de *shpe*·ra waiting room

— de estar de *shtaar* foyer

— de provas de *pro*·vash change room

— de trânsito de *trang*·zee·too
transit lounge

salão de beleza m sa·*lowng* de
be·*le*·za beauty salon

saldo m *saal*·doo balance (account)

saltar saal·*taar* jump

sandália ① sang·*daa*·lya sandal

sangue m *sang*·ge blood

santo/santa m/① *sang*·too/*sang*·ta
saint

santuário m sang·too·*aa*·ryoo shrine

sapato m sa·*paa*·too shoe

sarampo m sa·*rang*·poo measles

S

saúde ① sa-*oo*-de health
se se if
secar se-*kaar* dry
seco/seca ⓜ/① *se*-koo/*se*-ka dried • dry • stale
seda ① *se*-da silk
sedento/sedenta ⓜ/① se-*deng*-too/se-*deng*-ta thirsty
seguir se-*geer* follow
segundo ⓜ se-*goong*-doo second (time)
segundo/segunda ⓜ/① se-*goong*-doo/se-*goong*-da second
seguro ⓜ se-*goo*-roo insurance
— social soo-see-*aal* welfare
seguro/segura se-*goo*-roo/se-*goo*-ra safe
seios ⓜ pl *say*-oosh breasts
selo ⓜ *se*-loo stamp (postage)
sem seng without
semáforo ⓜ se-*maa*-foo-roo traffic light
semana ① se-*ma*-na week
sempre *seng*-pre always
Senhor se-*nyor* Mr
Senhora se-*nyo*-ra Mrs • Ms
senhoria se-nyoo-*ree*-a landlady
senhorio se-nyoo-*ree*-oo landlord
sensação ① seng-sa-*sowng* feeling (physical)
sensível seng-*see*-vel emotional
sensual seng-soo-*aal* sensual
sentar seng-*taar* sit
sentimentos ⓜ pl seng-tee-*meng*-toosh feelings
separado/separada ⓜ/① se-pa-*raa*-doo/se-pa-*raa*-da separate
ser ser be (ongoing)
seringa ① se-*reeng*-ga needle (syringe)
sério/séria ⓜ/① *se*-ryoo/*se*-rya serious
serviço ⓜ ser-*vee*-soo service
sexo ⓜ *sek*-soo sex
— protegido proo-te-*zhee*-doo safe sex
SIDA ① *see*-da AIDS

sim seeng yes
simpático/simpática ⓜ/① seeng-*paa*-tee-koo/seeng-*paa*-tee-ka nice
simples *seeng*-plesh simple
sinal ⓜ see-*naal* sign
— da linha telefónica da *lee*-nya te-le-*fo*-nee-ka dial tone
sintético/sintética ⓜ/① seeng-*te*-tee-koo/seeng-*te*-tee-ka synthetic
sobre *so*-bre on
sobremesa ① soo-bre-*me*-za dessert
sobretudo ⓜ soo-bre-*too*-doo overcoat
só de ida so de *ee*-da one-way (ticket)
sogra ① *so*-gra mother-in-law
sogro ⓜ *so*-groo father-in-law
sol ⓜ sol sun
solteiro/solteira ⓜ/① sol-*tay*-roo/sol-*tay*-ra single (person)
solto/solta ⓜ/① *sol*-too/*sol*-ta loose
sombra ① *song*-bra shadow
somente so-*meng*-te only
sonho ⓜ *so*-nyoo dream
sonolento/sonolenta ⓜ/① soo-noo-*leng*-too/soo-noo-*leng*-ta sleepy
sorrir so-*rreer* smile
sorte ① *sor*-te luck
soutien ⓜ soo-tee-*eng* bra
sozinho/sozinha ⓜ/① so-*zee*-nyoo/so-*zee*-nya alone
subir soo-*beer* climb
— a bordo a *bor*-doo board
suborno ⓜ soo-*bor*-noo bribe
suficiente soo-fee-see-*eng*-te enough
sujo/suja ⓜ/① *soo*-zhoo/*soo*-zha dirty
superstição ① soo-persh-tee-*sowng* superstition
surdo/surda ⓜ/① *soor*-doo/*soor*-da deaf
surpresa ① soor-*pre*-za surprise

T

tabacaria ① ta·ba·ka·*ree*·a tobacconist

tabaco ⓜ ta·*baa*·koo tobacco

talheres ⓜ pl ta·*lye*·resh cutlery

talvez tal·*vesh* maybe

tamanho ⓜ ta·*ma*·nyoo size

também tang·*beng* also

tampão ⓜ tang·*powng* plug (bath) • tampon

tampões para os ouvidos ⓜ pl tang·*poyngsh* pa·ra oosh oh·vee·doosh earplugs

tapete ⓜ ta·*pe*·te rug

tarde ① *taar*·de afternoon

tarifa postal ① ta·*ree*·fa poosh·*taal* postage

taxa ① *taa*·sha fee • tax

— de aeroporto de a·e·ro·*por*·too airport tax

— de câmbio de *kang*·byoo exchange rate

— de serviço de ser·*vee*·soo service charge

teatro ⓜ te·*aa*·troo theatre

tecido ⓜ te·*see*·doo fabric

teclado ⓜ te·*klaa*·doo keyboard

técnica ① *tek*·nee·ka technique

teimoso/teimosa ⓜ/①
tay·*mo*·zoo/tay·*mo*·za stubborn

teleférico ⓜ te·le·*fe*·ree·koo chairlift (skiing)

telefonar te·le·foo·*naar* telephone

telefone ⓜ te·le·*fo*·ne telephone

— público poo·*blee*·koo public phone

telemóvel ⓜ te·le·*mo*·vel cell/mobile phone

telescópio ⓜ te·lesh·*ko*·pyoo telescope

televisão ① te·le·vee·*zowng* television

temperatura ① teng·pe·ra·*too*·ra temperature (weather)

tempestade ① teng·pesh·*taa*·de storm

tempo ⓜ *teng*·poo time • weather

— inteiro eeng·*tay*·roo full-time

tenda ① *teng*·da tent

ténis ⓜ *te*·neesh tennis

— de mesa de *me*·za table tennis

tensão arterial ① teng·*sowng* ar·te·ree·*aal* blood pressure

tensão pré-menstrual ① teng·*sowng* pre·meng·*shtroo*·aal premenstrual tension

tentar teng·*taar* try (attempt)

ter ter have

— saudades sow·*daa*·desh miss (feel absence of)

terminar ter·mee·*naar* finish

terra ① *te*·rra land

terramoto ⓜ te·rra·*mo*·too earthquake

terrível te·*rree*·vel terrible

terrorismo ⓜ te·rroo·*reezh*·moo terrorism

tesoura ① sg te·*zoh*·ra scissors

teste ⓜ *tesh*·te test

— de gravidez de gra·vee·*desh* pregnancy test kit

— nuclear noo·klee·*aar* nuclear testing

teu/tua ⓜ/① te·*oo*/*too*·a your (one thing) inf sg

teus/tuas ⓜ/① te·*oosh*/*too*·ash your (more than one thing) inf sg

tia ① *tee*·a aunt

tigela ① tee·*zhe*·la bowl

tímido/tímida ⓜ/① *tee*·mee·doo/*tee*·mee·da shy

típico/típica ⓜ/① *tee*·pee·koo/*tee*·pee·ka typical

tipo ⓜ *tee*·poo type

título de registo do automóvel ⓜ *tee*·too·loo de rre·*zheesh*·too doo ow·*too*·mo·vel car owner's title

toalha ① *twaa*·lya towel

— de mesa de *me*·za tablecloth

— de rosto de *rrosh*·too face cloth

tocar too·*kaar* feel (touch) • play (guitar, etc) • touch

todo/toda ⓜ/① *to*·doo/*to*·da all • every

todos/todas ⓜ/① *to*·doosh/*to*·dash everyone

tomada ⓕ too·*maa*·da plug (electricity)

tonto/tonta ⓜ/ⓕ *tong*·too/*tong*·ta dizzy

torneira ⓕ toor·*nay*·ra faucet • tap (sink)

tornozelo ⓜ toor·noo·*ze*·loo ankle

torre ⓕ *to*·rre tower

tossir too·*seer* cough

tourada ⓕ toh·*raa*·da bullfight

touro ⓜ *toh*·roo bull

toxicodependente tok·see·ko·de·peng·*deng*·te drug user

trabalhador/trabalhadora ⓜ/ⓕ tra·ba·lya·*dor*/tra·ba·lya·*do*·ra labourer

trabalhar tra·ba·*lyaar* work

trabalho ⓜ tra·*baa*·lyoo work

— num bar noong baar bar work

— doméstico doo·*mesh*·tee·koo housework

— temporário teng·poo·*raa*·ryoo casual work

traduzir tra·doo·*zeer* translate

tráfico ⓜ *traa*·fee·koo traffic

— de drogas de *dro*·gash drug trafficking

traição ⓕ tra·ee·*sowng* cheat

tranca ⓕ *trang*·ka lock

trancado/trancada ⓜ/ⓕ trang·*kaa*·doo/trang·*kaa*·da locked

traseiro/traseira ⓜ/ⓕ tra·*zay*·roo/tra·*zay*·ra rear (location)

travão ⓜ tra·*vowng* brake (car)

trazer tra·*zer* bring

treinador/treinadora ⓜ/ⓕ tray·na·*dor*/tray·na·*do*·ra coach • manager (sport)

treinamento ⓜ tre·na·*meng*·too workout

tribunal ⓜ tree·boo·*naal* court (legal)

trilho de montanha ⓜ *tree*·lyoo de mong·*ta*·nya mountain path

triste *treesh*·te sad

trocar troo·*kaar* change (money) • exchange

trocos ⓜ pl *tro*·koosh loose change

trombose ⓕ trong·*bo*·ze stroke (health)

trovoada ⓕ troo·voo·*aa*·da thunderstorm

tu too you inf sg

tudo ⓜ *too*·doo everything

tumor ⓜ too·*mor* tumour

túmulo ⓜ *too*·moo·loo grave

tuna ⓜ *too*·na (university) music group

turista ⓜ&ⓕ too·*reesh*·ta tourist

último/última ⓜ/ⓕ *ool*·tee·moo/*ool*·tee·ma last (final)

ultrasom ⓜ ool·tra·*song* ultrasound

uma vez oo·ma vezh once

um outro/uma outra ⓜ/ⓕ oong oh·troo/oo·ma oh·tra another

universidade ⓕ oo·nee·ver·see·*daa*·de university

universo ⓜ oo·nee·*ver*·soo universe

urgente oor·*zheng*·te urgent

usar oo·*zaar* wear

útil *oo*·teel useful

vaca ⓕ *vaa*·ka cow

vacina ⓕ va·*see*·na vaccination

vaga ⓕ *vaa*·ga vacancy

vagão cama ⓜ va·*gowng* ka·ma sleeping car

vagão restaurante ⓜ va·*gowng* rresh·tow·*rang*·te dining car

vagarosamente va·ga·ro·za·*meng*·te slowly

vagina ⓕ va·*zhee*·na vagina

vago/vaga ⓜ/ⓕ *vaa*·goo/*vaa*·ga vacant

validar va·lee·*daar* validate

valioso/valiosa ⓜ/ⓕ va·lee·o·*zoo*/va·lee·o·za valuable

valor ⓜ va·*lor* value

varanda ⓕ va·*rang*·da balcony

vários/várias ⓜ/ⓕ *vaa*·ryoosh/*vaa*·ryash many • several

vazio/vazia ⓜ/ⓕ va·zee·oo/va·zee·a empty

vegetariano/vegetariana ⓜ/ⓕ ve·zhe·ta·ree·a·noo/ve·zhe·ta·ree·a·na vegetarian n&a

veia ⓕ vey·a vein

vela ⓕ ve·la candle

velho/velha ⓜ/ⓕ ve·lyoo/ve·lya old (age)

velocidade ⓕ ve·loo·see·daa·de speed (velocity)

— do filme doo feel·me film speed

vencedor/vencedora ⓜ/ⓕ veng·se·dor/veng·se·do·ra winner

vender veng·der sell

venenoso/venenosa ⓜ/ⓕ ve·ne·no·zoo/ve·ne·no·za poisonous

vento ⓜ veng·too wind

ventoínha ⓕ veng·too·ee·nya fan (machine)

ver ver see • watch (television)

verão ⓜ ve·rowng summer

verde ver·de green

verificar ve·ree·fee·kaar check

vermelho/vermelha ⓜ/ⓕ ver·me·lyoo/ver·me·lya red

vestido ⓜ vesh·tee·doo dress

via aérea ⓕ vee·a a·e·ree·a airmail

viagem ⓕ vee·aa·zheng journey

— de negócios de ne·go·syoosh business trip

viajar vee·a·zhaar travel

vício ⓜ vee·syoo addiction

— da droga da dro·ga drug addiction

vida ⓕ vee·da life

vigiar vee·zhee·aar watch (look after)

VIH ⓜ ve ee a·gaa HIV

vinha ⓕ vee·nya vineyard

vinho ⓜ vee·nyoo wine

violação ⓕ vee·oo·la·sowng rape

vir veer come

virar vee·raar turn

vírus ⓜ vee·roosh virus

visitar vee·zee·taar visit

vista ⓕ veesh·ta view

visto ⓜ veesh·too visa

vitamina ⓕ vee·ta·mee·na vitamin

voar voo·aar fly

vocês vo·sesh you inf pl

vóleibol ⓜ vo·lay·bol volleyball (sport)

— de praia de prai·a beach volleyball

voltar vol·taar return

voo ⓜ vo·oo flight

vosso/vossa ⓜ/ⓕ vo·soo/vo·sa your (one thing) inf pl

vossos/vossas ⓜ/ⓕ vo·soosh/vo·sash your (more than one thing) inf pl

votar voo·taar vote

voz ⓕ vosh voice

X

xadrez ⓜ sha·dresh chess

Z

zangado/zangada ⓜ/ⓕ zang·gaa·doo/zang·gaa·da angry

zona ⓕ zo·na shingles (illness)

Index

For topics that are covered in several sections of this book, we've indicated the most relevant page number in bold.